HARRAP'S

Book of
Humorous Quotations

HARRAP'S BOOK OF

HUMOROUS

QUOTATIONS

Cartoons by

Chosen and introduced by
G. F. *Lamb*

London

First published in Great Britain 1990
by HARRAP BOOKS Ltd
Chelsea House, 26 Market Square, Bromley BR1 1NA

© Geoffrey Lamb 1990

Illustrations © Harrap Books Ltd

ISBN 0 245-55073-9

Printed and bound in Great Britain
by The Bath Press, Avon

FOREWORD

There are few writings as humourless as an erudite discourse on humour. This foreword will therefore be both brief and free from erudition.

Humour is wide-ranging, and covers anything from the belly-laugh to the inward smile. I have chosen quotations which reflect this diversity, and have drawn them, for instance, from music-hall and radio comics (such as Lauder and Howerd), from professional humorists (such as Muir, Boothroyd, and Coren), from serious authors in less serious mood (such as Wells and Huxley), as well as from many other kinds of mirth-providers.

Nearly two hundred authors are presented, and about three thousand quotations. The book does not pretend to be fully comprehensive, but it is perhaps fair to say that most notable humorists who have expressed themselves in English or American (the two are not necessarily the same) have been included. Not everybody will find every item amusing, nor should anyone expect to. One man's chuckle is another man's yawn.

The book is intended to be read for pleasure, especially by incorrigible browsers. Sources are given wherever possible, but it is not an academic reference book. Humorous writing begins to be easily intelligible when English begins to be a modern language. This is roughly around the beginning of the eighteenth century, so I go no further back than Congreve and

Vanbrugh, who are modern enough to make modern audiences laugh. However, quotations from the present century predominate.

As well as offering material for browsing, I have aimed at providing ammunition for public and private speakers. A topic index is therefore included. Assuming that readers of such a book as this will not be helpless simpletons needing to be led by the hand all the way, I have given only the page numbers to indicate where relevant quotations may be found. The reader's own intelligence should enable him to select which items he needs.

G.F. LAMB

GEORGE ADE

George Ade (1866–1944), American humorist and dramatist, wrote for the *Chicago Record,* and was author of several Broadway shows, e.g. *The College Widow* (1904) and books, e.g. *Bang! Bang!* (1928).

1   "Whom are you?" he said, for he had been to night school. *Bang! Bang!*

2   He had been kicked in the head when young and believed everything he read in the Sunday papers. *The America of George Ade*

3   In the city a funeral is just an interruption of traffic; in the country it is a form of entertainment. *Cosmopolitan Magazine (February, 1928).*

4   Ade's Law: Anyone can win – unless there happens to be a second entry.

5   If it were not for the presents, an elopement would be preferable to a wedding. *Forty Modern Fables*

6   For parlour use, the vague generality is a life-saver. *Ib.*

7   The time to enjoy a European tour is about three weeks after you unpack. *Ib.*

8   Draw your salary before spending it. *Ib.*

9   One can only rest after plenty of practice. *Ib.*

10   Be it ever so humble, there's no place like home for wearing what you like. *Ib.*

11   Do unto yourself as your neighbours do unto themselves. *Hand-Made Fables*

12   Familiarity breeds contentment. *Ib.*

13   One man's poison ivy is another man's spinach. *Ib.*

14   Every man is the architect of his own fortunes, but the neighbours superintend the construction. *Ib.*

15   A bird in the hand may be worth two in the bush but it's a positive embarrassment to anyone not in the poultry business. *Fables*

16   She was a soprano of the kind often used for augmenting grief at a funeral. *Ib.*

17   A rose by any other name would smell as sweet, but wouldn't cost half as much. *Ib.*

18   The music teacher came twice a week to bridge the awful gap between Dorothy and Chopin.

19   Posterity is what you write for after being turned down by many publishers.

20   It is no time for mirth and laughter,
The cold grey dawn of the morning after.
The Sultan of Sulu

FRED ALLEN

Fred Allen (1894–1956), American comedian who at one time
appeared as a juggler in vaudeville, but achieved his greatest
fame as a satirical commentator on radio. *Treadmill
to Oblivion* (1954) was his autobiography.

1   A celebrity is a person who works hard all his life to become
    known, then wears dark glasses to avoid being recognized.
    Treadmill to Oblivion

2   A man who is paid in the dark can't make light of his salary. *Ib.*

3   (Of Jack Benny)
    His arm looks like a buggy whip with fingers. *Ib.*

4   Echo men are important in advertising. They follow in the
    wake of the big executive and echo his sentiments. *Ib.*

5   In show business there are more chorus girls kept than
    promises. *Ib.*

6   The grass is always greener in the other fellow's field – so let
    him worry about cutting it. *Ib.*

7   How do you stop a dead fish from smelling? Cut off its nose.
    Much Ado About Me

8   The last time I saw him he was walking down Lovers' Lane,
    holding his own hand. *Ib.*

9   When they lit all the candles on her birthday cake, six people
    were overcome with the heat. *Ib.*

10 He's a good boy. Everything he steals he brings home to his
    mother. *Ib.*

11 Money talks. It's the only conversation worth hearing when
    times are bad. *Ib.*

12   The penguin flies backwards because he doesn't care to see where he's going but wants to see where he's been. *The Backward View*

13   I have just returned from Boston. It's the only thing to do if you find yourself there. *Letter to Groucho Marx (1953)*

14   A committee is a group of people who individually can do nothing but as a group decide that nothing can be done.

15   Most of us spend the first six days of the week sowing wild oats, and then go to church on the Sunday to pray for a crop failure.

16   A gentleman is a man who wouldn't hit a woman with his hat on.

17   I don't want to own anything that won't fit into my coffin.

WOODY ALLEN

As an actor this American comedian (1935–) tends to appear as a misfit for whom things usually go wrong. In life, he has directed, written, and acted in a number of successful screenplays, e.g. *What's New Pussycat?* (1965), *Annie Hall* (1977), mostly wryly humorous.

1   Not only is there no God, but try getting a plumber at weekends. *Getting Even*

2   Eternal nothingness is O.K. if you're dressed for it. *Ib.*

3   I don't believe in an afterlife, but I'm bringing a change of underwear. *Ib.*

4   If man were immortal, do you realize what his meat bills would be? *Ib.*

5   Is knowledge knowable? If not, how do we know this? *Ib.*

6   Suffering is really God's will, though why He gets such a kick out of it is beyond me. *Ib.*

7   The sun, which is made of gas, can explode at any moment, sending our entire planetary system hurtling to destruction. Students are advised what the average citizen can do in such a case. *Ib.*

8   Most criminals actually work long hours, frequently in buildings without air-conditioning. *Ib.*

9   One of the best ways of combatting organized crime is telling the criminals you are not at home. *Ib.*

10   I finally wound up getting sued by a fictional character. *Ib.*

11   Death is one of the few things that can be done as easily lying down. *Without Feathers*

12   The lion and the calf may lie down together, but the calf won't get much sleep. *Ib.*

13   Money is better than poverty, if only for financial reasons. *Ib.*

14   My brain – it's my second favourite organ. *Sleeper*

15   I'm really a timid person. I was beaten up by Quakers. *Ib.*

16   Bisexuality immediately doubles your chances of a date on Saturday night. *New York Herald Tribune (1975)*

17   It's not that I'm afraid to die. I just don't want to be there when it happens. *Newsweek (1975)*

18   Mankind faces a crossroads. One path leads to despair and hopelessness. The other to total extinction. Let us hope we have the wisdom to choose correctly. *Side Effects*

19   Even as a kid I always went for the wrong women. When we went to see *Snow White* everyone fell in love with Snow White. I immediately fell for the wicked queen. *Annie Hall*

20   Sex is the most fun I ever had without laughing. *Ib.*

21 I think crime pays. The hours are good and you travel a lot.
Take the Money and Run

22 Making a funny film provides all the joy of getting your leg
caught in the blades of a threshing-machine. *Esquire*

23 My wife was immature. I'd be at home in the bath and she'd
come in and sink my boats.

24 If only God would give me some clear sign! Like making a
large deposit in my name at a Swiss bank.

KINGSLEY AMIS

Kingsley Amis (1922–), educated at the City of London School
and Oxford, was a university lecturer at Swansea, Princeton,
and Peterhouse, Cambridge. He achieved great success with his
novel *Lucky Jim* (1954), since when he has become a leading
contemporary novelist, and also a critic and poet.

1 I got the laundry to render up a shirt of mine that they had
been sitting on, if not wearing, for a couple of months.
Girl, 20

2 He handed me a small tumbler containing what I tried, with
some success, not to think of as a urine sample from one
gravely ill. *Ib.*

3 The real trouble with liars...was there could never be any
guarantee against their occasionally telling the truth. *Ib.*

4 Vivienne was wearing a fearful trouser-suit that looked as if it
had been made out of the seat-covers of some excitingly
new motor-coach. *Ib.*

5 Roy paid the taxi, crying out like a man in a film falling off a
high building when a coin rolled over the edge of his
hand. *Ib.*

6 "At least they didn't have pop music in the Black Hole of
Calcutta," said Roy. *Ib*

7   Nothing short of physical handicap has ever made anyone turn over a new leaf. *The Green Man*

8   A naked woman out of doors is either a sun-worshipper or a rape victim; a man in the same state is either a sexual criminal or a plain lunatic. *Ib.*

9   Haven't you noticed how we all specialize in what we hate most? *Lucky Jim*

10   Dixon felt like a man who knows he won't be able to jump on to the moving train if he stops to think about it. *Ib.*

11   Women are all keen on marrying men they don't much like. *Ib.*

12   He wished this set of dances would end; he was hot, his socks seemed to have been sprayed with fine adhesive sand, and his arms ached like those of a boxer keeping his guard up after fourteen rounds. *Ib.*

13   He must see if he could somehow restore his financial position from complete impossibility to its usual level of merely imminent disaster. *Ib.*

14   Welch's driving seemed to have improved slightly; at any rate, the only death Dixon felt himself threatened by was death from exposure to boredom. *Ib.*

15   He was of the faith chiefly in the sense that the church he currently did not attend was Catholic. *One Fat Englishman*

16   It was no wonder that people were so horrible when they started life as children. *Ib.*

17   Work was like what cats were supposed to be; if you disliked and feared it and tried to keep out of its way, it knew at once and sought you out. *Take a Girl Like You*

18 She had exercised a mysterious attraction and then an unmysterious repulsion on two former husbands, the second of whom had had to resort to fatal coronary disease to get away from her. *Jake's Thing*

19 Once there had been an exit on this side of the station, but it had been discovered...that the only people who benefited were passengers. *Ib.*

20 He dreamed he had to go on parade but couldn't find his boots, equipment, rifle or cap, and didn't know the way to the parade ground. *Ib.*

21 Death has something to be said for it:
There's no need to get out of bed for it.
Collected Poems

22 Fifty today, old lad?
Well, that's not doing so bad.
Ib. (*Ode to Me*)

ANONYMOUS

1 A minor operation is one performed on somebody else.

2 I know two things about the horse,
And one of them is rather coarse.

3 Curry gives me indiagestion.

4 Sex is bad for one – but it's good for two.

5 Horse power was fine when only horses had it.

6 One good turn gets most of the blanket.

7 It isn't how you win or lose
But how you place the blame.

8 (Notice in rear window of a Mini)
When I grow up I want to be a Rolls.

9   (Notice in car window)

Overtaker! See you at the Undertaker's!

10 (Advertisement in *Guardian* for job vacancy)

We aim to develop a non-sexist approach to working with young people...Applicants must be female.

11 (Notice on front gate)

Doberman guard dog on premises. Survivors will be prosecuted.

12 (Sign outside a do-it-yourself shop)

Special offer – disappearing loft ladders. Only two left.

13 My boss has boots so shiny I can see my face in them.

14 The only way to avoid making mistakes is to gain experience. The only way to gain experience is to make mistakes.

15 The French national anthem is The Mayonnaise.

16 "Hi, mister! Want to buy some pornographic postcards?"
    "No thanks, I haven't got a pornograph."

17 An Irishman found his wife unfaithful and threatened to shoot himself unless she gave up her lover. She only laughed. "You may laugh," he told her, "but you're next!"

18 Wife: "What would you do if you came home one day and found me in bed with another man?"
    Husband: "I'd give him a good bashing – with his white stick."

19 "Waiter! This coffee tastes like mud!"
    "Well, sir, it was ground only a few minutes ago."

20 To err is human, but to foul things up completely requires a computer.

REGINALD ARKELL

Reginald Arkell (d. 1959), English author, journalist, and dramatist, wrote many revues and musical comedies, e.g. *The Last Waltz* (1922), and was even better known for his light verse on gardening themes, e.g. *Green Fingers* (1934).

1 Of every single garden pest
  I think I hate the Green Fly best.
  Green Fingers

2 There was one Green Fly, I recall;
  I hated him the most of all.
  He sat upon my finest rose
  And put his fingers to his nose. *Ib.*

3 I'd rather have a skylark
  Than a parrot at the Zoo. *Ib.*

4 The Japanese
  Grow tiny trees
  About so high.
  I wonder why.
  More Green Fingers

5 How doth the little optimist
  Walk round the Chelsea Show,
  And scribble in a little book
  The things he means to grow. *Ib.*

6 I wonder why
  Some flowers will never try. *Ib.*

7 "Anyone with any sense
  Is certain to agree
  That English names for English flowers
  Is good enough for we." *Ib.*

8   The ground is so hard that you can't do a thing
But read about gardens and wait for the Spring.
Green Fingers Again

9   "If winter comes," the old-time lyric ran,
"Can Spring be far behind?" You bet it can! *Ib.*

10   I had just begun to like work in a garden
When all my arteries started to harden. *Ib.*

11   If you have got a microscope,
Look closely and you'll find
A midge can bite you from in front
Or sting you from behind. *Ib.*

12   Spinach *is* good for you.
It purifies the blood –
And looks like green mud.
And a Green Thumb

13   Croquet is all very well in its way,
If you hate all the people you happen to play.
But don't be discouraged – though starting as friends,
You'll hate them like poison before the game ends. *Ib.*

14   When you get a gardener
You'll discover very soon
That although you pay the piper
You will never call the tune. *Ib.*

15   Suppose you planted *people* in a row...
Suppose they were inspected every day
And all the weedy ones were thrown away! *Ib.*

16   I have never met any countryman who crept quietly along a
hedge, unless it was to shoot something. *Richard Jefferies*

17   When was there a prophet who found honour in his own
country until he was very rich or very dead? *Ib.*

RICHARD ARMOUR

Richard Armour (1906–), was born in California, USA and educated at Harvard. A university professor, he was also author of over twenty books, many of them humorous, and countless magazine articles.

1   I was born in the early hours of the morning, and had breakfast in bed. *Pills, Potions – and Granny*

2   "If you have blue blood in your veins there's something wrong with your circulation," my father used to say. *Ib.*

3   My father could never have run a filling station. Giving free air, or even directions, would have left him apoplectic. *Ib.*

4   My father's people were impressed only by money in the bank. Their only interest was interest. *Ib.*

5   Unaccustomed as she was to seeing my father in the role of a wounded hero, my mother rose to the occasion when he was carried in, and acted as any brave woman would. She fainted. *Ib.*

6   The corseting of those days pulled her in at the middle and correspondingly spread her out above and below. *Ib.*

7   Armour's Cold Cure Tablets were such large, bright red tablets that they made you feel better just to look at them. *Ib.*

8   My grandmother had a way of saying one thing *for* a person and ten things against, a formula which maintained her reputation for fairness. *Ib.*

9   A triumph of my father's salesmanship was the time he sold a Mexican both an ice pack and a hot water bottle, neither of which he came in for. *Ib.*

10   The greatest boon to his practical joking was electricity... But his fellow students did not turn against him till he electrified the toilet seats in the fraternity house. *Ib.*

11   The field was covered with the usual Southern California topsoil, in other words ninety-nine percent stones. *Ib.*

12   That money talks
     I'll not deny.
     I heard it once:
     It said "Goodbye".

ANTHONY ARMSTRONG

George Anthony Armstrong Willis (1897–1976) was born in Canada but educated at Uppingham and Cambridge. After serving in the regular Army he became a prolific writer for *Punch.* He also wrote crime novels and plays, e.g. *Ten Minute Alibi* (1931).

1   Montague is our oldest mule...He is content to meditate on his youth, and what a lad he was for kicking, and how hay isn't what it used to be in his young days. *Livestock in Barracks*

2   There is no rule to say that dog-racing must be done by greyhounds. In fact, there is no reason why one shouldn't have Pekinese chasing an electric éclair. *Ib.*

3   Two excited cats, composed principally of voice and claws, are not easy to hold. *Ib.*

4   The cats clung to Pullthrough as though he owed them money. *Ib.*

5   James, to whom the cats were now clinging, was having as much success in getting rid of them as a child trying to throw away a flypaper in a high wind. *Ib.*

6   He observed a small black and grey puppy chewing his boot to the accompaniment of subdued but blood-curdling growls, as from one who would stand no nonsense whatever from an insolent boot that passed remarks at others. *Ib.*

7   Our R.S.M. has been known to stop a clock by looking at it. *Ib.*

8   The Adjutant was hard at work on a scheme to relieve unemployment amongst subaltern officers. *Ib.*

9   The strain allowed him to lift his arm far enough to swallow other people's port, but not so far as to reach the electric bell pendant to ring for a round of his own. *Ib.*

10   His uncle, a celebrated back-bencher, told him the only way to get anything done in a democracy was to take someone out to lunch. *Punch (1941)*

ARTHUR ASKEY

Arthur Askey (1900–82), diminutive English comedian, born in Liverpool, worked his way up from seaside concert parties to stardom in films, plays, and pantomimes. His fame really began when he was invited (with Richard Murdoch) to be leading performer in the BBC radio show *Band Wagon* (1938).

1   My name was in large type, right across the bottom of the bill declaring that I was "The Popular Comedian". The first bill I saw displayed on a hoarding was close to the ground, and the local dogs had already given their opinion of me. *Before Your Very Eyes*

2   At Brighton we appeared twice daily at the Aquarium. At the matinees there were far more fish than patrons, but at least the fish gave us something to play to. *Ib.*

3   I never worked for Sir Thomas Beecham, but I admit that his family's products sometimes worked for me. *Ib.*

4   There were still some hurdles to be overcome, but fortunately with my height I felt I could run beneath them. *Ib.*

5   In those days at the BBC, if you said "the" instead of "but" you were hauled over the coals. *Ib.*

6   I suggested that as I was tagged the "Resident Comedian" I should pretend I lived on the premises. *Ib.*

7   By this time we had installed Lewis the goat in the flat...the point being that we could use the gag: "A goat in the flat? What about the smell?" "Oh, he'll get used to that." *Ib.*

8   "Have you any fresh salmon, waiter?"
     "I think it will be fresh, sir."
     "What do you mean, you *think* it will be fresh?"
     "Well, we won't know until we open the tin." *Ib.*

9   A girl went around for years doing auditions with no success at all. One day...the manager called her back and told her she had got the job. She looked at him in amazement. "I'm sorry," she said, "I only do auditions." *Ib.*

10   The commandant at Preston thanked me for organising the military hospital show. I said, "We don't want thanking – after all these lads did for us at Dunkirk."
     "Oh, none of them have been further than under the pier at Blackpool," he replied. "This is a V.D. hospital!" *Ib.*

11   There is only one motive for the racegoer, and that is how to make money without working for it. *Ib.*

12   Having seen the Grand National, it was always my ambition to throw a saddle over Mrs Mirabelle Topham [the owner of the course] and ride her over the appalling Aintree fences. *Ib.*

16

LADY ASTOR

Nancy Witcher Astor, née Langhorne (1879–1964), American wife of Viscount Astor, was the first woman member of the House of Commons (1919).

1 Nobody wants me as a Cabinet Minister and they are perfectly right.

2 Grass is growing on the Front Bench.
Quoted in *Observer, 1953*

3 (Deciding not to accept an invitation to play bridge with Edward VII)
I wouldn't know the King from the Knave.

4 One reason I don't drink is that I want to know when I'm having a good time.

5 The only thing I like about rich people is their money.

6 It isn't the common man who is important. It's the uncommon man.

7 I am the kind of woman I would run away from.

JANE AUSTEN

Jane Austen (1775–1817), British novelist, who was born and died in Hampshire. Her books, notable for their quiet humour, include *Pride and Prejudice* (1813) and *Emma* (1815).

1 It is a truth universally acknowledged, that a single man in possession of a good fortune must be in want of a wife.
Pride and Prejudice

2   Next to being married, a girl likes to be crossed in love a little now and then. *Ib.*

3   My mother's deafness is very trifling...by only raising my voice and saying anything two or three times over, she is sure to hear. *Emma*

4   One has no great hopes from Birmingham. I always say there is something direful in the sound. *Ib.*

5   A woman, if she have the misfortune of knowing anything, should conceal it as well as she can. *Northanger Abbey*

6   My sore throats are always worse than anyone's. *Persuasion*

7   People always live for ever when there is any annuity to be paid to them. *Sense and Sensibility*

8   I could not be happy with a man whose taste did not in every point coincide with my own. *Ib.*

9   Remember, my love, that you are not seventeen. It is too early in life to despair of happiness. *Ib.*

ALAN AYCKBOURN

Alan Ayckbourn (1939–), is a popular playwright, who was educated at Haileybury. He has worked in the theatre all his life, including repertory companies. He joined the Stephen Joseph theatre at Scarborough in 1957, and most of his many well-known plays were originally written for it.

1   Fishing is a way of life. It's like Transcendental Meditation. *Taking Steps*

2   If you want to know the time, don't bother asking a policeman, go to a watchmaker. *Ib.*

3   When you don't know what it is you want to do with your life, people make you feel guilty...They keep suggesting things. *Ib.*

4   She keeps falling asleep. Have you seen those tablets she's on? About fifteen a day. She sucks them like cough sweets. *Ten Times Table*

5   You can't rely on the police. They'll be hiding in doorways along with everybody else. *Ib.*

6   I've had a look round their house. You can tell a great deal from people's bedrooms. *Bedroom Farce*

7   How do these nurses do it? They're saints. I'd go stark raving mad and strangle all the patients. *Ib.*

8   Suddenly I've lost all my identity. Some mornings I say, "Who am I?" And I don't know. *Ib.*

9   You're the one who makes me violent. I was a pacifist until I met you. *Ib.*

10   She is a woman who has known her share of suffering and is anxious others should know about it too. *Woman in Mind*

11   God, in his infinite wisdom and with the entire cosmos to choose from, is unlikely to base the Kingdom of Heaven around Muriel's bedroom. *Ib.*

12   Sixteen years old and, until I told him, he thought his bed got damp at night because the roof leaked! *Ib.*

13   You packed him off to that piddling public school where he never saw anything female aged under 55 or weighing less than fifteen stone. *Ib.*

14   I do try to watch interesting programmes but I find them all so boring. *Ib.*

15   I feel like a man who's just spent his wedding night with an electrified steam shovel. *A Chorus of Disapproval*

16   They have microphones now that can pick up the sound of a
     pin dropping on Venus. *A Small Family Business*

17   Whatever you do, keep clear of thin women. They're trouble.
     Ib.

18   Eating is an obscene act...people sitting in front of each
     other in public, shovelling food into their mouths! *Ib.*

19   If you're going to be a criminal you've got to have some sort
     of brain. *Ib.*

20   He asked me for a play which would make people laugh
     when their seaside holidays were spoilt by the rain and
     they came into the theatre to get dry...This seemed to me
     as worthwhile a reason as any for writing a play. *Relatively
     Speaking (Introduction)*

PAM AYRES

Pam Ayres made a reputation reciting her unusual humorous
verses on TV, in her own inimitable rural accent. They have
also proved popular on LPs. Her first published collection was
Some of Me Poems (1976).

1   It is statistically proven,
    In chapter and in verse,
    That in a car-and-hedgehog fight
    The hedgehog comes off worse.
    All Pam's Poems

2   I wish I was a pop star,
    Colourful and brash,
    With me earoles full of crotchets
    And me wallet full of cash. *Ib.*

3   He would always take her hand
     And hold it like a cold dead fish
     Washed up along the strand. *Ib.*

4   No, it's white fish for me, no milk in me tea,
     And if we don't like it we lump it,
     No figs or sultanas, no mashed-up bananas,
     No pleasure and no buttered crumpet.
     Ib. (*The Slimming Poem*)

5   What other single comment
     Causes panic and despair
     Like someone saying, "Keep still!
     There's a wasp caught in your hair!"

6   Why do your rusty headlamps
     Look like sad, reproachful eyes?
     Ib. (*Good-bye Worn Out Morris 1000*)

7   Oh bring back the roly-poly pudding,
     Bread and butter pudding...Spotted Dick! *Ib.*

8   Ears pierced for improved rear vision. *Ib.*

9   Last night I ate that gastro-enteritis on a plate.
     I thought I'd make it to the Ladies'
     But no, I was too late. *Ib.*

10   I cannot give my telephone
     That's hazardous I know
     But if anyone will have me
     It is Bognor 410. *Ib.*

11   She'd have been the best girl there
     If it wasn't for her face, her feet,
     Her figure and her hair.
     The Ballad of Bill Spinks' Bedstead and Other Poems

12   Now some women fantasise nightly
     Of erotic adventures and steam
     But without sounding drab, all I want to grab
     Is a bucket or two of ice-cream. *Ib.*

'BALAAM'

'Balaam' (1914–) had a good many years' experience as teacher and training-college lecturer. *Chalk in My Hair* (1953) is a frank account of his teaching experiences; *Chalk Gets in Your Eyes* (1955) deals with his own education. *Come Out to Play* (1958) is a humorous novel of a teacher's life.

1 Outside the school on my first morning a horde of over two hundred boys was swarming in the road, many of them clinging to the railings as if they were an angry Parisian mob trying to pull down the gates of the Bastille. *Chalk in My Hair*

2 A certain type of child is innately backward. His dullness is not due to any outward cause: it is just an Act of God, and God only knows how to cure it. *Ib.*

3 This boy could not count beyond one and one, and even this sum he was liable to get wrong. *Ib.*

4 I find it hard to believe that the scientific mind could not, if persuaded, invent a silencer for street drills. *Ib.*

5 The school building was not that combination of Wandsworth Prison and Wellington Barracks which seemed to the architect who designed most London schools such a happy blend of significant styles. *Ib.*

6 When he took Shakespeare with a class he acted all the parts himself, including dancing and singing. Before singing he took out his false teeth and placed them on his table. His classroom was always in a state of excited uproar. *Ib.*

7 There are not a few teachers kidding themselves that they are modern when the fact is that they are merely incompetent. *Ib.*

8 Bishop's College smothered and choked me, like the embrace of an octopus. *Ib.*

9 You should not omit to leap after you have taken the precaution of looking. *Ib.*

10 Any boy seen walking behind the fives-courts was automatically suspected of loitering with intent to smoke. *Ib.*

11 A headmaster who feels that he has a teacher in his power is a more dangerous beast than any at the Zoo. *Ib.*

12 The school Sports Day is a purgatory of tedium. Exciting finishes are rare oases in a vast desert of dullness, and always happen while I am looking at something else. *Ib.*

13 I know a school which labels its four streams, respectively, 5A, 5 Alpha, 5 One, and Form 5. The device deceives no one but the headmaster himself. *Ib.*

14 I have seen a student trying to teach history who hardly knew whether the Armada was a town in Brazil or a winner of the Derby. *Ib.*

15 The parent who "wants a word with teacher" usually comes armed with a good many words, most of them bad ones. *Ib.*

16 Teachers have been giving lessons on Citizenship for years. They are just as effective in preventing juvenile delinquency as a lesson on Tolerance would be in preventing dogs from chasing cats. *Ib.*

17 My classics never soared above the elementary but bewildering pages of Kennedy's *Shorter Latin Primer*, which the heavy-handed wit from whom I had inherited the book had transformed into the *Shortbread Eating Primer*. It might almost as well have been the one as the other as far as I was concerned. *Chalk Gets in Your Eyes*

18 He was never quite so absent-minded as the Oxford professor who, according to tradition, pinned the notice "OUT" to his door as he went to take a lecture, returned to fetch a forgotten book, saw the "OUT" notice, and turned sadly away. *Ib.*

19 However carefully a pupil studies his errors in a composition on how to mend a puncture, he cannot be sure of getting a word-perfect answer on how to boil an egg. *Ib.*

20 A member of Parliament is no more required to pass an exam in standard speech than he is required to take an intelligence test. *Ib.*

21 The Head of a school is often chosen by a group of people who really know very little about it (the governors) from a group of people who usually know nothing about it (the candidates). *Ib.*

22 No statement about education is too fantastic to be believed. People have even been known to suppose that Eton is a comprehensive school. *Ib.*

23 Producing a school play is a simple way of qualifying for admission to a mental hospital. *Come Out to Play*

24 "The mere fact," said the headmaster, "that tennis is played with a soft ball has, I think, a certain enfeebling effect upon boys." *Ib.*

25 "As the newest master," said Mr Rodway, "you'll naturally be given the smallest room. I had it when I began twelve years ago. It has a dressing-table and a cupboard. If I remember rightly, you have to lift them on to the bed before you can open the door." *Ib.*

26 It is one of the many ironies of education that the less hostile a new master is towards his class, the more hostile they are likely to be towards him. *Ib.*

27 A tedious railway journey was made in a train that seemed to stop every few minutes to admire the scenery. *Ib.*

R. H. BARHAM

Richard Harris Barham (1788–1845), educated at St Paul's School and Oxford, was a minor canon of St Paul's Cathedral, but is now mainly remembered for his fluent light verses, collected as *The Ingoldsby Legends* (1840–47).

1   The Cardinal rose with a dignified look,
    He called for his candle, his bell, and his book.
    In holy anger, and pious grief,
    He solemnly cursed that rascally thief!
    The Jackdaw of Rheims

2   He cursed him in eating, he cursed him in drinking,
    He cursed him in coughing, in sneezing, in winking;
    He cursed him in sitting, in standing, in lying;
    He cursed him in walking, in riding, in flying! *Ib.*

3   Never was heard such a terrible curse!
    But what gave rise
    To no little surprise,
    Nobody seemed one penny the worse! *Ib.*

4   Heedless of grammar, they all cried, "THAT'S HIM!" *Ib.*

5   He would pore by the hour
    O'er a weed or a flower,
    Or the slugs that come crawling out after a shower.
    The Knight and the Lady

6   Though his cassock was swarming
    With all sorts of vermin,
    He'd not take the life of a flea!
    The Lay of St Aloys

7   But when the Crier cried "O Yes!" the people cried
    "O No!" *Misadventures at Margate*

8   And when you go to Margate next, just stop and ring the bell,
     Give my regards to Mrs Jones, and say I'm pretty well. *Ib.*

9   She drank Prussic acid without any water,
     And died like a Duke-and-a-Duchess's daughter!
     The Tragedy

10   "Look at the Clock!" quoth Winifred Pryce...
     "Out all night!
     Me in a fright!
     Staggering home as it's just getting light!
     You intoxified brute! – You insensible block! –
     Look at the Clock! – Do! – Look at the Clock!"
     The Milkmaid's Story

11   The vowels made use of in Welsh are so few
     That the A and the E, the I, O, and the U,
     Have really but little or nothing to do. *Ib.*

12   To conclude, Mrs Pryce was not over young,
     Had very short legs, and a very long tongue. *Ib.*

J. M. BARRIE

Sir James Matthew Barrie (1860–1937), novelist and playwright,
was born in Scotland and educated at Edinburgh University.
He settled in London as a journalist and then wrote a number
of successful novels, e.g. *The Little Minister* (1891) and plays, e.g.
Quality Street (1902), *Peter Pan* (1904).

1   I wish I had the whipping of the man who invented Latin.
     Quality Street

2   Algebra is X minus Y equals Z plus Y – and things like that.
     And all the time you are saying they are equal, you feel in
     your heart, "Why should they be?" *Ib.*

3   There is one very fine chair, but, heavens, not for sitting on;
     just to give the room a social standing. *What Every Woman
     Knows*

4   A young Scotsman of your ability let loose upon the world
     with £300, what could he not do? Especially if he went
     among the English. *Ib.*

5   "You're not a totaller, I hope?"
     "I'm practically a totaller."
     "So are we. How do you take it?" *Ib.*

6   Men are nervous of remarkable women. *Ib.*

7   A clergyman who plays cricket and can break both ways is sure to get on in England. *The Admirable Crichton*

8   His lordship may compel us to be equal upstairs, but there will never be equality in the servants' hall. *Ib.*

9   How shall we ever know if it's morning if there's no servant to pull up the blinds? *Ib.*

10   Life is like a cup of tea; the more heartily we drink, the sooner we reach the dregs. *Ib.*

11   If I was sure I were going to die tonight I would repent at once. *Sentimental Tommy*

12   Hogmanay, like all festivals, is a bank from which we can only draw what we put in. *Ib.*

13   In love-making, as in other arts, those do it best who can't tell how it's done. *Tommy and Grizel*

14   The room abounds in the little feminine touches that are so often best applied by the hand of man. *Dear Brutus*

15   Lady Caroline is lately from the enormously select school where they are all taught to pronounce their r's as w's; nothing else seems to be taught, but for matrimonial success nothing else is necessary. *Ib.*

16   I have seen him out there among his flowers, petting them, talking to them, coaxing them till they simply *had* to grow. *Ib.*

17   At Oxford he was runner-up for the presidentship of the Union and only lost it because the other man was less brilliant. *Ib.*

18   Ye canna expect to be both grand and comfortable. *The Little Minister*

19   Some of my plays peter out and some pan out.

20   I do not know whether Bacon wrote the works of Shakespeare, but if he did not it seems to me that he missed the opportunity of his life.

JOHN BARRYMORE

John Barrymore (1882–1942), American romantic actor and personality, was the matinee idol of his day. Later he achieved success as a film actor.

1   One of my chief regrets during my years in the theatre is that I couldn't sit in the audience and watch me.

2   There are a lot of Methods. Mine involves a lot of talent, a glass, and some cracked ice.

3   The good die young because they can see it's no use living if you've got to be good.

4   He neither drank, smoked, nor rode a bicycle. He lived frugally, saved his money, and died early, surrounded by greedy relatives. It was a great lesson to me.

5   (On smoking)
     Women have no pockets so they have to find something to do with their hands.

6   (Of his ex-wife)
     She's the kind of girl who won't go anywhere without her mother.

7   You never realize what a short time a month is until you pay alimony.

8   In Genesis it says it's not good for a man to be alone, but it can be a great relief.

MAX BEERBOHM

Sir Max Beerbohm (1872–1956), British writer and caricaturist, was born in London, and educated at Charterhouse and Oxford. He made his reputation as contributor to the *Yellow Book* of the nineties, as dramatic critic and essayist, and as author of an extravagantly fantastic Oxford novel, *Zuleika Dobson* (1911).

1   (On the Boat Race)

   Why does this annual fervour pervade all London? At Oxford the prospect of the race excites never more than a very mild interest. *Daily Mail (1897)*

2   The Squadron (at Cowes), with its thick battlements and its array of little brass cannons pointed across the Solent, gives one a sense of security from an English invasion. *Saturday Review (1898)*

3   You will think me lamentably crude: my experience of life has been drawn from life itself. *Zuleika Dobson*

4   On another small table stood Zuleika's library. Both books were in covers of dull gold. *Ib.*

5   Women who love the same man have a kind of bitter freemasonry. *Ib.*

6   Both Zuleika and the Duke were ravenously hungry, as people always are after the stress of any emotional crisis. *Ib.*

7   There are five ghosts permanently residing in the right wing of the house. *Ib.*

8   Beauty and the lust for learning have yet to be allied. *Ib.*

9   The loveliest face in the world will not please you if you see it suddenly, eye to eye, at a distance of half an inch from your own. *Ib.*

10   He held, in his enlightened way, that Americans have a
      perfect right to exist. But he did often find himself
      wishing that Mr Rhodes had not enabled them to exercise
      that right in Oxford. *Ib.*

11   She told him that she knew nothing about music really, but
      that she knew what she liked. As she passed him up the
      aisle, she said it again. People who say it are never tired of
      saying it. *Ib.*

12   Why should a writer never be able to mention the moon
      without likening her to something else – usually
      something to which she has not the faintest resemblance?
      Ib.

13   For people who like that kind of thing, that is the kind of
      thing they like. *Ib.*

14   It is the umbrella that has made Englishmen what they are.
      Saturday Review (1898)

BRENDAN BEHAN

Brendan Behan (1923–64), Irish playwright, was a Borstal boy,
but later developed into a lively and effective dramatist with *The
Quare Fellow* (1956) and *The Hostage* (1958). *Borstal Boy* (1958) is
autobiographical. Alcoholism led to his early death.

1   Most of us grow up to be the kind of men our mothers warned
     us against. *The Wit of Brendan Behan*

2   Whisky is too good to be sullied with water. *Ib*

3   I only take a drink on two occasions – when I'm thirsty and
     when I'm not. *Ib.*

4   Not all the sins of my past life passed in front of me but as
     many as could find room in the queue. *Ib.*

5   How's my health? If I felt any better I couldn't stand it. *Ib.*

6   She looked like a woman who looked under her bed hoping to find a man there but only found a collar-stud. *Ib.*

7   If there were only three Irishmen left in the world you'd find two of them in a corner talking about the other. *Ib.*

8   When a girl marries in Hollywood she throws the bridegroom away before she throws the bouquet. *Ib.*

9   Killing your wife is a natural class of thing could happen to the best of us. *The Quare Fellow*

10 Do you mean we're getting food with our meals today? *Ib.*

11 There's only one brand of tobacco allowed here – "Three Nuns". None today, none tomorrow, and none the day after. *Ib.*

12 She was fined for having concealed about her person two Thompson sub-machine guns, three Mills bombs, and a stick of dynamite. *Ib.*

13 The Bible was a consolation to a fellow alone in the old cell. The lovely thin paper with a bit of mattress coir in it, if you could get a match, was as good a smoke as ever I tasted. *Ib.*

14 The left leg is bad one day and the right is bad the next. It's only the mercy of God I'm not a centipede. *Ib.*

15 It's my belief that they bought the books for the prison by weight. I once got... Selfridge's furniture catalogue for my non-fiction or education book. *Borstal Boy*

16 I wish I'd been a mixed infant. *The Hostage*

17 PAT. Where the hell were you in 1916 when the real fighting was going on?
    MEG. I wasn't born.
    PAT. You're full of excuses. *Ib.*

18 Anyone would think you was doing God a good turn, speaking well of Him. *Ib.*

19 I was court-martialled [by IRA headquarters] in my absence

and sentenced to death in my absence. So I said, right,
you can shoot me in my absence. *Ib.*

20 Never throw stones at your mother,
You'll be sorry for it when she's dead,
Never throw stones at your mother,
Throw bricks at your father instead. *Ib.*

21 There's no one, no one, loves you like yourself. *Ib.*

22 I think weddings is sadder than funerals because they remind
you of your own wedding. You can't be reminded of your
own funeral because it hasn't happened. *Richard's Cork Leg*

HILAIRE BELLOC

Joseph Hilaire Pierre Belloc (1870–1953), French-born British
writer, was educated at Oxford, and became a Liberal M.P. His
prolific writings include nonsense verse, historical works,
novels, travel books, and essays. He was an ardent Roman
Catholic.

1 Lord Hippo suffered fearful loss
By putting money on a horse
Which he believed, if it were pressed,
Would run far faster than the rest:
For someone who was in the know
Had confidently told him so.
More Peers

2 The chief defect of Henry King
Was chewing little bits of string
At last he swallowed some that tied
Itself in ugly knots inside.
Cautionary Tales

3 Always keep a-hold of Nurse
For fear of finding something worse. *Ib.*

4   It happened to Lord Lundy then,
     As happens to so many men:
     Towards the age of twenty-six
     They shoved him into politics. *Ib.*

5   Godolphin Horne was nobly born;
     He held the human race in scorn. *Ib.*

6   Young Algernon, the Doctor's Son,
     Was playing with a Loaded Gun.
     He pointed it towards his sister,
     Aimed very carefully, but Missed her! *Ib.*

7   The Lion from the burning slopes
     Of Atlas lives on Antelopes,
     And only adds the flesh of men
     By way of relish now and then.
     New Cautionary Tales

8   John Vavassour De Quentin Jones
     Was very fond of throwing stones...
     Like many of the Upper Class
     He liked the sound of Broken Glass. *Ib.*

9   As a friend to the children commend me the Yak.
     You will find it exactly the thing:
     It will carry and fetch, you can ride on its back,
     Or lead it about with a string.
     The Bad Child's Book of Beasts

10   The Llama is a woolly sort of fleecy hairy goat,
     With an indolent expression and an undulating throat
     Like an unsuccessful literary man.
     More Beasts for Worse Children

11   The Rich arrived in pairs
     And also in Rolls Royces;
     They talked of their affairs
     In loud and strident voices.
     Ladies and Gentlemen

12   I'm tired of Love: I'm still more tired of Rhyme.
But money gives me pleasure all the time.
Epigrams

13   When I am dead, I hope it may be said:
"His sins were scarlet, but his books were read." *Ib.*

14   I always like to associate with a lot of priests because it makes
me understand anti-clerical things so well.
Letter to E.S.P.Haynes

15   You might imagine that people in biographies...would be
more or less like human beings – but they never are. *On
Anything*

16   If you try to laugh and say "No" at the same time it sounds
like neighing – yet people are perpetually doing it in
novels. *Ib.*

17   They loved each other like brothers, yet they quarrelled like
Socialists. *Hills and the Sea*

18   The only fish that can swim backwards is an eel. This I have
proved by observation, and I challenge any fisherman to
deny it. *Ib.*

ROBERT BENCHLEY

Robert Charles Benchley (1889–1945), American humorist and
actor, was for a time dramatic critic for the *New Yorker*. He wrote
and acted in many film comedies, and published several books
of humorous articles, e.g. *My Ten Years in a Quandary* (1936);
One Minute Please (1945).

1   The actual physical discomfort of travelling with the kiddies is
not so great, though you do emerge from it looking as if
you had just moved the piano upstairs, single-handed. *One
Minute Please*

2   There are moments when babies are asleep. Oh yes, there are. There *must* be. *Ib.*

3   It is a rule of all children to look with disfavour on any attentions from strangers. The only people they want to play with are those who hate children. *Ib.*

4   What do people care for winter breezes so long as they have the Little Colonel oil-heater in the front room, to make everything cosy and warm within a radius of four inches. *Ib.*

5   Breaking the ice in the pitcher seems to be a feature of the early lives of all great men. *Ib.*

6   The English language may hold a more disagreeable combination of words than "The dentist will see you now". I am willing to concede something to the question: "Have you anything to say before the current is turned on?" That may be worse for the moment but it doesn't last so long. *Ib.*

7   There is probably no moment more appalling than that in which the tongue comes suddenly upon the ragged edge of a space from which the old familiar filling has disappeared. *Ib.*

8   If you look at eggs, you will see that each one is *almost* round but not *quite*...Nature's way of distinguishing eggs from large golf balls. *Ib.*

9   The derivation of one colour from two other colours is not generally considered a sexual phenomenon, but that is because the psycho-analysts haven't got around to it yet. *Ib.*

10   There was a time, beginning with the Oscar Wilde era, when... even the butlers were wits, and served epigrams with the cucumber sandwiches. *Ib.*

11   No boat of less than four thousand tons ever sailed on time. *Around the World Backwards and Sideways*

12 No matter where you settle yourself [aboard an excursion boat], by the time the boat has started, the position turns out to be too sunny or too windy. *Ib.*

13 In the Sargasso Sea the eels' eggs are deposited and (pardon me) fertilized, and here the happy event takes place. Or perhaps it should be happy events, since they hatch out in litters of ten million per mother. *Ib.*

14 At this point the parents die, evidently disgusted at the prospect of cutting up food and picking up toys for ten million babies. *Ib.*

15 I should think that any self-respecting eel would resent being caught and ''banded'' and then tossed back, making him a figure of fun among the other eels. *Ib.*

16 I can go on a beach and stand perfectly upright...for four minutes, with my hands held high above my head, and at the end of that time there will be sand in my pockets, on the back of my neck, around my belt line (inside), and in my pipe. *Ib.*

17 I have never stretched myself on a beach for an afternoon's nap that a dog, fresh from a swim, did not take up a position just to the left of my tightly closed eyes, and shake himself. *Ib.*

18 No matter how late you arrive for a matinee, the curtain has never gone up. *Ib.*

19 Woman, however lovely she may be in stooping to folly in individual cases, is never so unlovely as when giggling at it in a group over boxes of chocolates at a matinee. *Ib.*

20 Drawing on my fine command of language, I said nothing. *Chips Off the Old Benchley*

21 Even nowadays a man can't step up and kill a woman without feeling just a bit unchivalrous. *Ib.*

22 A dog teaches a boy fidelity, perseverance, and to turn round three times before lying down.

ALAN BENNETT

Alan Bennett (1934–), writer of plays and screenplays, was educated at Oxford. He first made his name as performer and part-author of the satirical revue *Beyond the Fringe* (1960). Plays include *Forty Years On* (1969), *Habeas Corpus* (1975). TV plays include the monologue series *Talking Heads* (1989).

1   When a society has to resort to the lavatory for its humour, the writing is on the wall. *Forty Years On*

2   Standards are always out of date. That's what makes them standards. *Ib.*

3   "Her legs leave something to be desired."
"All legs leave *something* to be desired. That is part of their function and part of their charm." *Ib.*

4   I am not a spinster. I am unmarried. *Habeas Corpus*

5   We had to remove from our railway compartment three times to avoid a clergyman who was looking up my daughter's legs under cover of the *Daily Telegraph*. *Ib.*

6   My surgery is full of girls expecting something and they don't know who it's from. *Ib.*

7   You don't look like a doctor to me. You haven't any trousers on. *Ib.*

8   In a few moments I shall ask you to remove your clothes in their entirety (but) I shall be as far from desire as a plumber uncovering a manhole. *Ib.*

9   If you choose to commit suicide on a doctor's afternoon off, that's your funeral. *Ib.*

10   "I've just taken fifty sleeping pills. The pink ones." "Those aren't sleeping pills. They're laxatives." *Ib.*

11   He only went into the Army in order to put his moustache to good purpose. *Ib.*

12 I've known for years our marriage has been a mockery. My body lying there night after night in the wasted moonlight. I know now how the Taj Mahal must feel. *Ib.*

13 When art comes in the door, manners go out of the window. *Talking Heads*

14 You see the spear come out of his back, killing him, and ruining his dinner jacket. *Ib.*

15 I ought to have a Ph.D. in the number of flower arrangement classes I've been to, but still my efforts show as much evidence of art as walking-sticks in an umbrella stand. *Ib.*

16 If you can't get compared with the Queen Mother, the Virgin Mary's the next best thing. *Ib.*

17 When somebody in a novel says something like "I've never been in an air crash", you know this means that five minutes later they will be. *Ib.*

18 There are some lace curtains popular nowadays that are gathered up for some reason in the middle. They look to me like a woman who's been to the lav and got her underskirt caught up behind her. *Ib.*

19 One learnt early the valuable lesson that life is generally something that happens elsewhere. *Ib.*

20 He's been had up for exposing himself in a Sainsbury's doorway...Tesco's you could understand it. *Ib.*

21 "We met the problem with love," he said, as though love was some all-purpose antibiotic. *Ib.*

22 The best way to avoid a broken hip is to have a flexible mind. *Ib.*

23 There is invariably something queer about women who wear ankle socks. *The Old Country*

24 Why is it that only teeth decay?...You don't have to go to the doctor's to have holes in your arm stopped up, do you? *Getting On*

ARNOLD BENNETT

Enoch Arnold Bennett (1867–1931), was an English journalist, critic, and novelist. His novel *The Old Wives' Tale* (1908), together with his stories of the Potteries, made him a leading novelist of his time.

1   The freelance writer is a tramp touting for odd jobs. *The Truth About an Author*

2   The pay was bad, as it too often is where a paper has ideals. *Ib.*

3   My profits from this first novel...exceeded the cost of having it typewritten by one sovereign...I got a new hat out of it. *Ib.*

4   A speculative builder, in too much of a hurry to use a measure, stepped out the foundations of fifteen cottages with his own bandy legs. *These Twain*

5   There's nothing like an unsatisfactory holiday for reconciling us to a life of toil. *Mr Prohack*

6   For him, hell was a place where the inhabitants always had to keep an eye on the clock. *Ib.*

7   Journalists say a thing they know isn't true in the hope that if they keep on saying it long enough it will be true. *The Title*

8   It is only people of small stature who need to stand on their dignity. *Journals*

9   The price of justice is eternal publicity. *Things That Have Interested Me*

MICHAEL BENTINE

Michael Bentine (1922–), of Peruvian extraction, was a
leading British humorist after the war. He was one of the
Goons in the programme's early years, and wrote material for
many well-known comedians, besides presenting his own TV
shows (e.g. *It's a Square World*).

1   One British Olympic sports commentator described a U.K.
     runner who was lagging far behind the field as: "Coming
     in confidently and supremely fit – a gallant sixteenth."
     Sports Commentators

2   That roar of ecstatic welcome was for Her Royal Highness
     riding Kinky... Just coming up to the water jump... Good
     heavens, Kinky's *refused*. But her Royal Highness has
     accepted!... What a brilliant swimmer she is! *Ib.*

3   "Have you any concrete evidence of ghosts?"
     "No. Very few ghosts are made of concrete." *The Best of
     Bentine*

4   In radio, or sound effects off-stage, all staircases are wooden.
     Ib.

5   Regularly, in celebration of the thwarting of Guy Fawkes in his
     attempt to blow up the Houses of Parliament, many
     innocent men, women, and children gravely injure or
     even kill themselves with British fireworks. *Ib.*

6   I once played to a large mirror in order to reach the audience
     in an L-shaped cabaret room. *Ib.*

7   As the old actor's adage has it: "Learn the lines, speak them
     clearly, don't bump into the furniture, but first, check that
     your flies aren't undone." *The Shy Person's Guide to Life*

8   Tommy Trinder gave me invaluable advice about hecklers.
     "Always get them to repeat what they have said," he told
     me, "because nothing sounds quite so funny or offensive
     when it is repeated." *Ib.*

9   When television writers of soap operas are seized by writer's block they usually rework an earlier favourite script episode into an offering for one of the hospital sagas. *The Hospital Syndrome*

10   Our next-door neighbour turned out to be a funeral furnisher...During a bitterly cold winter he would lean over the garden fence. "Terrible weather," he'd say with a radiant smile. "They're dropping like flies." *Conversation Piece*

11   The reluctance of the British to communicate with each other is legendary. It is also true. *Ib.*

12   Real life can't be beaten when it comes to belly laughs. *The Best of Bentine*

13   Of all the synthetic professions created for the luxury trade, the Toast Master's is probably the most dispensable. *The Toast Master*

E. C. BENTLEY

Edmund Clerihew Bentley (1875–1956) is best known as the originator of the Clerihew, a four-line humorous verse form with irregular metre, often dealing with a particular person. He also wrote a notable detective novel, *Trent's Last Case* (1913).

1   Sir Christopher Wren
     Said, "I am going to dine with some men.
     "If anybody calls
     "Say I am designing St Paul's."
     Biography for Beginners

2   The Abbé Liszt
     Hit the piano with his fist.
     That was the way
     He used to play. *Ib.*

3   Karl Marx
     Was completely wrapped up in his sharks
     The poor creatures seriously missed him
     While he was attacking the capitalist system. *Ib*

4   The novels of Jane Austen
     Are the ones to get lost in. *Ib.*

5   What I like about Clive
     Is that he is no longer alive.
     There is a great deal to be said
     For being dead. *Ib.*

6   To have enriched and refined
     The universal mind
     Affords me some measure
     Of not ignoble pleasure. *Ib.*

7   The digestion of Milton
     Was unequal to Stilton
     He was only feeling so-so
     When he wrote *Il Penseroso*.
     More Biography

8   It only irritated Brahms
     To tickle him under the arms.
     What really helped him compose
     Was to be stroked on the nose. *Ib.*

9   Henry the Eighth
     Took a thucthethion of mateth.
     He inthithted that the monkth
     Were a lathy lot of thkunkth. *Ib.*

10   "Susaddah!" exclaimed Ibsen,
     "By dose is turdig cribson!
     "I'd better dot kiss you.
     "Atishoo! Atishoo!" *Ib.*

11   The moustache of Hitler
     Could hardly be littler
     Was the thought that kept recurring
     To Field Marshal Goering.
     Clerihews

12   Howling the chorus of a comic song
         I stagger home to bed at half-past three.
     A spirited performance on the gong
         Brings down my maiden aunt in *robe de nuit.*
     Ballade of Vain Delight

13   Last Thursday evening, feeling like a spree,
         (Although my conscience told me it was wrong)
     I put some strychnine in my parents' tea...
         Who is there now to love and comfort me? *Ib.*

JEFFERY BERNARD

Jeffery Bernard (1932–), journalist, was educated at
Pangbourne Naval College (which he hated). He developed a
taste early on for horse-racing, pubs, and Soho, and for many
years has contributed to the *Spectator* a "Low Life" column.

1   I've met a better class of person in the gutter than I have in
    the drawing-room. *Low Life*

2   Playing Dante to a Beatrice isn't my idea of fun. *Ib.*

3   Had the Last Supper been held at the Hilton the bill would
    have come to £500. *Ib.*

4   I'm definitely not going to heaven. I'm sure it's very white and
    cold, sparsely furnished, with maybe a bit of shining
    chrome here and there. *Ib.*

5   Take my tip and stay out of Wales even if you are the Prince of
    it. *Ib.*

6   Typing at a table in a sunshine-filled garden is nearly always
     impracticable...There is always a wasp lurking behind me,
     like a sadistic schoolmaster, wanting to see what I've
     written. *Ib.*

7   All the medical advice columns in print are for women.
     There's no doctor I can write to to ask why my hands
     shake, why I forget my own telephone number, and why
     the bed keeps catching fire. *Ib.*

8   My French stinks. It seems that when I asked somebody for a
     light I asked them to set me on fire. *Ib.*

9   Whenever you meet a pretty teenage girl always make a
     beeline for the mother. I've found it to be usually very
     rewarding. *Ib.*

10   A couple of them [medical students] couldn't diagnose a
     decapitation, but I gather they'll qualify. *Ib.*

11   Women (should have) labels on their foreheads saying,
     "Government Health Warning: women can seriously
     damage your brains, genitals, current account,
     confidence, razor blades, and good standing among your
     friends." *Ib.*

12   160 kilometres in a taxi? It made my wallet break out in a
     sweat. *Ib.*

13   I once had a cup of coffee at Epsom that had soup in it. *Daily
     Telegraph (24 March 1986)*

14   You never see a pretty unattached girl on a race-course. *Ib.*

15   Playing poker with the bookmakers in the train all the way to
     York is one of the most hazardous occupations there is. *Ib.*

JOHN BETJEMAN

Sir John Betjeman (1906–84), poet and journalist, was educated at Marlborough and Oxford. A great champion of Victorian and Edwardian architecture and taste, and a popular poet, he was appointed Poet Laureate in 1972. *Summoned By Bells* (1960) was a poetical autobiography.

1   There's something about a 'varsity man that distinguishes him
    from a cad:
    You can tell by his tie and blazer he's a 'varsity undergrad.
    The 'Varsity Students' Rag

2   It's something to become a bore,
    And more than that, at twenty-four.
    The Wykehamist

3   Come, friendly bombs, and fall on Slough,
    It isn't fit for humans now,
    There isn't grass to graze a cow.
    Slough

4   Gracious Lord, oh bomb the Germans.
        Spare the women for Thy sake;
    And if that is not too easy
        We will pardon Thy mistake.
    In Westminster Abbey

5   Maud was my hateful nurse who smelt of soap
    And forced me to eat chewy bits of fish.
    Summoned By Bells

6   Still on the bedroom wall, the list of rules:
    Don't waste the water. It is pumped by hand.
    Don't throw old blades into the W.C.
    Don't keep the bathroom long, and don't be late
    For meals... Ib.

7   "Breathe in the ozone, John. It's iodine."
    But which is iodine and which is drains? *Ib.*

8   ...We learned by heart
Those patriotic lines of Oxenham
"What can a little chap do
For his country and for you – "
"He can boil his head in the stew",
We added. *Ib.*

9   As one more solemn of our number said:
"Spiritually I was at Eton, John."

10   (At Oxford)
For while we ate Virginia hams,
Contemporaries passed exams. *Ib.*

11   Failed in Divinity! O towers and spires! *Ib.*

12   A prep-school master teaching Games,
      Maths, French, Divinity.
Harsh hand-bells harried me from sleep
For thirty pounds a term and keep. *Ib.*

13   It's awf'lly bad luck on Diana,
      Her ponies have swallowed their bits;
She's fished down their throats with a spanner
      And frightened them all into fits.
Hunter Trials

14   Oh! would I were the racket press'd
With hard excitement to her breast.
The Olympic Girl

15   Here among long-discarded cassocks,
Damp stools, and half-split-open hassocks,
here where the Vicar never looks
I nibble through old service books.
Diary of a Church Mouse

16   We spray the fields and scatter
      The poison on the ground,
So that no wicked wild flowers
      Upon our farms are found.
Farmer's Weekly

17 Pam, I adore you, Pam, you great big mountainous sports girl,
Whizzing them over the net, full of the strength of five.
Pot Pourri from a Surrey Garden

18 Bournemouth is one of the few English towns that one can
safely call "her". *First and Last Loves*

19 We are told that we live in the age of the common man... He
is not the common man, but the average man, which is far
worse. *Ib.*

20 The suburbs which once seemed to me so lovely with their
freckled tennis girls and their youths in club blazers have
spread so far in the wake of the motor-car that there is
little but suburb left. *Ib.*

21 History must not be written with bias, and both sides must be
given, even if there is only one side. *Ib.*

AMBROSE BIERCE

Ambrose Bierce (1842–1913?) fought in the American Civil
War and then drifted into humorous journalism, writing for
Britain's *Fun* as well as for American journals. His satirical and
cynical *Devil's Dictionary* has enjoyed lasting popularity. In 1913
he disappeared in Mexico.

1   An absurdity is a statement or belief manifestly inconsistent
with one's own opinion. *The Devil's Dictionary*

2   An acquaintance is a person whom we know well enough to
borrow from, but not well enough to lend to. *Ib.*

3   "The man was in such deep distress,"
Said Tom, "that I could do no less
Than give him good advice." Said Jim:
"If less could have been done for him
I know you well enough, my son,
To know that's what you would have done." *Ib.*

4   The most affectionate creature in the world is a wet dog. *Ib.*

5   In law, to appeal is to put the dice back in the box for another
throw. *Ib.*

6   Armour is the kind of clothing worn by a man whose tailor is a
blacksmith. *Ib.*

7   Astrology is the art of making the dupe see stars. *Ib.*

8   An auctioneer is a man who proclaims with a hammer that he
has picked a pocket with his tongue. *Ib.*

9   Bacchus was a convenient deity invented by the ancients as an
excuse for getting drunk. *Ib.*

10   Among the Romans the censor was an inspector of public
morals, but the public morals of modern nations will not
bear inspection. *Ib.*

11   Thou shalt not covet thy neighbour's wife,
     For she would bring thee naught but strife. *Ib.*

12   A deposit is a charitable contribution to the support of a
     bank. *Ib.*

13   Desertion: an aversion to fighting as exhibited by
     abandoning an army or a wife. *Ib.*

14   Dispatches offer a complete account of all the murders,
     outrages, and other disgusting crimes which take place
     everywhere, disseminated daily by an Associated Press.

15   Dice are small polka-dotted cubes of ivory, constructed like a
     lawyer to lie on any side. *Ib.*

16   But heed the warning words the sage hath said:
     A woman absent is a woman dead. *Ib.*

17   A baby is a misshapen creature of no particular age, sex, or
     condition. *Ib.*

18   Bigot: one who is obstinately and zealously attached to an
     opinion that you do not share. *Ib.*

19   In our civilization, and under our republican (American)
     form of government, brain is so highly honoured that it is
     rewarded by exemption from the cares of office. *Ib.*

20   A cynic is a blackguard whose faulty vision sees things as they
     are, not as they ought to be. The Scythians used to pluck
     out a cynic's eyes to improve his vision. *Ib.*

21   An ingenious instrument known as a barometer tells us what
     kind of weather we are having. *Ib.*

22   A prudent man is one who believes half of what he sees, a
     quarter of what he reads, and ten per cent of what he
     hears. *Ib.*

23   Clairvoyant: a person who has the power of seeing what is
     invisible to the patron – namely, that he is a blockhead. *Ib.*

24   To consult is to seek another person's approval of a course
     already decided on. *Ib.*

25 Don't steal; thou'lt never thus compete
Successfully in business. Cheat. *Ib.*

26 An elector is a person who enjoys the sacred privilege of
voting for the man of another man's choice. *Ib.*

27 Duty is that which sternly impels us in the direction of profit,
along the lines of desire. *Ib.*

28 The ancient philosophies were of two kinds – *exoteric*, those
which philosophers themselves could partly understand,
and *esoteric*, those that nobody could understand. *Ib.*

29 A fork is an instrument used chiefly for the purpose of
putting dead animals into the mouth. *Ib.*

30 A heathen is a benighted creature who has the folly to
worship something that he can see and feel. *Ib.*

31 Idiot: a member of a large and powerful tribe whose
influence on human affairs has always been dominant. *Ib.*

32 In matrimony a similarity of tastes, particularly the taste for
domination, is known as incompatibility. *Ib.*

33 Loquacity is a disorder which renders the sufferer unable to
curb his tongue when you wish to talk. *Ib.*

34 Love: a temporary insanity curable by marriage. *Ib.*

35 Money is a blessing that is of no advantage to us except when
we part with it. *Ib.*

36 Man's chief occupation is extermination of other animals
and his own species, which, however, multiplies with such
rapidity as to infest the whole habitable earth – and
Canada. *Ib.*

37 Philosophy is a route of many roads leading from nowhere to
nothing. *Ib.*

38 When we call a thing self-evident we mean it is evident to
ourselves but to nobody else.

39   In diplomacy an ultimatum is the last demand before resorting to concessions. *Ib.*

40   What is worth doing is worth the trouble of asking somebody to do it. *Ib.*

41   Railroads. The chief of many mechanical devices enabling us to get away from where we are to where we are no better off. *Ib.*

42   (On weather forecasts)

Once I dipt into the future far as any eye could see,
And I saw the Chief Forecaster, dead as anyone can be –
Dead and damned and shut in Hades as a liar from his
   birth,
With a record of unreason seldom paralleled on earth. *Ib.*

GEORGE A. BIRMINGHAM

James Owen Hannay (1865–1950), an Irish clergyman educated at Haileybury and Dublin, wrote a number of humorous novels set in Ireland, under the pen-name George Birmingham. Many of them feature either an eccentric and persuasive Irish clergyman or an artful Irish doctor.

1   Subscribers to *The Times* have been educated into an unworthy kind of scepticism. *General John Regan*

2   If a man cannot go to sleep over a back number of a weekly paper there is no use his trying to go to sleep at all. *Ib.*

3   If he happened to be selling an archangel a pair of wings it would turn out afterwards that the feathers were dropping out. *Ib.*

4   Horse dealing is a thing apart...Honesty, in the common sense of the word, does not enter into it. *Ib.*

5 "Aren't you a newspaper editor?...Don't you spend your whole life writing on subjects that you know nothing about?" *Ib.*

6 The things that are told about the boyhood of great men are all invented. Nobody expects them to be true. *Ib.*

7 Few things are more attractive to tourists than ruins. *Ib.*

8 The Connaught farmer is like the rest of the human race in his dislike of being asked to subscribe to anything. *Ib.*

9 He was a practised orator and could make a very small amount of information go a long way. *Ib.*

10 Nothing is more gratifying to the prophet of evil than the fulfilment of his own prediction. *Ib.*

11 Tact is simply a delicate form of lying. *Ib.*

12 As yachtsmen often do, he began the day by tapping the barometer. *Spanish Gold.*

13 No one can rise otherwise than awkwardly out of the depths of a hammock-chair. *Ib.*

14 A statement isn't a lie if it proves itself in actual practice to be useful. *Ib.*

15 Did you ever notice that a woman, when she gets her blood up, is twice as reckless as a man? *Ib.*

16 Like everyone else in the West of Ireland, cleric or layman, Meldon had a keen taste for making money out of a stranger. *Ib.*

17 It wouldn't be the slightest use telling the literal truth. People wouldn't believe you. *Ib.*

18 The law, especially in Ireland, is a curious thing. *The Simpkins Plot*

19 Miss King was accustomed to talk about her art. Literary people who might have known better, and critics who certainly did know better, encouraged her. *Ib.*

20   When people start talking about art, it simply means that they are dead to all sense of morality. *Ib.*

21   Mr Simpkins had a busy and vigorous mind of a sort not uncommon among incompetent people. *Ib.*

22   Galileo hit upon the fact that the earth goes round the sun, and it struck him as immensely important. He gassed on about it until everybody got so tired of the subject that the authorities had to put him in prison and keep him there until he said it wasn't true. *Ib.*

23   We'd all be doing exactly the same things we are doing today if Galileo had never made his beastly telescope. *Ib.*

24   "You can rear a child," said the doctor, "on pretty near anything, so long as you give it enough of whatever you do give it." *Ib.*

25   "There is one appeal that is never made in vain to Englishmen, and that is the appeal to duty. Wasn't that the meaning of the signal Nelson hoisted just before he asked Hardy to kiss him. And what did Hardy do? Kissed him at once, though he can't possibly have liked it." *Ib.*

26   It's a curious thing that when a man is really satisfied with himself he gets to look like a sheep. *Ib.*

BASIL BOOTHROYD

John Basil Boothroyd (1910–88) began his career in a bank, but then began writing humorous articles for *Punch*, of which he later became assistant editor (1952–70). He was also an accomplished broadcaster and speaker. Prince Philip chose him as his biographer, *Philip* (1971).

1   The older you get in China, the more you're revered and respected and made a fuss of...whereas in the West we're

more inclined to concentrate on getting the old folks out of our hair and into a nice little Eventide Home. *Boothroyd at Bay*

2 In my own family circle everyone says, "Don't let your father mend it, he'll only make it worse". *Ib.*

3 Instant cooking is a must (for husbands). Wives may get a kick out of slaving all morning over a hot stove: husbands want something you can pour water on and it's a meal. *Ib.*

4 Feed the birds. But don't expect any gratitude. All you'll get in return is those decorations all over the car, mostly down in the headlight crannies where you can't get at them *Ib.*

5 Horses are rather nice, silly, harmless creatures if only they were left to mind their own business...But all these men and women have to be for ever clambering up on top of them in special costume, and making them jump over things. *Ib.*

6 The most annoying guide for my money is the chap...who not only gives you a microphone commentary on places of interest, but drives the coach with the other hand. *Ib.*

7 I suppose some people like to know that you could get sixteen and a half London buses into the dome of St Paul's Cathedral, but it isn't really what Sir Christopher Wren had in mind. *Ib.*

8 Throwing a couple of dice...is a trick I've never mastered, I don't know why. I always get one of them up my sleeve, or under the table. Sometimes I lose one altogether, and wreck the game. *Ib.*

9 Christmas comes but once a year – I think that's generally established. *Ib.*

10 Each September the shops start putting their bits of plastic holly in the windows, and sticking labels saying "Useful Gift" on everything from workmen's boots to bicycle pumps. *Ib.*

11 Watch out for Blackberryitis. Scientists say that one of the early symptoms is a dark discolouration all round the mouth and chin. *Ib.*

12 There's nothing worse than turning up to auction a cake and finding you're down to make a thirty-minute speech. Unless it's turning up with a thirty-minute speech and finding you're only down to auction a cake. *Accustomed As I Am*

13 It's no joke having to talk to an audience composed of children and grown-ups. If you say anything complicated the grown-ups won't understand it. *Ib.*

14 It was a hotel whose character could be deduced from its wardrobe. One door wouldn't stay open and the other wouldn't stay shut. *Ib.*

15 The time-honoured question, can you hear at the back...always seems to me a pretty silly question, because if you can't hear at the back you can't hear me asking you if you can hear at the back. *Ib.*

16 The whole business of pet keeping is difficult. Pets mean vets. Also kennels, baskets, harnesses, rubber balls, animal crockery, brushes and combs, and the re-french polishing of gnawed TV table-legs. *The Whole Thing's Laughable*

17 It is well known that pocket contents expand to fill all pockets available. *Ib.*

18 We wrote off (to a famous mail-order house) for a dozen yards of Regency stripe curtain damask, and in response to our valued order received two candlewick bedspreads. *Ib.*

19 I keep all my drinks at the bottom of the sideboard, and I can't get at them till I've asked the fattest guest to get out of the armchair I've just put him in. *To My Embarrassment*

20 You don't expect to take a wife shopping with you and just come out with what you went in for. *Let's Stay Married*

21   Every man expects his marriage to be different, and it's
      naturally a shock to find it's like everybody else's. *Ib.*

VICTOR BORGE

Victor Borge (1909–), is a Danish musician who became a
popular and amusing entertainer at the piano. *My Favourite
Intervals* (1974) contains accounts of several notable composers
and operas, written in lively style.

1   Handel wrote a lovely Funeral Ode for Queen Caroline, but
      she didn't live to appreciate it. *My Favourite Intervals*

2   Mozart once proposed to Marie Antoinette. (They were seven
      years old at the time, so the romance never really
      amounted to much.) *Ib.*

3   Since he was a little on the lazy side, Mozart didn't start
      writing operas until he was twelve. *Ib.*

4   Rossini used to wear two or three wigs, one on top of the
      other, so he wouldn't have to bother taking the bottom
      one off. *Ib.*

5   On his 70th birthday Rossini's friends collected twenty
      thousand francs to erect a monument. "What a waste of
      money," the composer groaned. "Give me the cash, and
      I'll stand on the pedestal myself!"

6   Estelle was tall, shapely, beautiful, had a dazzling smile, and
      wore pink boots. Berlioz had never seen pink boots
      before, so he fell madly in love with her. *Ib.*

7   Harriet turned him down at first, but...Berlioz swallowed some
      poison right in front of her to prove that his intentions
      were honourable. *Ib.*

8   Everything went right for Bizet until the day he was born. *Ib.*

9   He was the kind of fellow who stayed up nights to finish an
      opera by the deadline, only to find out afterwards that the
      production had been postponed for a year. *Ib.*

10   At the University of Leipzig...Wagner majored in gambling, duelling, drinking, and making love. When he learned that he was supposed to attend classes too, he quit. *Ib.*

NEIL BOYD

Peter de Rosa, formerly a Roman Catholic priest, became a BBC producer. He has written several semi-humorous books under the name Neil Boyd, including *Bless Me, Father* (1979) and *Bless Me Again, Father* (1981). The former was also a London TV series.

1   Women are almost as difficult to comprehend as nuns. *Bless Me, Father*

2   Run the hot water for a minute or two. It comes eventually if you pray hard to St Anthony. *Ib.*

3   Pray mightily for the success of our Bazaar. Sometimes the Lord is hard of hearing. *Ib.*

4   "All priests go to confession every fortnight."
     "Nuns too?"
     "Every eight days."
     "Good gracious me! What *do* they get up to, locked in behind them high walls?" *Ib.*

5   Giorgio made it sound as if the Church's system of indulgences was a protection racket invented by the Mafia. *Ib.*

6   No Sicilian does what he is expected to do, otherwise they'd never be able to trust each other. *Ib.*

7   It was a bit like shaking hands with a tired sausage. *Ib.*

8   An Irishman only feels like everyone else when he's different. *Bless Me Again, Father.*

9   When Father Duddleswell...asked my honest opinion of anything I had to watch my step. *Ib.*

10   Every evening sermon was practically a guided tour of the nether regions. *Ib.*

11   If ever a man opens a car door for a woman, it's because he has either a new woman or a new car. *Ib.*

12   Her description of him as having a bay-window belly and a French-loaf sort of face was exact. *Ib.*

13   I'm delighted to find after all these years [my tennis] has not deteriorated. It's just as bad as before. *Ib.*

14   Teetotalism is against nature. Like a bishop waiting at a bus stop or a hen laying eggs at midnight. *Ib.*

WILLIAM BOYD

William Boyd (1952–), born in Ghana and educated at Gordonstoun and Oxford, has been book reviewer, TV critic, and lecturer in English at St Hilda's College, Oxford. His first novel, *A Good Man in Africa* (1981), won the Whitbread and Maugham awards.

1   Morgan detested the sight of the man's little Welsh knees peeking out between the hem of his shorts and the top of his socks like two bald, wrinkled babies' heads. *A Good Man in Africa*

2   Her nose was long and thin and turned up sharply at the end like a ski-jump. *Ib.*

3   These occasions had the same effect on him as weddings: they were awash with false sincerity, hypocrisy, and a dreadful backslapping bonhomie. *Ib.*

4   [It was] the final insult from a bourgeois, ex-public school God. *Ib.*

5   Set in undulating tropical rain forest, from the air the town resembled nothing so much as a giant pool of crapulous vomit on somebody's expansive unknown lawn. *Ib.*

6   Morgan never thought of her as Chloe, and only seldom as
     Mrs Fanshawe. Usually the kindest epithets were Fat Bitch,
     or the Old Bag. *Ib.*

7   She had a chest like an opera singer, a single wedge of heavily
     trussed and boned undergarmentry from which the rest of
     her body tapered gradually. *Ib.*

8   "Goodness me," Celia said. "What on earth did you do to
     offend her?"
     "God knows," Morgan said uncomfortably. "Something
     to do with being alive, I think." *Ib.*

9   One day Morgan had come across a lunatic, wearing a filthy
     loin cloth... Spontaneously he had thrust a pound note
     into his calloused hand. The madman turned his yellow
     eyes on him for a brief moment before stuffing the note
     into his wide moist mouth where he chewed it up with
     salivating relish. *Ib.*

10   A haggard country-and-western chanteuse... had a repertoire
     consisting solely of... suicide, abortion, adultery, desertion,
     mental and physical cruelty, alcoholism, and terminal
     illness. *Stars and Bars*

11   His eyes throbbed painfully, as if they had been removed
     from their sockets, bounced up and down on the floor,
     and reinserted. *Ib.*

12   He saw the international language of sexual gesticulation
     being covertly practised as if they were a gathering of
     randy deaf-mutes. *On the Yankee Station.*

13   You write fiction and what are you doing? You're telling lies.
     Ib.

MALCOLM BRADBURY

Malcolm Bradbury (1932–), English academic, novelist, and
critic, was educated at University College, Leicester, Queen

Mary College, London, in the USA and Manchester. He has
been a lecturer at the universities of Birmingham and East
Anglia. His novels include *Eating People is Wrong* (1954), *The
History Man* (1975) and *Rates of Exchange* (1983).

1   The room is a simple rectangle, with unpainted breeze-block
    walls, described in the architectural journals as proof of
    the architect's honesty. *The History Man*

2   The new buildings all had toilets with strange modern symbols
    of man and woman on them, virtually indistinguishable. *Ib.*

3   Students no longer look like an intellectual élite; indeed, what
    they resemble this autumn is rather the winter retreat of
    Napoleon's army from Moscow. *Ib.*

4   There are two studies...Howard's downstairs, where he writes
    books, and Barbara's upstairs, where she means to. *Ib.*

5   The secretaries...are at their first serious duty of the day,
    watering the potted plants. *Ib.*

6   I've noticed your hostility towards him...I ought to have
    guessed you were friends. *Ib.*

7   Marriage is the most advanced form of warfare in the modern
    world. *Ib.*

8   Treece was uneasily aware that his tone was that of a man who
    had been reading from Dr Spock's book on baby care.
    Eating People is Wrong

9   "I suppose you know a lot of writers," she said. "I know
    some," said Treece, "but I think I prefer people." *Ib.*

10 Poor man, he has tried to show us all that foreigners aren't
    funny, but they are. *Ib.*

11 In the lounge of the hotel were huge leather armchairs that
    looked like cows. *Ib.*

12 If I had any children, I'd lock them up in a cage until they
    could prove that they were moral creatures...Man is a
    moral animal, and children aren't. *Ib.*

13 The church she attended made a practice of public confession, so that...you not only had the pleasure of *doing* the sin, but the second, more sophisticated, pleasure of talking about it afterwards. *Ib.*

14 He carries his soul around in a paper bag as if he'd just bought it at Marks and Spencer's. *Ib.*

15 He had written two well-known novels, and the royalties were scarcely enough, as he put it, to keep him in condoms. *Ib.*

16 Life in hospital was so arduous that it was a pity it had to happen to sick people; at least they should let them go home, now and then, for a rest. *Ib.*

17 As with most modern living, there were snags; as Rita sometimes complained, the only place you were really entitled to hang out your washing was in your car. *Who Do You Think You Are?*

18 I signed and notarized a document in which I promised not to overthrow the American government by force – a promise I have carefully kept to this day. *Stepping Westward*

19 He had long held to one of the most fundamental of all literary convictions, that the world owed him a living. *Ib.*

20 It was known, even to him, that he was a married man. *Ib.*

21 He always felt that one day she would pick him up, shove him in her handbag, and click the fastening to. *Ib.*

22 Elaine always said "your writing" as other wives of generous character might have said "your drinking", and probably in her mind the two peccadilloes were of pretty much the same order. *Ib.*

BERTOLT BRECHT

Bertolt Brecht (1898–1956), influential German Marxist dramatist, amongst whose numerous plays were *The Threepenny Opera* (1928) and *The Caucasian Chalk Circle* (1948).

1   I don't trust him. We're friends. *Mother Courage*

2   "We're in God's hands now."
    "I hope we're not as desperate as that." *Ib.*

3   As a grown man, you should know better than to go around
    advising people. *Ib.*

4   What happens to the hole when the cheese is gone? *Ib.*

5   Don't tell me peace has broken out. *Ib.*

6   Fearful is the seductive power of goodness. *The Caucasian
    Chalk Circle*

7   I love the people...It's only that their smell brings on my
    migraine. *Ib.*

8   Life is short and so is money. *The Threepenny Opera*

CARYL BRAHMS & NED SHERRIN

Caryl Brahms (1901–82), born Doris Abrahams, journalist,
ballet critic, script writer, and novelist, wrote her novels in
collaboration with either S. J. Simon or Ned Sherrin. *Ooh
La-La!* (1973) is based on the French farces of Georges Feydeau.
Ned Sherrin (1931–) TV producer who made his name
directing *That Was the Week That Was* (1963), has also produced
several films, e.g. *Virgin Soldiers* (1969).

1   Give her the sack! That'll teach her to wake me up when I've
    left instructions for her to wake me up! *Ooh! La-La!*

2   Lucky Australians! They can go on sleeping for another seven
    hours and still pass as early risers. *Ib.*

3   He smiled his irresistible smile, but Dora found it highly
    resistible. *Ib.*

4   It must be someone collecting for charity. Respectable women
    never call on the family for any other reason. *Ib.*

5   "When is your birthday?"
     "May 22nd."
     "The same as last year?" *Ib.*

6   "Cor!" If ever a throatful of sound could be said to dig
     someone in the ribs, it was this one. *Ib.*

7   An operation is never a waste of time. There is always
     something to be gained from it, even if it is only the fee. *Ib.*

8   I've been discovered more times than America! *Ib.*

9   He must study. Unfortunately he has no inclination for it. It
     means he'll have to learn to write. *Ib.*

10   Singers worth their while must watch it;
     Always count your dotted crotchet.
     Rappel 1910

11   Choristers you must be braver
     With your demi-semi-quaver. *Ib.*

12   Outside the band was playing "Pomp and Circumstance" to
     keep the people quiet or else to drown the noise they were
     making. *Ib.*

13   The King [Edward VII] had a quick look at the Royal
     Academy pictures and privately thanked his Maker that he
     had to be in Sandringham that week-end and wouldn't
     have to listen to the speeches at the banquet. *Ib.*

14   They had voices like the rattle of an empty coal-scuttle. *Ib.*

CARYL BRAHMS & S.J. SIMON

S. J. Simon (d. 1948), a Russian émigré and professional bridge
player, collaborated with Caryl Brahms in several novels, such
as *A Bullet in the Ballet* (1937), and *No Bed for Bacon* (1941).

1   "Managing monarchs," Burghley began, "is like forecasting the weather." *No Bed For Bacon*

2   "Not a rag to wear," rasped Elizabeth. She was standing in front of a great wardrobe containing the ample folds of three hundred and sixty dresses. *Ib.*

3   "With the Queen" (said Drake) "one must speak first of the profits and only then of the cost." *Ib.*

4   "The trouble with your plays, Will," said old man Burbage, "is that you leave far too many characters alive at the end." *Ib.*

5   "By the way, Will," Bacon said, "I almost forgot. When you've a moment to spare, you might polish up this essay..." *Ib.*

6   Since it is probable that any book flying a bullet in its title is going to produce a corpse sooner or later – here it is. *A Bullet in the Ballet* (opening sentence)

7   His private secretary could be relied on to bustle in briskly and completely misunderstand what was wanted of him. *Envoy on Excursion*

8   The sun, heavy-eyed from lack of sleep, owing to the system of a staggered summer time, stumbled into the heavens, and with a heavy sigh set about its duties. *Ib.*

9   This was the dress rehearsal. Only naturally the dresses had not arrived. *Ib.*

10   In all his experience no one had yet called him a man of the world without trying to put something across him immediately afterwards. *Ib.*

11   It is only the decadent who know how to live well. *Ib.*

12   In his study the miser opened his safe, pulled out a bag of gold, and practised trickling it through his fingers. He was getting better at it. *Ib.*

13   To the ordinary train passenger the trek to nourishment is

made up of a fine collection of bruises, a recurring vista of disappointment, and an ecstasy of "Pardons". *Ib.*

14   "Vot" asked George I courteously, "is the difference between a public nuisance and a public convenience?" *No Nightingales*

HAROLD BRIGHOUSE

Harold Brighouse (1882–1958) was born and educated in Manchester, and was on the staff of the *Manchester Guardian*. He wrote novels and numerous plays, chiefly Northern comedies, the most enduring being *Hobson's Choice* (1916).

1   Breakfast? After a Mason's meeting last night! *Hobson's Choice*

2   I hate bumptiousness like I hate a lawyer. *Ib.*

3   You're pretty, but you can lie like a gas-meter. *Ib.*

4   Beware of roaring at women, Henry. It's like trying to defeat an army by banging a drum. *Ib.*

5   It's a thing I've noticed about wenches. Get one wedding in a family, and it goes through the lot like measles. *Ib.*

6   I suppose lawyers are like doctors. They've a secret language of their own. If you get a letter from one lawyer, you've got to take it to another to get it read. *Ib.*

7   Think of that! To have your name in the *Guardian*! It's very near worth while to be ruined for the pleasure of reading about yourself in a printed paper! *Ib.*

8   Other people's troubles is mostly what folks read the paper for, and it's twice the pleasure when it's the trouble of a man they know. *Ib.*

9   I've thrown my razor through the window. Had to, or I'd have cut my throat. *Ib.*

10   She's not the sort that wants the truth wrapped round with a feather-bed for fear it hits her hard. *Ib.*

ART BUCHWALD

Art Buchwald (1923–), American journalist and humorist, is a columnist for the *New York Herald Tribune*. His numerous books include *I Chose Caviar* (1957), *How Much Is That In Dollars?* (1962), and *I Never Danced at the White House* (1973). His humour is often ironical.

1   If I call a character Chuck or Jack, my readers are going to expect him to punch somebody in the nose, but if I call him Harry or Fred or Louie, the reader is going to expect him to *be* punched in the nose. *I Never Danced in the White House*

2   Too much time, money, and advertising have gone into Christmas to have a small minority spoil it by going to church...We're against churches remaining open on the one day of the year that is sacred to our gross national product. *Ib.*

3   "Dad, you have to admit that wearing a tie, and a jacket that matches the pants, is a pretty funny idea." *Ib.*

4   Recently two Israeli researchers announced that they had been able to cure nose colds by chilling the big toes of patients' feet. *Ib.*

5   Any man who is married can appreciate why we have named our hurricanes after women. *Ib.*

6   When an editor asks one fiction writer to review another writer's new book, he is signing the latter's death warrant. *Ib.*

7   "We can lick the problem of the high cost of food if we make

one more slight sacrifice. I am asking every person in the nation...to stop eating." *Ib.*

8   "Dr Peters said it was one of the best operations he had ever seen." "So it was, except that you cut off the wrong leg." *Ib.*

9   "Your administration is involved in the obstruction of justice, the bribing of witnesses, the forging of papers, wire-tapping, perjury, and using the mails to defraud." "Good God, nobody's perfect!" *Ib.*

10 When I arrived in Paris fourteen years ago I had only one piece of luggage. I left with 34 pieces of luggage. I still had only one piece of luggage; my wife's clothes accounted for the others. *I Chose Capitol Punishment*

11 The perfect husband is one who can see his wife's faults, correct them if they need correcting, and show her what she is doing wrong. *Ib.*

12 Tax reform is when you take taxes off things that have been taxed in the past and put taxes on things that haven't been taxed before. *Ib.*

13 Every time I tune in to a commercial, I discover that it's interrupted by a programme. *Ib.*

14 In Paris...there are so many crises going on that half the time you would never know you were in one. *Ib.*

15 All my friends in Paris seemed very happy when I was leaving. To them they were not losing a friend but gaining an apartment. *Ib.*

16 Americans have been brought up to believe that everyone loves them for themselves. *Ib.*

17 Americans accept that a person can be an alcoholic, a dope fiend, a wife beater, and even a newspaperman, but if he doesn't drive there's something wrong with him. *How Much Is That In Dollars?*

18   It's easier to find a travelling companion than it is to get rid of one. *Vogue (1954)*

ANTHONY BURGESS

John Anthony Burgess Wilson (1917–), British novelist and critic, was born and educated in Manchester, and has been a teacher and lecturer. His books include *A Clockwork Orange* (1962) and *Inside Mr Enderby* (1966).

1   Doctors leave it to Nature to cure in her own time, but they take the credit. *Nothing Like the Sun*

2   There is a lot to be said for not being known to the readers of the *Daily Mirror. Inside Mr Enderby*

3   Laugh and the world laughs with you; snore and you sleep alone. *Ib.*

4   He said it was artificial respiration, but now I find I am to have his child. *Ib.*

5   Rome's just a city like anywhere else. *Ib.*

6   Would you try...a poem every week? Preferably set in the form of prose, so as not to offend anyone. *Ib.*

7   The best thing to do, when you've got a dead body and it's your husband's on the kitchen floor, and you don't know what to do about it, is to make yourself a good strong cup of tea. *One Hand Clapping*

8   You've no idea how pleasant it is not to have any future. It's like having a totally efficient contraceptive. *Honey for the Bears*

9   There is usually something wrong with writers the young like. *Playboy*

10   The US presidency is a Tudor monarchy plus telephones.

SAMUEL BUTLER

Samuel Butler (1835–1902), British writer, educated at
Shrewsbury and Cambridge, was the grandson of a famous
headmaster and son of a clergyman. His keen satirical humour
is shown in his novels *Erewhon* (1872), *The Way of All Flesh*
(1903) and in his *Note-Books* (1912).

1   It has been said that although God cannot alter the past,
    historians can. *Erewhon*

2   A man's friendships, like his will, are invalidated by his
    marriage. *The Way of All Flesh*

3   The advantage of doing one's praising for oneself is that one
    can lay it on so thick and exactly in the right places. *Ib.*

4   One reason why clergymen's households are generally
    unhappy is because the clergyman is so much at home. *Ib.*

5   A man is a fool to remember anything that happened more
    than a week ago unless it was pleasant. *Ib.*

6   It was perhaps as well that our prayers were seldom marked by
    any very encouraging degree of response. *Ib.*

7   He had the harmlessness of the serpent and the wisdom of the
    dove. *Ib.*

8   Nice people either never knew any Latin and Greek or forgot
    what they had learned as soon as they could. *Ib.*

9   The greater part of every family is always odious. If there are
    one or two good ones in a very large family it is as much as
    can be expected. *Ib.*

10 The best liar is he who makes the smallest amount of lying go
    the longest way. *Ib.*

11 It is far safer to know too little than too much. *Ib.*

12 We have all come short of the glory of making ourselves as comfortable as we easily might have done. *Ib.*

13 To himself everyone is an immortal; he may know that he is going to die, but he can never know that he is dead. *Note-Books*

14 Genius has been described as an extreme capacity for taking trouble...It might more fitly be described as a supreme capacity for getting its possessors into trouble. *Ib.*

15 It does not matter what a man hates as long as he hates something. *Ib.*

16 To live is like to love – all reason is against it, and all healthy instinct is for it. *Ib.*

17 Life is the art of drawing sufficient conclusions from insufficient premises. *Ib.*

18 All animals except man know that the principal business of life is to enjoy it. *Ib.*

19 God is love, I daresay. But what a mischievous devil Love is. *Ib.*

20 "Man wants but little here below" but likes that little good – and not too long in coming. *Ib.*

21 Man is the only animal that can remain on friendly terms with the victims he intends to eat. *Ib.*

22 Some men love Truth so much that they seem to be in continual fear lest she should catch a cold through over-exposure. *Ib.*

23 I do not mind lying, but I hate inaccuracy. *Ib.*

24 Justice is being allowed to do whatever I like. Injustice is whatever prevents my doing it. *Ib.*

25 The foundations of morality are like all other foundations; if you dig too much, the superstructure will come tumbling down. *Ib.*

26 Most of those who call themselves artists are really picture

dealers, only they make the pictures themselves. *Ib.*

27 Parents are the last people on earth who ought to have children. *Ib.*

28 When you have told anyone you have left him a legacy the only decent thing to do is to die at once. *Ib.*

29 Cannibalism is moral in a cannibal country.

30 The Ancient Mariner would not have taken so well if it had been called The Old Sailor.

LORD BYRON

George Gordon Noel Byron (1788–1824), poet, educated at Harrow and Cambridge, wrote poetry from an early age. He composed several poetic dramas, e.g. *Manfred* (1817), but his most enduring work, apart from short lyrics, is his fluent narrative satire *Don Juan* (1819–24).

1   I like the weather when it is not rainy,
       That is, I like two months of every year.
    Beppo

2   For most men (till by losing rendered sager)
    Will back their own opinions with a wager. *Ib.*

3   I've half a mind to tumble down to prose,
    But verse is more in fashion – so here goes. *Ib.*

4   One hates an author that's *all author. Ib.*

5   Our first parents never learn'd to kiss
       Till they were exiled from their earlier bowers,
    Where all was peace, and innocence, and bliss,
       (I wonder how they got through the twelve hours).
    Don Juan

6   'Tis pity learned virgins ever wed...
    But – Oh! ye lords of ladies intellectual,
    Inform us truly, have they not hen-peck'd you all? *Ib.*

7   What men call gallantry, and the gods adultery,
    Is much more common when the climate's sultry. *Ib.*

8   Coleridge, too, has lately taken wing...
    Explaining metaphysics to the nation –
    I wish he would explain his Explanation. *Ib.*

9   Christians have burn'd each other, quite persuaded
    That all the Apostles would have done as they did. *Ib.*

10 Pleasure's a sin, and sometimes sin's a pleasure. *Ib.*

11 There's nought, no doubt, so much the spirit calms
    As rum and true religion. *Ib.*

12 Let us have wine and women, mirth and laughter,
    Sermons and soda-water the day after. *Ib.*

13 Dreading that climax of all human ills,
    The inflammation of his weekly bills. *Ib.*

14 He was the mildest manner'd man
    That ever scuttled ship or cut a throat. *Ib.*

15 As a boy, I thought myself a clever fellow,
    And wished that others held the same opinion. *Ib.*

16 That all-softening, overpowering knell,
    The tocsin of the soul – the dinner bell. *Ib.*

17 A lady of "uncertain age", which means
    Certainly aged. *Ib.*

18 Society is now one polished horde,
    Formed of two mighty tribes, the *Bores* and *Bored*. *Ib.*

19 Thus in the East they are extremely strict,
    And wedlock and a padlock mean the same. *Ib.*

20 There is a tide in the affairs of women
    Which, taken at the flood, leads – God knows where. *Ib.*

21   "Kiss" rhymes to "bliss" in fact as well as verse –
     I wish it never led to something worse. *Ib.*

22   St Peter sat by the celestial gate:
         His keys were rusty and the lock was dull,
     So little trouble had been given of late;
         Not that the place by any means was full...
         The devils had taken a longer, stronger pull.
     The Vision of Judgement

23   The angels all were singing out of tune,
         And hoarse with having little else to do. *Ib.*

24   (On George III).

     A better farmer ne'er brushed dew from lawn,
         A worse king never left a realm undone. *Ib.*

25   A man must serve his time to every trade
     Save censure – critics all are ready made.
     English Bards and Scotch Reviewers

C.S. CALVERLEY

Charles Stuart Calverley (1831–1884) was educated at Harrow, Oxford, and Cambridge, where he later became a Fellow. He is best remembered for his clever humorous poems and parodies, *Verses and Translations* (1862) and *Fly Leaves* (1886).

1   That mild, luxurious
     And artful beverage, Beer. How the digestion
     Ever got on without it, is a startling question.
     Verses and Translations

2   What is coffee but a noxious berry
         Born to keep used-up Londoners awake? *Ib.*

3   Doctors have said it:
     How those who use fusees

All grow by slow degrees
Brainless as chimpanzees,
   Meagre as lizards;
Go mad, and beat their wives,
Plunge (after shocking lives)
Razors and carving-knives
   Into their gizzards.
Ib. (Ode to Tobacco) A fusee is a large-headed match for lighting cigarettes, etc. in a wind.

4   All the theology we knew
       Was that we musn't play on Sunday. *Ib.*

5   Bed at Ostend at 5 a.m.
       Breakfast at 6, and train 6.30,
    Tickets to Konigswinter (mem.
       The seats unutterably dirty).
    Ib. (Dover to Munich)

6   By many a tidy little town,
       Where tidy little Fraus sit knitting;
    (The men's pursuits are, lying down,
       Smoking perennial pipes, and spitting).

7   (The cook's kitchen)

    Never durst the missis enter here until I've said
       "Come in":
    If I saw the master peeping, I'd catch up the
       rolling-pin. *Ib.*

8   "Under the trees!" Who but agrees
    That there is magic in words such as these?
    Lads and "fair shes" (that is Byron, and he's
    An authority) lie very much at their ease...
    Talking of all things, from earthquakes to fleas.
    Fly Leaves

9   I've read in many a novel that unless they've
       souls that grovel

Folks *prefer* in fact a hovel to your dreary
marble halls. *Ib.*

PATRICK CAMPBELL

Patrick Campbell (Lord Glenavy) (1913–80), journalist and TV
personality, was educated at Rossall and Oxford. He wrote a
humorous column for various papers, but is perhaps best
remembered for his TV appearances (e.g. *Call My Bluff*).

1   Experts used to study birds and bees and ants. Now they study
motorists. *All Ways on Sundays*

2   The only rewarding moments to be found in the grey wastes of television interviews are when the destined victim turns upon his persecutors and has them for dinner. *All Ways on Sundays*

3   What will not come to pass in my lifetime, as sure as misery, is a cure for the common cold. *Ib.*

4   Public houses – and they are increasing in number – where semi-professional caterwauling is provided on purpose by the management. *Ib.*

5   I am a writer, an observer of and commentator upon the human scene, and therefore unfortunately cut off from playing any active part in the productive life of the nation. *Ib.*

6   The British motorist likes to fight, to give no quarter, to arrive at his destination in the certain knowledge that he has given to all other road users as good as, if not better than, he got. *Ib.*

7   I put on the white alpaca jacket and the openwork shoes. I looked like the driver of a coach on an outing to Folkestone on August Bank Holiday. *35 Years On the Job*

8   There is no such thing as getting anywhere by aeroplane in a couple of hours. Strikes, civil unrest, and faulty radio beacons get in the way. *Ib.*

9   When we left the restaurant at about four o'clock I didn't immediately recognize the fixed grin and the glittering, glassy eye that met me in a mirror. *Ib.*

10   (In New York)

     It would be absolutely magical if we could alleviate our hunger with something that tasted of food. *Ib.*

11   Everything in France shuts from midday until 2.30 p.m. *Ib.*

12   The only people I've ever given working orders to have been occasional charwomen, and mostly I've told them not to bother, that I'd do it myself. *My Life and Easy Times*

13   These Rotary lunches were the only kind of straight
      reporting I was ever able to do, thanks to my failure to
      learn shorthand. I am deeply indebted to my lack of it. It
      probably saved me from a lifetime of hard work. *Ib.*

IAN CARMICHAEL

Ian Carmichael (1920–) was born in Yorkshire and educated
at Bromsgrove School and RADA. He began as a light
comedian in Herbert Farjeon revues, but after the war
developed his career in various plays, e.g. *The Tunnel of Love*
(1959), in films, e.g. *Brothers in Law* (1957) and on TV, e.g. *The
World of Wooster* (1965).

1   At soccer I played in goal, and during the term I held that
      responsible position...I let in more goals than most people
      have had the proverbial hot suppers. *Will the Real Ian
      Carmichael...*

2   (Aids to memory in a school play.)
      Pages from the script were removed and secreted all over the
      set – behind an ornament, on the mantelpiece, flat on a
      desk, even inside a performer's hat. *Ib.*

3   The drum kit included a bass drum, which Mr Moses
      pronounced as if it were a bottle of beer. *Ib.*

4   The teenage gregarious male, I have come to the conclusion,
      can be a very unpleasant person indeed. *Ib.*

5   We were now Officer Cadets, and so the stream of N.C.O.
      invective was always followed by the word "Sir". *Ib.*

6   I look back with pride at having passed through the Royal
      Military College...and to think that it took an evil,
      paranoic, First World War Austrian corporal and
      peacetime housepainter to get me there! *Ib.*

7   When you get rain and tanks together you also get mud. *Ib.*

8   I had deliberately chosen the demob suit that I considered
     would be the most useful for playing – with the greatest
     respect to their esteemed callings – either impecunious
     City clerks or third grade Civil Servants.

9   *New Faces* was the show in which that celebrated nightingale
     started singing in Berkeley Square, and from which,
     regardless of traffic jams and petrol fumes, it seems to
     have been warbling ever since. *Ib.*

10   The first thing he did was to lock all the doors of the
     limousine on the inside. When I asked why, I was
     informed that it was always the safest way to travel in New
     York. *Ib.*

LEWIS CARROLL

Charles Lutwidge Dodgson (1832–1898), clergyman and
mathematician, wrote, in addition to his two famous *Alice*
books, clever nonsense poems, such as *The Hunting of The Snark*
(1876).

1   If you drink much from a bottle marked "poison" it is almost
     sure to disagree with you. *Alice in Wonderland*

2   Everything's got a moral if only you can find it. *Ib.*

3   We called him Tortoise because he taught us. *Ib.*

4   I only took the regular course...the different branches of
     Arithmetic – Ambition, Distraction, Uglification, and
     Derision. *Ib.*

5   "That's the reason they're called lessons," the Gryphon
     remarked: "because they lessen from day to day." *Ib.*

6   The further off from England the nearer is to France –
     Then turn not pale, beloved snail, but come and join the
     dance. *Ib.*

7   The jurors are putting down their names for fear they should forget them before the end of the trial. *Ib.*

8   "Write that down," the King said to the jury, and the jury eagerly wrote down all three dates on their slates, and then added them up, and reduced the answer to shillings and pence. *Ib.*

9   "Where shall I begin, please, your Majesty?" he asked. "Begin at the beginning," the King said gravely, "and go on till you come to the end: then stop." *Ib.*

10   Curtsy while you're thinking what to say. It saves time. *Alice Through the Looking-Glass*

11   The sun was shining on the sea,
         Shining with all his might...
     And this was odd because it was
         The middle of the night. *Ib.*

12   "The time has cone," the Walrus said,
     "To talk of many things:
     Of shoes – and ships – and sealing-wax –
         Of cabbages – and kings." *Ib.*

13   It's one of the most serious things that can possibly happen to one in a battle – to get one's head cut off. *Ib.*

14   The rule is, jam tomorrow and jam yesterday – but never jam today. *Ib.*

15   It's a poor sort of memory that only works backwards. *Ib.*

16   "One can't believe impossible things," said Alice. "I daresay you haven't had much practice," said the Queen. "When I was your age I always did it for half-an-hour a day. Why, sometimes I've believed as many as six impossible things before breakfast." *Ib.*

17   "When *I* use a word," Humpty-Dumpty said in rather a scornful tone, "it means just what I choose it to mean – neither more nor less." *Ib.*

18   "As to poetry, you know," said Humpty-Dumpty..."*I* can repeat poetry as well as other folk, if it comes to that – " "Oh, it needn't come to that," Alice hastily said. *Ib.*

19   "I see nobody on the road," said Alice. "I only wish *I* had such eyes," the King remarked in a fretful tone. "To be able to see Nobody! And at that distance too!" *Ib.*

20   "This is a child!" Haigha said, coming in front of Alice..."It's as large as life, and twice as natural." *Ib.*

21   "I've got a plan for keeping your hair from falling off," said the White Knight. "First you take an upright stick. Then you make your hair creep up, like a fruit tree. Now the reason hair falls off is because it hangs *down* – things never fall upwards, you know." *Ib.*

22   The more head-downwards I am, the more I keep inventing new things. *Ib.*

23   But I was thinking of a plan
To dye one's whiskers green,
And always use so large a fan
That they could not be seen. *Ib.*

24   And now, if e'er by chance I put
My fingers into glue,
Or madly squeeze a right-hand foot
Into a left-hand shoe...
I weep, for it reminds me so
Of that old man I used to know. *Ib.*

25   A child's more important than a joke, I hope. You couldn't deny that, even if you tried with both hands. *Ib.*

26   He thought he saw an Elephant,
That practised on a fife:
He looked again, and found it was
A letter from his wife.
Sylvie and Bruno

27   The loss of his clothes hardly mattered, because
         He had seven coats on when he came,
      With three pairs of boots – but the worst of it was
         He had wholly forgotten his name.
      The Hunting of the Snark

28   His intimate friends called him "Candle-ends",
      And his enemies, "Toasted-cheese". *Ib.*

JOYCE CARY

Arthur Joyce Lunel Cary (1888–1957), educated at Clifton and
Oxford, became a successful novelist after a brief colonial
experience in Nigeria. His novels include *The African Witch*
(1936), *Mister Johnson* (1939), and *The Horse's Mouth* (1944).

1   My canvas was two feet off the floor, which just suited me. I
     like to keep my pictures above dog level. *The Horse's Mouth*

2   I hate God. It wasn't fair to make a girl and give her a face like
     mine. *Ib.*

3   "You want only joy and love and peace that passeth all
     understanding." "So it does," said Coker. "It passed mine
     long ago." *Ib.*

4   "If you find life a bit dull at home," I said, "and want to
     amuse yourself, put a stick of dynamite in the kitchen
     fire." *Ib.*

5   It's not really a kick when done by an expert. It's a push with
     the foot. *Ib.*

6   Sara could commit adultery at one end and weep for her sins
     at the other, and enjoy both operations at once. *Ib.*

7   No woman really gets old inside until she's dead or takes to
     bridge. *Ib.*

8   I never could stand doctors. Well, they've got to find
     something wrong, haven't they? It's only professional. *Ib.*

9 "Academy artist?" I said. "Since when? I may be dead, but I haven't admitted it." *Ib.*

10 I don't care for people to admire my pictures unless they like them. *Ib.*

11 "He had a face like what Cardinal Newman's would have been if he'd gone into the army instead of the Church, grown an Old Bill moustache, lost most of his teeth, and only shaved on Saturdays." *Ib.*

12 After all, what else could anyone do with a stranger, except fleece him? *Mister Johnson*

13 There has never been a mail robbery in Fada [Nigeria], and there never will be until civilization and private enterprise are much further advanced. *Ib.*

14 The office, the centre of Fada government, is a two-roomed mud hut with a mud porch and half a new roof. *Ib.*

HENRY CECIL

Henry Cecil Leon (1902–1976), lawyer and humorous novelist, educated at St Paul's School and Cambridge, was appointed a County Court Judge in 1949. He wrote many light-hearted novels, mainly with a legal background, notably *Brothers in Law* (1955).

1 The first thing for a barrister to learn in going into chambers in the Temple is the importance of the clerk. *Brothers in Law*

2 What he said was excellent, but there can be too much of an excellent thing. *Ib.*

3 The system of cleaning was for a lady called a laundress to come in every morning, make herself a cup of tea, and go on to the next set of chambers. *Ib.*

4 Justice is a funny thing. Sometimes the poorer counsel wins a case just because he's so bad that the judge has to step in. *Ib.*

5   Justice must not only be done but must appear to be done –
     and must be paid for being done. *Ib.*

6   He won't send briefs to barristers who aren't any good. He has
     an old-fashioned notion about studying the interests of his
     clients. *Ib.*

7   There are such lovely things to be seen at Ascot, some with
     two legs and some with four. *Ib.*

8   A sort of Jekyll and Hyde stood to receive his sentence.
     "Counsel has argued," said the judge, "that you are really
     two people. All I can say is that you must both go to
     prison." *Ib.*

9   If everyone were reasonable and good there'd be no need for
     us lawyers. *Friends at Court*

10   "Horses are less predictable than judges – though I've
     known a few decisions which could be classed as rank
     outsiders." *Ib.*

11   Never before in his career had Mr Justice Kingsdown wanted
     to take off his wig and throw it at counsel. *Ib.*

12   Customers occasionally grow a bit red in the face when they
     have been kept waiting three-quarters of an hour and are
     then told that everything is off except cottage pie and
     prunes and rice. But as for bringing an action for breach
     of contract – well, it is hardly ever heard of. *Sober as a Judge*

13   In hotel brochures the picture of the lounge is often taken at
     such an angle that you might imagine it was the length of
     a cricket pitch, whereas in fact two men with long arms
     could span it from wall to wall. *Ib.*

14   Mr Justice Darling once observed that..."although an
     itinerant vendor need not cry 'stinking fish', yet, if he
     knows his fish do stink, he is not entitled to cry 'fresh
     fish' ". *Ib.*

15   What was served to the plaintiff was a soggy mess, but that
     apparently is all the Englishman expects of cabbage. *Ib.*

16 I used to play forward at Rugger, and everyone says I dance like it. *Ib.*

17 I hardly ever listened to what Gladys said. She said so much and she said it all the time. *Portrait of a Judge*

18 Faces can lie, but not necks. Look at a horse's teeth and a woman's neck. *Ib.*

19 It is easy to say what you would do in given circumstances if you know perfectly well that those circumstances will never arise. *Truth With Her Boots On*

20 If there were perfect justice, the man in the right would always win...There would be no need for any law courts. *Ib.*

21 Ordinary social lies are told by almost everyone. One cannot imagine even an Archbishop, on being asked if he liked the soup, saying that it was undrinkable. *Ib.*

22 A party at which you can hear what is said to you is a failure from the start. *Ib.*

23 He peppered most of his statements with such phrases as "I'll tell you the truth" and "to be perfectly honest" and "I won't tell you a lie", which are often the signs that a person is not telling the truth, is not perfectly honest, and *is* telling a lie. *Ib.*

HAROLD CHAPIN

Harold Chapin (1884–1915), was an American who devoted himself to the English theatre as actor and playwright, and who died as a British soldier in the First World War. His comedy *The New Morality* (1920), posthumously produced, was admirably written.

1 Tell a husband what you're giving him hell for? Why, he'd forgive himself in two minutes and crawl out! *The New Morality*

2   A man always thinks you're fearfully unjust if you're not patting him on the head. *Ib.*

3   "He isn't a brute."

"I know he isn't. That's why it's so gratifying to call him one." *Ib.*

4   "I believe men are the noblest creatures God ever made – the cowards!" *Ib.*

5   I've seen lots of these platonic friendships. The man thinks he's a hero and looks like a fool, and the woman goes about with that damn-conceited look of having got something for nothing. *Ib.*

6   In a case of libel never let your client meet the plaintiff in your presence – or you may yourself be called as a witness for further libels! *Ib.*

7   In the eyes of a British jury, for a woman to offer a reason for doing anything only makes her offence the blacker. *Ib.*

8   There can be very few people at the present day who are really without a working knowledge of bad language. *Ib.*

9   You really ought to have been in prison. A barrister ought to know his profession from the bottom up. *Ib.*

G. K. CHESTERTON

Gilbert Keith Chesterton (1874–1936) attended St Paul's School and the Slade School of Art. A clever journalist, essayist, novelist, detective-story writer, poet, critic and religious writer, he was notable for his sense of fun and his love of paradox.

1   God rest you merry gentlemen,
     May nothing you dismay:
     On your reposeful cities lie
     Deep silence, broken only by

The motor horn's melodious cry
    The hooter's happy bray.
A Christmas Carol

2   The gallows in my garden, people say,
       Is new and neat and adequately tall...
    But just as all the neighbours – on the wall –
       Are drawing a long breath to shout "Hurray",
    The strangest whim has seized me – after all
       I think I will not hang myself today.
A Ballade of Suicide

3   The villas and the chapels where
       I learned with little labour
    The way to love my fellow-man
       And hate my next-door neighbour.
The World State

4   John Grubby, who was short and stout
    And troubled with religious doubt,
    Refused about the age of three
    To sit upon the curate's knee.
The New Freethinker

5   I remember my mother, the day that we met,
    A thing I shall never entirely forget;
    And I toy with the fancy that, young as I am,
    I should know her again if we met in a tram.
Songs of Education

6   Before the Romans came to Rye or out of Severn strode
    The rolling English drunkard made the rolling English
       road.
The Rolling English Road

7   Nebuchadnezzar the King of the Jews
    Suffered from new and original views,
    He crawled on his hands and knees, it's said,
    With grass in his mouth and a crown on his head.
Pioneers, O Pioneers

8 And Noah he often said to his wife when he sat down to dine, "I don't care where the water goes if it doesn't get into the wine."
Wine and Water

9 And Noah he cocked his eye and said, "It looks like rain, I think." *Ib.*

10 I reluctantly tore myself away from the task of doing nothing in particular. *Tremendous Trifles*

11 I always get wrong in drawing the hind legs of quadrupeds, so I drew the soul of the cow. *Ib.*

12 The cows stared at me and called a committee. *Ib.*

13 The cab did not like me; it threw me out violently in the middle of the Strand. *Ib.*

14 I found myself crawling out from underneath the cab in attitudes so undignified that they must have added enormously to that great cause...the pleasures of the people. *Ib.*

15 We talk of wild animals, but the wildest animal is man. *Ib.*

16 Lying in bed would be an altogether perfect and supreme experience if only one had a coloured pencil long enough to draw on the ceiling. *Ib.*

17 I have met Ibsenite pessimists who thought it wrong to take beer but right to take prussic acid. *Ib.*

18 I am always meeting idealists with very long necks. *Ib.*

19 He said to me: "A man can't get on by hanging about with his hands in his pockets". I made reply with the quite obvious flippancy that perhaps a man got on by having his hands in other people's pockets. *Ib.*

20 Bruges belfry is an unnaturally long-necked animal, like a giraffe. *Ib.*

21 Keeping a bar is much better than writing a book. Many an English writer has wished he kept a pub instead of a publisher. *The Spice of Life*

22 No one has yet had the star-defying audacity to hint at a separation between bread and cheese. *Ib.*

23 "The poet delights in disorder only. If it were not so the most poetical thing in the world would be the Underground Railway."
   "So it is," said Mr Syme. *The Man Who Was Thursday*

24 What is there poetical about being in revolt? You might as well say that it is poetical to be sea-sick. Being sick is a revolt. *Ib.*

25 "What education I had was very rough and old-fashioned."
   "Where did you have it?" asked Syme.
   "Oh, at Harrow." *Ib.*

26 I defended capital with so much intelligence that any fool could see I was quite poor. *Ib.*

27 The most dangerous criminal now is the entirely lawless modern philosopher. *Ib.*

28 "Secretary," said the president seriously, "if you'd take your head home and boil it for a turnip it might be useful. I can't say. But it might." *Ib.*

29 Thieves respect property; they merely wish it to become their property. *Ib.*

30 The human race, to which so many of my readers belong, has been playing at children's games from the beginning. *The Napoleon of Notting Hill*

31 "Do you know a shop where they cut your hair properly? I keep on having my hair cut but it keeps on growing again." *Ib.*

32 He was very fond of children, like all people who are fond of the ridiculous. *Ib.*

33 To be clever enough to get all that money, one must be stupid enough to want it. *The Innocence of Father Brown*

34 A man generally makes a small scene if he finds salt in his coffee. *Ib.*

35 The room was used by the proprietor for delicate and important matters, such as lending a duke a thousand pounds or declining to lend him sixpence. *Ib.*

36 Journalism largely consists in saying "Lord Jones Dead" to people who never knew he was alive. *The Wisdom of Father Brown*

37 "Do you believe in curses?"
"I don't believe in anything; I'm a journalist."
The Incredulity of Father Brown

38 White ermine was meant to express moral purity; white waistcoats were not. *What's Wrong with the World*

JOHN CLEESE & CONNIE BOOTH

John Cleese (1939–), actor and writer, educated at Cambridge, was a prominent member of the TV show *Monty Python's Flying Circus* (1969–74). He was later co-author with Connie Booth (his first wife, and actress in the series) of *Fawlty Towers*, and script writer and director of the film *A Fish called Wanda*.

1 When I asked you to build me a wall I was rather hoping that instead of just dumping the bricks in a pile you might have found time to cement them together. *Fawlty Towers*

2 She can kill a man at ten paces with one blow of her tongue. *Ib.*

3 I have seen better organized creatures than you running round farmyards with their heads cut off. *Ib.*

4 Have you seen the people in Room Six? They've never even sat on chairs before. *Ib.*

5 BASIL. I fought in the Korean War, you know. I killed four men...
SYBIL. He was in the catering corps. He poisoned them. *Ib.*

6 It's all right when old people have the life force, but mother, well, she's got more of the death force. *Ib.*

7 MR JOHNSON. Is there anywhere they do French food?
BASIL. Yes, France, I believe. They seem to like it there. *Ib.*

8 You're either crawling all over them licking their boots, or spitting poison at them like some Benzedrine puff-adder. *Ib.*

9 AMERICAN GUEST. Took five hours from London, Couldn't find the freeway. Had to take some little back street called the M5. *Ib.*

10 After a hard day's slaving under the hair-dryer she needs to unwind. *Ib.*

WILLIAM CONGREVE

William Congreve (1670–1729), born in England but brought up in Ireland, was the most distinguished writer of what is loosely called Restoration Comedy. His plays, noted for their wit and style, include *Love for Love* (1695) and *The Way of the World* (1700).

1 I could never look long upon a monkey without very mortifying reflections. *Concerning Humour in Comedy*

2 If a playwright should steal a dialogue of any length from the extempore discourse of the two wittiest men upon earth, he would find the scene but coldly received by the audience. *Ib.*

3   I thought a contemplative lover could no more have parted
     with his bed in a morning than he could have slept in it.
     The Old Bachelor

4   If the husband be out of the way, it will do well for the wife to
     show her fondness and impatience of his absence by
     choosing a lover as like him as she can. *Ib.*

5   My talent is that of speaking truth, which I don't expect ever
     to recommend me to people of Quality. *Ib.*

6   I find we are growing serious, and then we are in great danger
     of growing dull. *Ib.*

7   Courtship is to marriage as a very witty prologue to a very dull
     play. *Ib.*

8   Married in haste, we may repent at leisure. *Ib.*

9   Critics avaunt! For you are fish of prey,
     And feed, like sharks, upon an infant play.
     The Double-Dealer (Prologue)

10   There is nothing more unbecoming a man of Quality than to
     laugh. *Ib.*

11   Though marriage makes man and wife one flesh, it leaves
     'em still two fools. *Ib.*

12   No mask like open truth to cover lies. *Ib.*

13   I have no money; and therefore resolve to rail at all who
     have. *Love for Love*

14   I know that's a secret, for it's whispered everywhere. *Ib.*

15   He that first cries out "Stop Thief" is often he that has stolen
     the treasure. *Ib.*

16   I am no married man, and thou canst not lie with my wife. I
     am very poor, and thou canst not borrow money of me.
     Then what use am I as a friend? *Ib.*

17   I'd no more play cards with a man that slighted his ill-fortune
     than I'd make love to a woman who undervalued the loss
     of her reputation. *The Way of the World*

18 Here she comes, i'faith, full sail, with her fan spread and streamers out, and a shoal of fools for tenders. *Ib.*

19 Let us be as distant as if we had been married a great while; and as well-bred as if we were not married at all. *Ib.*

20 I nauseate walking. 'Tis a country diversion. *Ib.*

21 "Do you pin up your hair with all your letters?"

"Only with those in verse. I never pin up my hair with prose." *Ib.*

22 I won't be called Names after I'm married... as Wife, Spouse, My Dear, Joy, Jewel, Love, Sweetheart, and the rest of that nauseous cant. *Ib.*

23 If I continue to endure you a little longer, I may by degrees dwindle into a wife. *Ib.*

JILLY COOPER

Jilly Cooper (1937–), British journalist and novelist, is married to publisher Leo Cooper. After working on provincial newspapers and in publishing, she became a columnist for the *Sunday Times* and *Mail on Sunday,* and has often appeared on TV. Her novels include *Prudence* (1978) and *Rivals* (1988), and her non-fiction *Men and Super Men* (1972) and *Class* (1979).

1 Singers have the most marvellous breath control and can kiss for at least ten minutes without stopping. *Men and Super Men*

2 The most indolent women have been seen running to catch a boss. *Ib.*

3 On the whole barristers are more interested in their briefs than in a girl's. *Ib.*

4   The male is a domestic animal which, if treated with firmness and kindness, can be trained to do most things. *Ib.*

5   (On Painters)
     Don't be fooled by that line about seeing you as a beautiful form not as a sexual object. It's the easiest way I know to get a woman to remove her clothes. *Ib.*

6   Lovers behave far more respectably than married couples. Have you ever heard of a mistress-swapping party? *Ib.*

7   Cars are a complete sex substitute. Why else do men refer to the beastly things as "she"? *Ib.*

8   Virginity is supposed to be something you give your husband, like engraved cuff-links, on your wedding-day. *Women and Super Women*

9 Rugger wives deserve a chapter in Foxe's *Book of Martyrs*. If they're not washing rugger shirts and having their best suitcases stolen to accommodate revolting towels and rugger boots, they're freezing on the touchline crying "Come on!" *Ib.*

10 A Ms is as good as a male. *Ib.*

11 Tall girls stand about at parties looking gentle and apologetic, like Great Danes. *Ib.*

12 Nowhere does Parkinson's Law operate so efficiently as in the house: mechanical gadgets don't cut down the time spent, they just mean you wash sweaters after you've worn them once instead of scraping the food blob off with your fingernail. *Ib.*

13 Australia is a land of harsh rules, which everyone breaks. *Jolly Marsupial*

14 One is reminded of the exquisite pre-war comment on Hitler: "If the fellow's going to raise his right arm so much, he really ought to go to a decent tailor." *Ib.*

15 Dance partners should be changed often, like nappies. *Ib.*

16 "You worked in an office once didn't you, Jill?" a feminist once asked earnestly. "Did men ever harass you?" "Yes," I replied, "but not nearly enough." *Ib.*

17 There would never be any stigma to an [aristocratic] young man going into the Church, because the upper classes have to believe in God. *Class*

18 Anthony Eden's father once hurled a barometer out of the window into the pouring rain, yelling, "See for yourself, you bloody thing!" *Ib.*

19 They live in a council house with walls so thin that you can hear the budgie pecking its seed next door. *Ib.*

20 "I work in Harrods," said a pale girl, "but in the book department," as though that made it better. *Prudence*

21   "Nice hair. Is it natural?"
"Of course. I'm too young to dye." *Ib.*

22   I felt just about as wanted as a Christmas Tree on Twelfth Night. *Ib.*

23   Alimony is the root of all evil. *Ib.*

24   Henley was so wet this year it should have been rechristened Duckley. *Turn Right at the Spotted Dog*

25   The trouble with nudist beaches is that everyone hides behind books trying to pretend they're not looking at everyone else. *Ib.*

26   At Henley, only male crews may compete in the Ladies Plate. *Ib.*

27   The only animal I really identify with... is a dog – probably a rather rotund, jolly, slightly unkempt mongrel who bounces up to people, wagging its tail. *Telegraph Sunday Magazine (13 March 1986)*

TOMMY COOPER

Tommy Cooper (1921–84), a six-foot-four ex Guardsman turned comedian, made his performing debut at the Windmill Theatre. His stage act was based on wildly despairing (and comic) attempts to perform magic. He made many TV appearances in his own series.

1   I knew a cannibal...who had been influenced by Catholic missionaries. On Fridays he ate only fishermen. *Just Like That*

2   I never wanted to be a footballer. I didn't like all that kissing and cuddling. *Ib.*

3   The corporal said he had been born in the saddle. It must have been hard on his mother. *Ib.*

4   I had just taken my exam for the Magic Circle...One of the tricks I had to perform was with marked cards. I nearly failed. My marks weren't high enough. *Ib.*

5   One of them asked me if I knew what good clean fun was. "I give up," I said. "What good is it?" *Ib.*

6   There was a man who couldn't resist driving cars away. He said he was just motorvated. *Ib.*

7   A dentist got married to a manicurist. They fought tooth and nail. *Ib.*

8   I'm a master of the meaningful silence – a wizard at the meaningless utterance. *Ib.*

9   I once had a job painting the white lines down roadways, but I packed it in before I went round the bend. *Ib.*

ALAN COREN

Alan Coren (1938–), deputy editor and editor of *Punch* (1969–87), has also been a TV critic, a frequent broadcaster, and has written novels, plays, and short stories.

1   I find everything about James Bond believable...the girls, the fights, the villains, the plots, they're all exactly like my own domestic life. *The Cricklewood Diet*

2   I do not know why this book is called *The Cricklewood Diet*. All I know is that it is something to do with a great breakthrough in publishing. *Ib.*

3   Alexander the Great was born in 356 BC...He had great difficulty in working out how old he was, since (given that by the time he was twelve it was 344 BC) he seemed to be growing younger every year. *Ib.*

4   That night Alexander saw his first alligator. He rushed
     screaming to his tent, where he told the distraught
     Callisthenes that he was being pursued by four-legged
     handbags. *Ib.*

5   "Six days!" exclaimed the man. "To make a *world?*
     It would take that long to order the nails!"
     "He's God!" shouted Moses. "You think he has to hang
     around waiting for planning permission?" *Ib.*

6   You leave your body behind in a box and upon arrival at what
     we call Heaven's Gate you get a cloakroom ticket. This
     enables you to claim your body when the Resurrection
     comes. *Ib.*

7   By the time I get to our pears they are brown and flat and wet,
     not unlike small cowpats with wasps in. *Ib.*

8   It's cannibal country. I didn't find out till the fifth day when I
     went to complain to the courier about the food and found
     out it was him that had given me indigestion. *Punch*

9   When that Aprille with his taxe-forms drere
     Comes, draggynge in a new financial yeere,
     Thenne many folke loke round to see how theye
     May kepe the Inlande Revenue atte baye. *Ib.*

10   Democracy is choosing your dictators, after they've told you
     what you think it is you want to hear. *Daily Mail*

11   (On Holland)
     Apart from cheese and tulips, the main product of the country
     is advocaat, a drink made from lawyers. *The Sanity Inspector*

12   All I know of birds to this day is that sparrows are the ones
     that are not pigeons. *Tissues for Men*

13   We had decided that the only way to stop the children from
     nagging to be taken to Disneyworld was either to go, or to
     strangle them (a close decision). *Ib.*

14 There is absolutely no indication whatever [in Disneyworld] of the valuable part that the Red Indians played in the opening up of the American West, by getting wiped out. *Ib.*

15 The black sateen of her hobbled skirt tightened across her thigh like an overstuffed dustbin-liner. *Ib.*

16 The happy couple slipped away across the croquet lawn, pausing only to leave the offside front wing on an elderly yew. *Ib.*

17 You've come a long way, Bernie, from that one little shop in Fortune Green Road. You now have two little shops. *Ib.*

18 [There were] heartening reports from various tobacco companies that smoking cured baldness, enhanced virility, prevented foot odour, and made you taller. *Ib.*

19 I purchased one of the few tracts of genuine swamp in the New Forest, together with the small cottage sinking picturesquely into it. *Ib.*

20 There is nothing less feminine than a woman drinking out of a jug. *Bin Ends*

21 Many people do not realize that they are mentally disturbed until this is triggered off by an unexpected shock, like falling off a roof. *Ib.*

22 The nauseatingly foreign system of motorways is virtually at an end. A patriotic combination of dingbat design, unanticipated subsidence, shrewd mismanagement...and fourteen million orange cones has ensured that Britain now has no straight wide boring roads at all. *Ib.*

23 Can anything more sharply evoke the memory of imperial greatness than the rolling English road, eight feet wide at its blind corners, a cow standing in the middle of it. *Ib.*

24 I seem to remember reading somewhere about what a Supreme Being is entitled to do. *Something for the Weekend*

NOEL COWARD

Sir Noel Coward (1899–1973) began his career as a child actor. His early play *The Vortex* (1923) was serious, but subsequently his fame rested mainly on his gift for light comedy, with crisp dialogue. He also wrote words and music for revues and operettas, e.g. *Bitter Sweet* (1929), and wrote and produced several films, e.g. *Brief Encounter* (1945). He was knighted in 1970. *Present Indicative* (1937) is autobiographical.

1   There was a lavatory at the end of the garden, the door of which always had to be kept shut because the goat liked to use it as well as the family. *Present Indicative*

2   Mr Crawford directed rehearsals [of *Charley's Aunt*] with all the airy deftness of a rheumatic deacon producing *Macbeth* for a church social. *Ib.*

3   I reflected gleefully that for five hundred dollars I would gladly consider turning *War and Peace* into a music-hall sketch. *Ib.*

4   Alexander Woolcott, in a rage, has all the tenderness and restraint of a newly caged cobra. *Ib.*

5   The S. S. *Cedric*...was old and slow, and wallowed through the sea like a fat swimmer doing a perpetual breast stroke. *Ib.*

6   I sang every witty couplet with perfect diction and a wealth of implication which sent them winging out in the dark auditorium, where they fell wetly, like pennies into mud. *Ib.*

7   With all three plays running at once I was in an enviable position. Everyone but Somerset Maugham said I was a second Somerset Maugham. *Ib.*

8   She goes about using Sex as a sort of shrimping-net. *Hay Fever*

9   He has that innocent look that never fails to attract elderly women. *The Vortex*

10 I expect Florence will just go on and on, then suddenly become quite beautifully old, and go on and on still more. *Ib.*

11 I hate the very nicest type of Englishman. *Ib.*

12 Bruce Fairlight is an earnest dramatist, the squalor of whose plays is much appreciated by those who live in comparative luxury. *Ib.*

13 You and your mother are always trying to help lame dogs over stiles – even if they're not lame and don't want to go. *Easy Virtue.*

14 Joan used to walk across a ballroom as though she was trudging through deep snow. *Relative Values*

15 Everything that happens is chance. It was chance meeting you. It was chance falling in love. It's chance that we're here, particularly after your driving. *Private Lives*

16 "It doesn't suit women to be promiscuous."
"It doesn't suit men for women to be promiscuous." *Ib.*

17 "I believe that life is for living, don't you?"
"It's difficult to know what else one could do with it."
Nude with Violin

18 "Was he a heavy drinker?"
"Sometimes he would go for hours without touching a drop." *Ib.*

19 If I'm going to have champagne I must take off my hat. *Ib.*

20 I always bite people when I'm suddenly astonished. *Ib.*

21 She [the Mona Lisa] looked as if she had just been sick or was about to be. *Ib.*

22 "What did he think of Picasso?"
"He tried not to." *Ib.*

23 "One lives and learns, doesn't one?"
"That is certainly one of the more prevalent delusions." *Ib.*

24 Don't look martyred. It draws your mouth down at the corners. Like a weary old camel. *A Song at Twilight*

25 I really don't care to discuss false teeth during dinner. *Ib.*

26 There's always a crisis in Bulgaria, the same as there's always a haggis in Scotland. *The Young Idea*

27 I have never been able to take anything seriously after eleven o'clock in the morning. *Ib.*

28 I long ago came to the conclusion that nothing has ever been definitely proved about anything. *Blithe Spirit*

29 It's discouraging to think how many people are shocked by honesty and how few by deceit. *Ib.*

30 Nobody but a monumental bore would have thought of having a honeymoon at Budleigh Salterton. *Ib.*

31 Phoebe Lucas plays a glamorous courtesan with about as much sex appeal as a haddock. *Present Laughter*

32 Miss Erikson looked more peculiar than ever this morning. Is her spiritualism getting worse? *Ib.*

QUENTIN CRISP

Quentin Crisp (1908–), writer, broadcaster and performer, had a variety of jobs, including that of artist's model, before achieving success with his book *The Naked Civil Servant* (1968), an account of his homosexual life.

1 As soon as I stepped out of my mother's womb on to dry land, I realized that I had made a mistake – that I shouldn't have come. *The Naked Civil Servant*

2 The trouble with children is that they are not returnable. *Ib.*

3 Keeping up with the Joneses was a full-time job with my mother and father...When I lived alone I realized how much cheaper it was to drag the Joneses down to my level. *Ib.*

4   A fair share of anything is starvation diet to an egomaniac. *Ib.*

5   This school was on top of a hill so that God could see everything that went on. *Ib.*

6   The one thing I would not wish on my worst enemy is eternal life. *Ib.*

7   I don't hold with abroad and think that foreigners speak English when our backs are turned. *Ib.*

8   The world lay all before me – like a trap-door. *Ib.*

9   A reputation for wit is earned not by making jokes but by laughing at the pleasantries of others. *Ib.*

10   I wrote an anti-Pirandello play so bad that to this day I cannot see why it was never staged. *Ib.*

11   The movie business has a genius for bringing some kind of chaos out of order. *Ib.*

12   The telephone is my favourite musical instrument. *Daily Express (27 April 1989)*

13   My favourite food is Guinness. It's the only food that doesn't have to be cooked or kept in a refrigerator. *Ib.*

14   I once knew a woman with snakes that slithered to the door when the bell rang, like dogs. They spat at me, but at least one wasn't asked to stroke them. *Ib.*

15   I only keep books if they're signed for me, otherwise I throw them away. *Ib.*

WILL CUPPY

William Jacob Cuppy (1884–1949), American humorist and critic, reviewed detective fiction for the *New York Herald Tribune* for many years, and was author of several humorous books, e.g. *How to Tell Your Friends from the Apes* (1931) and *How to Become Extinct* (1941).

1   The apes are in cages. *How to Tell Your Friends from the Apes*

2   Orang-utans teach us that looks are not everything – but darned near it. *Ib.*

3   Young gorillas are friendly, but they soon learn. *Ib.*

4   The Chimpanzee is found in Equatorial Africa and in vaudeville. *Ib.*

5   Normal young tigers do not eat people. If eaten by a tiger you may rest assured that he was abnormal. *Ib.*

6   The Love Bird is one hundred percent faithful to his mate, who is locked into the same cage. *Ib.*

7   If an animal does something, we call it instinct. If we do the same thing for the same reason, we call it intelligence. *Ib.*

8   The hippopotamus is monogamous. He looks as if he would have to be. *Ib.*

9   You can't teach an old Gnu tricks. *Ib.*

10   The Dodo never had a chance. He seems to have been invented for the sole purpose of becoming extinct. *How to Become Extinct*

11   George I kept his wife in prison because he believed she was no better than he was. *Decline and Fall of Practically Everybody*

12   He is known as Alexander the Great because he killed more people of more different kinds than any other man. *Ib.*

13   *Sartor Resartus* is simply unreadable, and for me that always sort of spoils a book. *Ib.*

14   This world is full of people who are ready to think the worst when they see a man sneaking out of the wrong bedroom in the middle of the night. *Ib.*

HUNTER DAVIES

Hunter Davies (1936–), British author, contributor to *The Sunday Times* and other journals, lives in the Lake District and has written books about the area, including a biography of Wordsworth.

1   Since the arrival of Women's Lib, dads have been somewhat pushed into a corner. *Father's Day*

2   I don't watch television... I always seem to have something better to do, such as nothing. *Ib.*

3   All children love doing jobs, until they are capable of doing them. *Ib.*

4   (Catching trains)

Davies timing is running on to the platform just as the train is leaving, and throwing oneself into the last compartment. *Ib.*

5   Today, prices rise while you're standing at the check-out counter. *Ib.*

6   I can't bear not to buy special offers, even when I can see it's that funny-coloured coffee that tastes of dishwater and which no one will ever drink, even me. *Ib.*

7   Complete freedom can be very restricting. You alone make the decision about what to do next, or when and how you do it, and it can drive you mad. *Ib.*

8   It was so unbelievably quiet and peaceful on the plane that I did a very unusual thing. I read a book. You know, one of those bound things, pages full of words. *Ib.*

9   My son doesn't just read books – he attacks them, grinding back the spines so that they break instantly, punching them in the face, kicking hell out of their insides. *Ib.*

10   Fat people don't seem to age as much as thin people, not when you get close up and inspect the damage. *Ib.*

LES DAWSON

Les Dawson (1934–) was born in Manchester. After surviving poverty and a variety of jobs he became a popular TV comedian, at one time with his own show *Sez Les*. *A Clown Too Many* (1985) is his autobiography.

1   When she lightly kissed me upon my cheek, it felt as though I had been savaged by a frankfurter. *The Amy Pluckett Letters*

2   The memory of my wedding day is etched firmly in my mind – but they say time is a great healer. *Ib.*

3   The money meant luxuries such as food and shoes. *Ib.*

4   "I have been discharged from the [Mental] Institution" (she wrote) "and I'm back at my old job in a solicitor's office. I work there as a teapot." *Ib.*

5   The salesman who sold me the car told me I'd get a lot of pleasure out of it. He was right – it was a pleasure to get out of it. *Ib.*

6   The main hotel, the Splendide, was bombed during the last days of the war by the RAF. Apparently the Navigator had stayed there once and been charged double for a single room. *Ib.*

7   I left behind me at Bovington Camp...N.C.O.s whose brain energy was that of a retarded pit pony. *A Clown Too Many*

8   As a salesman I proved the truth of the old adage, "If at first you don't succeed, fail, fail again." *Ib.*

9   My wife's mother tells people I am effeminate. I don't mind because compared to her, I am. *Ib.*

10   I used to sell furniture for a living. The trouble was, it was my own. *Ib.*

11 I'm not saying the place is dirty, but you have to spray the kitchen with DDT before the flies will come in. *Ib.*

12 The neighbours love it when I play the piano. They break my window to hear me better. *Ib.*

CLARENCE DAY

Clarence Shepard Day (1874–1935) wrote several humorous autobiographical books from material first published in *The New Yorker, Harper's Magazine*, and other journals. *Life with Father* (1935) was dramatized (1939) with great success.

1 In the fight between Satan and God we had been told that God won. There were stray bits of evidence to the contrary lying around, but we accepted the official announcement. *Life with Father*

2 Any sufferings that Father ever had he attributed solely to God. Naturally, he never thought for a moment that God could mean him to suffer. God was just clumsy, not to say muddle-headed. *Ib.*

3 When the household expenses shot up very high...Father would yell his head off. He always did some yelling anyhow, merely on general principles. *Ib.*

4 Apart from a few odd words in Hebrew, I took it for granted that God had never spoken anything but the most dignified English. *Ib.*

5 The only Clarence in history was a duke who did something dirty in Tewkesbury, and who died a ridiculous death afterwards in a barrel of Malmsey. *Ib.*

6 One of the things Father specially detested about guests was the suddenness with which they arrived. *Ib.*

7 Father declared he was going to buy a new plot in the cemetery. "And I'll buy one in a corner," he added triumphantly, "where I can get out!" *Ib.*

8 "If you don't go to other men's funerals," General Anderson told Father, "they won't go to yours." *Ib.*

9 When Father lay stretched out on his sofa, his toes would begin stretching and wriggling in a curious way by themselves, as though they were seizing this chance to live a life of their own. *Ib.*

10 When people thought they were ill, Father declared, it didn't mean there was anything the matter with them; it was merely a sign of weak character. *Ib.*

11 While the gout was besieging him, Father sat in a big chair by the fire with his bad foot on a stool, armed with a cane. Not that he used it to walk with...When visitors entered he brandished it fiercely at them to keep them away from his toe. *Ib.*

12 When Father went to church and sat in his pew, he felt he was doing enough. Any further spiritual work ought to be done by the clergy. *My Father's Dark Hour*

13 Father and God usually saw eye to eye. They had perfect confidence in each other. The only exception was when God seemed to be neglecting His job. *Ib.*

14 He didn't actually accuse God of gross inefficiency, but when he prayed his tone was loud and angry, like that of a dissatisfied guest in a carelessly managed hotel. *Ib.*

15 I never felt at ease with the clergyman. He never seemed to speak to me personally but to a thing called My Child. *Ib.*

16 The one thing Father always gave up in Lent was going to church. *Ib.*

17 Father preferred to begin a discussion by stating his conclusion and by calling yours nonsense, and to end the debate then and there. *Ib.*

18   The Victorians had too much sense to converse with children
      as though they were human beings. *Life with Mother*

19   Mother seemed to expect the German language to behave
      like a gentleman and not be too hard on a busy woman
      who was studying it out of pure kindness. *Ib.*

20   Good, roaring, wet, tempestuous winds and rough seas gave
      Father pleasure. But the land was another matter entirely.
      Its duty was to bring forth fruits in abundance for Father.
      Ib.

21   This move of ours from No.251 to No.420 bulked as large in
      my mind as the flight of the Israelites from Egypt, and
      they didn't have to carry such heavy furniture as a
      Victorian family. *Ib.*

22   Mother never thought of the horse as the friend and
      companion of man. She looked at all horses suspiciously.
      They weren't really tame, like our dogs. Horses were too
      large to be trusted. *Ib.*

23   Who drags the fiery artist down?
      Who keeps the pioneer in town?
      Who hates to let the seaman roam?
      It is the wife, it is the home.

PETER DE VRIES

Peter De Vries (1910–), American journalist, was educated at
Calvin College, Michigan. He is co-editor of *Poetry Magazine*, as
well as being on the staff of *The New Yorker* and the author of
over twenty novels.

1   "Do you like codfish balls?"
     "I don't know, I've never attended any."
     The Mackerel Plaza

2   He was one of those doctors who run their practice on the firm theory that ninety-nine percent of their patients are quacks. *Ib.*

3   He had the one characteristic I always find it hard to cope with – piety. *Ib.*

4   Let us hope that a kind Providence will put a speedy end to the acts of God under which we have been labouring. *Ib.*

5   I learnt the meaning of words like putative and adumbrate and simulacrum...Though actual occasions for their use were all but inconceivable, they gave me a sense of security, like a gun kept loaded just in case. *Consenting Adults*

6   I met a young woman who said she married to get away from the furniture at home. *Ib.*

7   Being ordered into long woollen underwear was sometimes a mid-July punishment. *Ib.*

8   From the bathroom came the sound of my grandmother brushing her tooth. *Ib.*

9   (In a supermarket)
    Boxes of breakfast cereal [were] arranged in a construction with holes in it, like a Henry Moore sculpture. *Ib.*

10 Columbine never slept on her back. She was afraid a chunk of plaster might fall out of the ceiling and land on the bed. *Ib.*

11 I wondered whether any woman could be happy with a man who says "folderol". *Ib.*

12 He took little girls on Sunday botany hikes in organized tours of one. *Ib.*

13 I wanted to be bored to death, as good a way to go as any. *Comfort Me With Apples*

14 He was a deluge of words and a drizzle of thought. *Ib.*

15   There are times when parenthood seems nothing but feeding the mouth that bites you. *Tunnel of Love*

16   Everybody hates me because I'm so universally liked. *The Vale of Laughter*

CHARLES DICKENS

Charles John Huffam Dickens (1812–1870), was a master of humour, revealed particularly in *Pickwick Papers* (1837–9).

1   That punctual servant of all work, the sun, had just risen. *Pickwick Papers*

2   There are very few moments in a man's existence when he experiences so much ludicrous distress...as when he is in pursuit of his own hat. *Ib.*

3   "Success to the Mayor," cried a voice, "and may he never desert the nail and sarspan business." *Ib.*

4   It's not at all necessary for a crowd to know what they are cheering about. *Ib.*

5   Poverty and oysters always seem to go together. *Ib.*

6   Never sign a valentine with your own name. *Ib.*

7   The boy's always asleep. Goes on errands fast asleep, and snores as he waits at table. *Ib.*

8   If the principal tower of Rochester Castle had suddenly walked from its foundations and stationed itself opposite the coffee-room window, Mr Winkle's surprise would have been no greater. *Ib.*

9   "That horse wouldn't shy if he was to meet a vaggin-load of monkeys with their tails burnt off" [said the ostler]. *Ib.*

10   The tall quadruped evinced a decided inclination to back into the coffee-room window. "Only his playfulness, gen'l'men," said the head ostler encouragingly. *Ib.*

11   Mr Winkle's horse was drifting up the street in the most mysterious manner – side first, with his head towards one side of the way and his tail towards the other. *Ib.*

12   In the main street of Ipswich... the Great White Horse Inn is rendered the more conspicuous by a stone statue of some rampacious animal distinctly resembling an insane cart-horse. *Ib.*

13   As she had lived for the most part in the country, and never read the parliamentary debates, she was little versed in the refinements of civilized life. *Ib.*

14   Discontented or hungry jurymen always find for the plaintiff. *Ib.*

15   "Battledore and shuttlecock's a wery good game, when you an't the shuttlecock and two lawyers the battledores." *Ib.*

16   It came like magic in a pint bottle; it was not ecstasy but it was comfort. *Little Dorrit*

17   You can't make a head and brains out of a brass knob with nothing in it. *Ib.*

18   The word papa gives a pretty form to the lips. Papa, potatoes, poultry, prunes and prisms are all very good words for the lips. *Ib.*

19   "Do other men, for they would do you." That's the true Business precept. *Martin Chuzzlewit*

20   He'd make a lovely corpse. *Ib.*

21   Accidents will occur in the best-regulated families. *David Copperfield*

22   Fashions are like human beings. They come in, nobody knows when, why, or how; and they go out, nobody knows when, why, or how. *Ib.*

23   His hand felt like a fish, in the dark. *Ib.*

24   He'd be sharper than a serpent's tooth, if he wasn't as dull as ditch water. *Our Mutual Friend*

25　He had but one eye, and the popular prejudice runs in favour of two. *Nicholas Nickleby*

26　I am screaming out loud all the time I write and so is my brother. *Ib.*

27　Whenever a man dies without any property of his own, he always seems to think he has a right to dispose of other people's. *Ib.*

28　Into these bowls Mrs Squeers poured a brown composition which looked like diluted pincushions without the covers. *Ib.*

MONICA DICKENS

Monica Enid Dickens (1915–) is the great-granddaughter of Charles. Despite her education at St Paul's School for Girls, she decided to become a domestic servant, and later a nurse and a newspaper reporter. These experiences led her to write three autobiographical books. She has also written a number of novels.

1　The trouble with housework is that whatever you do seems to lead to another job to do or a mess to clear up. *One Pair of Hands*

2　It is a curious fact that good glass cracks at a touch, while cheap stuff can be hurled about with perfect safety. *Ib.*

3　"I take a look at me dream book" (said Polly), "and it says 'To dream of a kiss from the beloved one is a sign of impending stomach disorder'." *Ib.*

4　I went there [a school of French cookery] quite unable to boil an egg, and came out with Homard Thermidor and Crêpes Suzette at my fingertips. I was still unable to boil an egg, however. *Ib.*

5　A maid makes a good defenceless listener for people who want to talk about themselves. *Ib.*

6　Three a.m. is not the most propitious time for meditation. *Ib.*

7　My school reports used to say: "Not amenable to discipline; too fond of organizing", which was only a kind way of saying "Bossy". *One Pair of Feet*

8　The idea of nursing had always attracted me...It's one of those adolescent phases like wanting to be a nun. *Ib.*

9　The matron had asked me for references, so I dictated one or two to friends with solid-looking surnames. *Ib.*

10　I was frightened by the alien atmosphere of hospital. The smell alone makes you feel an outsider, and everyone is always too busy to be bothered with you. *Ib.*

11　Whatever nurses may look like individually, *en masse* they make an oddly pure effect, like a billowing flight of doves, which belies their conversation. *Ib.*

12　Women were not meant to live *en masse* – except in harems. *Ib.*

13　She sipped her drink as if it had been poured out for her by a Borgia. *Ib.*

14　She looked like one of those potatoes that people photograph and send to the papers because it bears a curious resemblance to a human face. *Ib.*

15　Imagine the hill on which the town is built as a rather squat pudding, and the town as a sauce which has been poured over and run down the sides. *Ib.*

16　When one of the first remarks of a new patient is: "Now I don't want to be any trouble," you can bet your shirt they are going to be more trouble than anyone else in the ward. *Ib.*

17　We were in league against the boss. One always is, however much one likes the boss and hates one's fellow workers. *My Turn to Make the Tea*

18 I lived with some friends. We thought we were friends, but when I had been there a few weeks we discovered we were not. *Ib.*

19 He always spoke of me as Her and She...as if I were a thing in a Zoo that had not been classified. *Ib.*

20 There were four magistrates...Next to the Colonel sat an old man who never contributed anything...He looked lost, but patient, as if his wife had sent him there to be out of the way until lunchtime. *Ib.*

21 She drank tea with so many fingers crooked that I was afraid she would drop the cup. *Ib.*

22 The rule of all competitions: never print the winning entry, so that no one can write in to claim that theirs was better. *Ib.*

23 Bigamists seldom look capable of getting one woman to marry them, let alone two. *Ib.*

PETER FINLEY DUNNE

Peter Finley Dunne (1867–1936), American humorist and journalist, at one time editor of *Collier's Weekly,* was the author of several books containing the pungent comments of a supposed Irish saloon-keeper, Mr Dooley.

1 All you've got to do is to believe what you hear, and if you do that enough, after a while you'll hear what you believe. *Mr Dooley Remembers*

2 Don't jump on a man unless he's down. *Ib.*

3 It doesn't make much difference what you study as long as you don't like it. *Ib.*

4 Many a man that couldn't direct ye to the drug store on the corner when he was thirty will get a respectful hearing whin age has further impaired his mind. *Mr Dooley on Making a Will*

5 If a man is wise he gets rich, an' if he gets rich he gets foolish, or his wife does. That's what keeps the money movin' around. *Observations by Mr Dooley*

6 Ye can always read a doctor's bill an' ye never can read his purscription. *Mr Dooley Says*

7 "Justice is blind." Blind she is, an' deaf an' dumb, and has a wooden leg. *Mr Dooley's Opinions*

8 Vice...is a creature of such hideous mien...that the more ye see it the better ye like it. *Ib.*

9 A fanatic is a man who does what he thinks the Lord would do, if He knew the facts of the case. *Ib.*

10 An appeal is when ye ask one court to show its contempt for another court. *Ib.*

11   Miracles are laughed at by a nation that reads thirty million newspapers a day. *Ib.*

12   The past always looks better than it was. It's only pleasant because it isn't here.

13   Swearing is a compromise between running away and fighting.

GERALD DURRELL

Gerald Durrell (1925–) was born in India. Youthful interest in animals led him to work at Whipsnade Zoo. He has led many animal-collecting expeditions, and written several lively books about his experiences with animals and people, e.g. *Beasts in My Belfry* (1973).

1   "She's so beautiful," said Sven, "that it almost makes me wish I weren't homosexual." *Fillets of Plaice*

2   "I always thought a yashmak was a bloody silly idea," said Larry. "If a woman's got a pretty face she should show it. The only thing I *would* advocate is a gag if she talked too much." *Ib.*

3   "I wonder if he knows how to saw a woman in half," said Larry thoughtfully. "I mean, so that you can get the half that functions but doesn't talk." *Ib.*

4   As in courts of law all over the world, you knew perfectly well that everybody was lying the hind leg off a donkey. *Ib.*

5   He took down the calendar of a woman in a voluptuous pose who was so obviously a mammal that it almost embarrassed *me. Ib.*

6   "Some people never let their right hand know what their left
      is doing."
      "My dear," said Ursula, shocked, "I never let either of my
      hands know what I'm doing." *Ib.*

7   If you take her out to lunch, keep her away from the menu,
      unless somebody's just died and left you a couple of
      hundred pounds. *Ib.*

8   "She became pregnant. She was going to have an illiterate
      baby." *Ib.*

9   She dropped bricks at the rate of an unskilled navvy helping
      on a building site. *Ib.*

10   The camel would stand towering over you...staring at you
      with disbelieving disgust as though you were a child-
      murderer. *Beasts in My Belfry*

11   The deer decided that between him and the safety of the
      garage lay a monstrous and probably dangerous enemy – a
      tea-trolley...He lowered his head and charged. *Ib.*

12   In those days money was worth money. Now it's a lot of
      lavatory paper. *Ib.*

13   Roger [the dog] worked his way over his hind quarters in
      search of a flea, using his front teeth like a pair of
      hair-clippers. *My Family and Other Animals*

14   He was obviously a scientist of considerable repute (I could
      have told this by his beard). *Ib.*

15   Mother [was] clad in the bathing-costume which made her
      look, as Larry pointed out, like a sort of marine Albert
      Memorial. *Ib.*

T. S. ELIOT

Thomas Stearns Eliot (1888–1965), American-born poet
domiciled in England, first achieved fame with *The Waste Land*

(1922). He was mainly a serious poet and literary critic but his humour emerged in the popular cat poems of *Old Possum's Book of Practical Cats* (1939). His verse plays include *Murder in the Cathedral* (1935) and the serious comedy *The Cocktail Party* (1949).

1   The naming of cats is a difficult matter. *Old Possum's Book of Practical Cats*

2   All day she sits upon the stair or on the steps or
        on the mat:
     She sits and sits and sits and sits – and that's
        what makes a Gumbie Cat! *Ib.*

3   The Rum Tum Tugger is a terrible bore;
     When you let him in, then he wants to be out;
     He's always on the wrong side of every door,
     And as soon as he's at home, then he'd like to get about.
     Ib.

4   [Growltiger] was the roughest cat that ever roamed
        at large...
     The Persian and the Siamese regarded him with fear –
     Because it was a Siamese had mauled his missing ear. *Ib.*

5   Macavity's a Mystery Cat: he's called the Hidden Paw –
     For he's the master criminal who can defy the Law.
     He's the bafflement of Scotland Yard, the Flying
        Squad's despair:
     For when they reach the scene of crime – *Macavity's
        not there! Ib.*

6   His manner is vague and aloof,
     You'd think there was nobody shyer –
     But his voice has been heard on the roof
     When he was curled up by the fire. *Ib.*

7   You now have learned enough to see
     That cats are much like you and me. *Ib.*

8   Before a cat will condescend
To treat you as a trusted friend,
Some little token of esteem
Is needed, like a dish of cream. *Ib.*

9   Now the Peke, although people may say what they please,
Is no British dog, but a Heathen Chinese. *Ib.*

10   This is the first time
I've ever seen you without Lavinia
Except for the time she got locked in the lavatory
And couldn't get out.
The Cocktail Party

11   It was perfectly infuriating
The way you *didn't* complain. *Ib.*

12   All cases are unique, and very similar to others. *Ib.*

H. F. ELLIS

Humphrey Francis Ellis (1907–), English humorous writer,
was assistant and then deputy editor of *Punch* for several years.
He also wrote for *The New Yorker*. He is perhaps best known as
creator of the pompous and rather ridiculous prep school
master, A. J. Wentworth.

1   I like to have two anxieties a week. To have more confuses the
mind. *Punch*

2   My mental picture of US Congress, as opposed to any accurate
knowledge, is tolerably clear. Its members sit in a circular
building on stepped-up benches, with desks in front of
them. They are all called Senator and they are all exactly
alike. *Ib.*

3   The report that astronomers in Texas have seen green spots
on Mars gives fresh impetus to the belief that some sort of
allotment system is in operation on the planet. *Ib.*

4   Gas-holders were probably the ugliest contrivances ever conceived. Nobody loved them, except at the Oval, where any landmark was welcome. *Ib.*

5   It is impossible to combine the heating of milk with any other pursuit whatsoever. *Ib.*

6   The speed at which boiling milk rises from the bottom of the pan to any point beyond the top is greater than the speed at which the human brain and hand can combine to snatch the confounded thing off. *Ib.*

7   Don't describe painting in terms of painting. Compare it with a piece of music, describing the latter as if it were a painting, and you will have the reader (or listener) so fogged in no time that he won't have the spirit to resist. *Ib.*

8   There is a monstrous misconception that in no circumstances is a master justified in throwing books etc. at his boys. *A.J. Wentworth B.A.*

9   A boy should be instructed to remove his spectacles before being assaulted. *Ib.*

10   Every mathematics master dreads the day when he will have to explain the Theory of Pythagoras to boys who have never met it before. *Ib.*

11   "Is a right-angled triangle likely to have a square on its hypotenuse?...I mean in real life." *Ib.*

12   Every schoolmaster knows how unnerving it is when the boys sit quietly in their places and watch you in a silly expressionless way. *Ib.*

13   I strode at once to my desk to get my punishment-book but when I opened the lid a pigeon flew out. *Ib.*

14   It was easy to see that Maeterlinck, expounding his mystical symbolism in a language no one could understand, would test the endurance of the keenest lecturegoer. *A Bee in the Kitchen*

15   The British, for all their loss of prestige, are not yet afraid of small turtles. *Ib.*

16   He looked at the man with the sort of untroubled loathing one might give a snake known to have its fangs removed. *Ib.*

GEORGE FARQUHAR

George Farquhar (1678–1707), was an Anglo-Irish writer of what are loosely called Restoration comedies, contemporary with Congreve and Vanbrugh. His last and best was *The Beaux' Stratagem* (1707).

1   She has cured more people in and about Lichfield within ten years than the doctors have killed in twenty. *The Beaux' Stratagem*

2   He says little, thinks less, and does – nothing at all. *Ib.*

3   There's no form of prayer in the Liturgy against bad husbands. *Ib.*

4   Did you ever see a poet or a philosopher worth ten thousand pounds? *Ib.*

5   No woman can be a beauty without a fortune. *Ib.*

6   There's no scandal like rags, nor any crime so shameful as poverty. *Ib.*

7   "Madam, I've brought you a whole *packet* of news...I asked who the gentleman was; they said they never saw him before. I inquired what countryman he was, and they replied 'twas more than they knew. I demanded whence he came, and their answer was, they could not tell. Lastly, I asked whither he went, and they replied they knew nothing of the matter." *Ib.*

8   It is a maxim, that man and wife should never have it in their power to hang one another. *Ib.*

9   I hate all that don't love me and slight all that do. *The Constant Couple*

10   She dresses up a sin so religiously that the Devil would hardly know it. *Ib.*

11   "What makes him so gay?"
"Why, he's in mourning for his father. The old man broke his neck in fox-hunting, so the son has broken his indentures." *Ib.*

12   He is an honest fellow, and will be faithful to any roguery that is trusted to him. *The Recruiting Officer*

HERBERT FARJEON

Herbert Farjeon (1887–1941), dramatic critic to *Sunday Pictorial, Daily Herald, Vogue,* and other journals, was the author and director of several revues, especially at the Little Theatre, London. He was a cricket lover from his youth.

1   Is it part of an umpire's obligation to submit to being festooned with sweaters and cardigans by an inconsiderate fielding side? And would he be within his rights in demanding a cloakroom fee? *Herbert Farjeon's Cricket Bag*

2   A batsman given to run-stealing need not open his mouth to gain the reputation of a wit. *Ib.*

3   I would like a bat with the words WHAT A ROTTEN WICKET-KEEPER stamped in large letters on the back of it. *Ib.*

4   I discovered to my surprise that the M.C.C. blazer was not red, white, and blue. *Ib.*

5   But when the ground is nearly drowned –
      Each May it is the same –
    You must agree cricket to be
      A most abandoned game! *Ib.*

6   I would no more let the ball go between my legs when fielding
than I would shake a lady's hand with my batting-gloves
on. *Ib.*

7   I felt as pleased with myself as the witness in the police court
who asked the magistrate if he would kindly speak up. *Ib.*

8   We all enjoy feeling sorry for players who get hurt.
Applauding them when they manfully continue is one of
the real pleasures of the game. *Ib.*

9   If the batsmen keep sitting on the splice,
      I'll take to knitting or breeding mice. *Ib.*

10   A gentleman is a man who never hurts anybody else
unintentionally. *Ib.*

11   The advantages of having two wickets instead of one are at
present practically non-existent. But would they not be
considerable if the bowlers and batsmen at both ends were
to bowl and bat simultaneously?

12   Most plays are content with a run but *The Bat* has scored a
boundary hit. *Sunday Pictorial*

13   (Review of Capek's play *R.U.R. – Rossum's Universal Robots*)
Not content with discoursing on supermen, the author presents
them in the flesh – or whatever it is they are made of. *Daily
Express (17 January 1923)*

W. C. FIELDS

William Claude Dukenfield Fields (1879–1946), American film
actor and director, began his career as a music-hall juggler, but

developed into a famous eccentric film comedian and writer,
often appearing as a sleazy alcoholic.

1   Rhino meat is as tough as broiled mother-in-law on the chef's
    night off. (Quoted in Carlotta Monti and Cy Rice's *W. C.
    Fields and Me*)

2   At Philadelphia there was little to do after dark, so he got
    married. *Ib*

3   Anyone smiling after curfew rang was liable to be arrested. If a
    woman dropped her glove on a street, she might be
    hauled before a judge for strip-teasing. *Ib*.

4   I was locked up only for petty crimes such as vagrancy,
    larceny, and murder. *Ib*.

5   It was a marriage of convenience, as my father had a blister on
    his big toe and couldn't travel far to find a girl. *Ib*.

6   In the beginning Adam and Eve were very happy and
    contented, as well they should have been with no work, no
    income tax, no lawyers, no doctors, no children, and no
    dogs. *Ib*.

7   I believe in tying the marriage knot, as long as it's round the
    woman's neck. *Ib*.

8   I've no objection to writers preparing my scripts as long as
    they don't let me see them. *Ib*.

9   Don't ever open your mouth first in a business deal.... The fish
    that opens its mouth gets caught. *Ib*.

10 (Entering a restaurant)
    Gee, the soup sounds good. (Quoted in *Abracadabra*)

11 Anyone who hates children and dogs can't be all bad
    (Quoted in *Radio Times*)

12 All my available funds are completely tied up in ready cash.
    (Quoted in Bennet Cerf's *Try and Stop Me*)

13   I am free of all prejudice. I hate everyone equally.
     (Quoted in *Saturday Review*)

14   We lived for days on nothing but food and water.

15   After two days in hospital I took a turn for the nurse.

16   It's a funny world: a man's lucky if he gets out of it alive.
     You're Telling Me

17   Thou shalt not take the name of the Lord thy God in vain
     unless you've used up all the other four-letter words.

RONALD FIRBANK

Arthur Ronald Firbank (1886–1926) was educated privately but
attended Cambridge University. He was well-to-do, and his early
novels were published with his own money and soon became
something of a cult, e.g. *Valmouth* (1919); *The Flower Beneath the
Foot* (1923).

1   "A shark, a shark!" was her way of designating anything that
    had fins, from a carp to a minnow. *The Flower Beneath the
    Foot*

2   She was looking, as the grammar-books say, "meet" to be
    robbed, beneath a formidable tiara, and wearing a dozen
    long strands of pearls. *Ib.*

3   "I could not be more astonished," the King declared, "if you
    told me there were fleas at the Ritz." *Ib.*

4   I feel his books are all written in hotels with the bed unmade.
    Ib.

5   I seem to *know*, when I talk to a man, the colour of his braces.
    Ib.

6   "Life is like that, dear," she would sometimes say, but she
      would never say what it was that life was like. *Ib.*

7   "I think I must undertake a convenience for dogs," the
      Archduchess crooned. "It is disgraceful that they have not
      got one already, poor creatures." *Ib.*

8   "I hate dancing with a fat man," Mlle de Nazinizi was saying,
      "for if you dance at all near him his stomach hits you." *Ib.*

9   Beneath the strain of expectation even the little iced-sugar
      cakes looked green with worry. *Ib.*

10   To behold the Englishman at his best one should watch him
      play tip and run. *Ib.*

11   She made a ravishing corpse. *The Eccentricities of Cardinal
      Pirelli*

12   I daresay you can't judge Egypt by *Aida*. *Ib.*

13   All millionaires love a baked apple. *Vainglory*

14   To be sympathetic without discrimination is so very
      debilitating. *Ib.*

15   There was really no joy in pouring out one's sins while he sat
      assiduously picking his nose. *Valmouth*

CYRIL FLETCHER

Cyril Fletcher (1913–), English variety comedian, pantomime
actor, radio and TV performer, regularly appeared in *That's
Life*. His own writing features the 'Odd Ode'.

1   For many years I was quite sure that thunder was the sound of
      God moving his beer barrels across the floor of the sky.
      Nice One Cyril

2   My act had to follow hers [his future wife's], and the audience
      really didn't want me at all...You might say that Betty

overwhelmed them. I followed and underwhelmed them. *Ib.*

3   Horses know if it is your first ride. *Ib.*

4   I never went to a university. Who was it that said, "After university it's a straight run through to the grave."? *Ib.*

5   At the Princes Theatre (now the Shaftesbury) I made a lady laugh so much she gave birth then and there, in the middle of an Odd Ode, to a child. *Ib.*

6   A bishop sat through a complete performance of *A Midsummer Night's Dream*, played entirely by the girls of the school of which he was Chairman of the Governors. Praising the girls' performance in his speech of thanks he said (innocently), "I think this is the first time I have ever seen a female Bottom". *Ib.*

7   Our first domestic servant seemed to be an old English sheepdog in maid's uniform, who needed to keep her feet up as much as possible. *Ib.*

8   I have a large voice. Large enough to fill the Albert Hall; or empty it. *Ib.*

9   Beneath the bridge we often caught trout for the table. Don't tell anyone, but we scooped them out of the stream in a wastepaper basket. *Ib.*

10   Once an old gentleman assailed me after one of my lunch-time speeches with, "I thought your material was very rude." "Which, sir, were the jokes that offended you?" "I couldn't tell you. I'm very deaf and they were laughing very loudly." *Ib.*

MICHAEL FRAYN

Michael Frayn (1933–), journalist and *Observer* columnist, has achieved his main fame with plays, several of which, e.g. *Donkey's Years* (1977), *Noises Off* (1982), received Best Comedy awards. He has also written novels and a number of TV plays and documentaries.

1   This doctor said that all medicine was really witchcraft pure and simple, and when he wrote out a prescription for pills it was no different from the old days when they recited a spell. *Alphabetical Order*

2   "Would you like me to die here, or shall I go outside?" *Ib.*

3   When anyone says they often think something it means they've just thought of it now. *Ib.*

4   People get what they've always wanted, and what they've always wanted turns out to be not what they want at all. *Ib.*

5   "I even have to help with the children's treat! And I haven't got any children! I hate children! I hate their parents too!" *Ib.*

6   Roddy used to eat cold peas and treacle for breakfast. *Donkey's Years*

7   It's not going to be much of a party if they don't throw toilet rolls out of the window. *Ib.*

8   There is a certain social barrier between the drunk and the sober which is very difficult to bridge. Especially on a narrow stairway. *Ib.*

9   They threw me in the river...I took it all in good part. I usually take my clothes off first, so it made a change. *Ib.*

10   Is there anything worse than speaking a foreign language to someone who turns out to be English? *Clouds*

12   The only thing my mosquito netting let through was the mosquitoes. *Ib.*

13   Everyone wants to be asked to tell the story of his life. *Ib.*

14   If he says he's coming tomorrow you can be sure of one thing – it won't be tomorrow. *Make and Break*

15 They put in dogs to stop the thieving, and what happened? Someone walked off with all the bloody dogs' food! *Ib.*

16 As the curtain rises the award-winning modern telephone is ringing. *Noises Off*

17 BURGLAR. No bars, no burglar alarms! They ought to be prosecuted for incitement. *Ib.*

A. G. GARDINER

Alfred George Gardiner (1865–1946), journalist and essayist, wrote many light articles and essays under the pen-name 'Alpha of the Plough'. For many years he was editor of the *Daily News*. Among his books were several collections of his articles, including *Pebbles on the Shore* (1915) and *Many Furrows* (1924).

1 Is not the title *As You Like It* a confession that Shakespeare had bitten his quill until he was tired of the vain search for a title? *Pebbles on the Shore*

2 If you eat brown bread you will never die, or at any rate you will live till everybody is tired of you. *Ib.*

3 I once hung a silk hat up in the smoking-room of the House of Commons. When I went to get it, it was gone. *Ib.*

4 Blackbirds and starlings have stripped the cherry-tree as clean as a bone. Their point of view is that the cherries are provided for them, and they are right. Our moral code is for us, not for them. *Ib.*

5 If you were offered beer out of a china basin you would feel that the liquor had somehow lost its attraction. *Ib.*

6 If Shakespeare were put in the dock and tried by the grammarians, he would be condemned as a rogue and a vagabond. *Ib.*

7   Sir Edward Clarke proposed that we should impose a tax on those who had names as well as numbers on their garden gates. *Ib.*

8   Ordinarily the wearing of a monocle seems like an announcement to the world that you are a person of consequence. *Ib.*

9   When one of the Rothschilds heard that a friend of his had died leaving a million of money he remarked: "Dear me, dear me! And I thought he was quite well off." *Ib.*

10 I cannot get rid of a secret conviction that the aim of railway trains is to give me the slip. *Ib.*

11 It was one of those stopping, leisurely trains that give you an understanding of eternity. *Selected Essays*

12   I flicked the mosquito off my nose, and he made a tour of the railway compartment, visited each window, fluttered round the light, decided there was nothing so interesting as that large animal in the corner, and came and had a look at my neck. *Ib.*

13   In spite of his military uniform and his formidable weapon, the wasp is not a bad fellow, and if you leave him alone he will leave you alone. *Ib.*

14   There is nothing so irresistible as the right sort of smile. It is better than a silver spoon in the mouth. *Ib.*

15   This body of mine is carried about on a pair of cunningly devised stilts, and waves a couple of branches with five flexible twigs at the end of each. *Ib.*

16   If we were sentenced to eternal life we would shriek for the promise of death. *Ib.*

17   A fine use of words does not necessarily mean a use of fine words. *Ib.*

18   It is difficult to find a name for anything, from a baby to a book. *Ib.*

19   I recall occasions when I have talked to myself. They have been remarks I have made on the golf links. *Ib.*

20   Though I am the perfect height of five-feet-nine-and-a-half I always feel depressed and outclassed in the presence of a man six-feet-two. *Ib.*

JOHN GAY

John Gay (1685–1732), English dramatist and poet, achieved great success with *The Beggar's Opera* (1728), a satirical play with songs based on traditional tunes. A sequel, *Polly* (1729), was banned for political reasons.

1   All men are thieves in love, and like a woman the better for being another's property. *The Beggar's Opera*

2   O Polly, you might have toyed and kissed,
By keeping men off, you keep them on. *Ib.*

3   POLLY. All my sorrows are at an end.

MRS PEACHAM. A mighty likely speech, in troth, for a wench who is just married! *Ib.*

4   Where is the woman who would scruple to be a wife if she had it in her power to be a widow? *Ib.*

5   How happy could I be with either
Were t'other dear charmer away! *Ib.*

6   Is there any power that could tear me away from you? You might sooner tear a fee away from a lawyer or a pretty woman from a looking-glass. *Ib.*

7   Am I not your wife? Your neglect of me proves it! *Ib.*

8   The necessaries of life?...Whether we can afford it or not, we must have superfluities! *Polly*

9   Leave morals and honesty to the poor, as they do in London. *Ib.*

10   Must we, if we love an apple,
Nevermore desire a peach? *Ib.*

11   'Tis better far to go without
Than to have too much of woman. *Ib.*

12   What are you about, putting the weapons in order so briskly? At this rate we shall be hard pressed to avoid the battle! *Ib.*

13   Those who in quarrels interpose
Must often wipe a bloody nose. *Fables*

14   And what's a butterfly? At best
He's just a caterpillar dressed. *Ib.*

15   In every age and clime we see
     Two of a trade can ne'er agree. *Ib.*

16   Envy is a kind of praise. *Ib.*

17   Life is a jest, and all things show it.
     I thought so once; but now I know it.
     My Own Epitaph

W. S. GILBERT

Sir William Schwenck Gilbert (1836–1911) was a Londoner,
educated at King's College. His fame rests on his comic operas,
with music by Sir Arthur Sullivan, which have enjoyed lasting
popularity. He also wrote other plays, e.g. *The Palace of Truth*
(1870) and light verse, e.g. *Bab Ballads* (1869).

1   I should have preferred to ride through the streets of Venice;
    but owing, I presume, to an unusually wet season, the
    streets are in such a condition that equestrian exercise is
    impractical. *The Gondoliers*

2   In enterprise of martial kind,
        When there was any fighting,
    He led his regiment from behind –
        He found it less exciting. *Ib.*

3   It's extraordinary what unprepossessing people one can love if
    one gives one's mind to it. *Ib.*

4   DUKE. May she make you happier than her mother has made
    me.
    DUCHESS. Sir!
    DUKE. If possible. *Ib.*

5   In short, whoever you may be,
    To this conclusion you'll agree –
    When everyone is somebodee,
        Then no one's anybody! *Ib.*

6   His mother is the wife of a highly respectable and
     old-established brigand who carries on an extensive
     practice in the mountains. *Ib.*

7   Hearts just as pure and fair
     May beat in Belgrave Square
     As in the lowly air
         Of Seven Dials.
     Iolanthe

8   Can a Lord Chancellor give his own consent to his own
     marriage with his own Ward? Can he marry his own Ward
     without his own consent? And if he marries without his
     own consent, can he commit himself for contempt of his
     own Court? *Ib.*

9   My learned profession I'll never disgrace
     By taking a fee with a grin on my face
     When I haven't been there to attend to the case. *Ib.*

10   But then the prospect of a lot
         Of dull M.P.'s in close proximity,
     All thinking for themselves, is what
         No man can face with equanimity. *Ib.*

11   When Wellington thrashed Bonaparte,
         As every child can tell,
     The House of Peers, throughout the war,
     Did nothing in particular,
         And did it very well. *Ib.*

12   No girl *could* care for a man who goes about with a mother
     considerably younger than himself! *Ib.*

13   You dream you are crossing the Channel, and tossing
         about in a steamer from Harwich –
     Which is something between a large bathing-machine
         and a very small second-class carriage –
     And you're giving a treat (penny ice and cold meat)
         to a party of friends and relations –
     They're a ravenous horde – and they all came aboard

at Sloane Square and South Kensington Stations. *Ib.*

14 You are very dear to me, George. We were boys together – at least *I* was. *Ib.*

15 Self-decapitation is an extremely difficult, not to say dangerous, thing to attempt. *The Mikado*

16 I can trace my ancestry back to a primordial atomic globule. Consequently my family pride is something inconceivable. *Ib.*

17 I have a left shoulder-blade that is a miracle of loveliness. People come miles to see it. *Ib.*

18 I forget the punishment for compassing the death of the Heir Apparent...I think boiling oil occurs in it, but I'm not sure. I know it's something humorous, but lingering. *Ib.*

19 I don't go about prepared to execute gentlemen at a moment's notice. I've never even killed a bluebottle! *Ib.*

20 What on earth is this love that upsets everybody, and how is it to be distinguished from insanity? *Patience*

21 It is my hideous destiny to be madly loved at first sight by every woman I come across. *Ib.*

22 You can't get high Aesthetic tastes, like trousers, ready made. *Ib.*

23 I know he is a truly great and good man, for he told me so himself. *H.M.S. Pinafore*

24 In spite of all temptations
To belong to other nations,
    He remains an Englishman! *Ib.*

25 Be careful to be guided by this golden rule –
    Stick close to your desks and never go to sea,
    And you all may be Rulers of the Queen's Navee. *Ib.*

26 Like precious stones, his sensible remarks
Derive their value from their scarcity!
Princess Ida

27   To everybody's prejudice I know a thing or two;
I can tell a woman's age in half a minute – and I do.
But although I try to make myself as pleasant as I can,
Yet everybody says I am a disagreeable man! *Ib.*

28   Isn't your life extremely flat
With nothing whatever to grumble at! *Ib.*

29   He's everything that I detest,
But if the truth must be confessed,
    I love him very dearly!
The Sorcerer

30   You've no idea what a poor opinion I have of myself, and
how little I deserve it. *Ruddigore*

31   I'm very well acquainted too with matters mathematical,
I understand equations, both the simple and quadratical,
About binomial theorem I'm teeming with a lot o' news –
With many cheerful facts about the square of the
                hypotenuse.
The Pirates of Penzance

32   When the enterprising burglar's not a-burgling,
When the cut-throat isn't occupied in crime,
He loves to hear the little brook a-gurgling,
And listen to the merry village chime. *Ib.*

33   When your humour they flout,
    You can't let yourself go;
And it *does* put you out
    When a person says "Oh,
I have known that old joke from my cradle".
The Yeomen of the Guard

34   LIEUT. Say that I had sat me down hurriedly on something
sharp? Can you give me an example?
JESTER. Sir, I should say that you had sat down on the
spur of the moment. *Ib.*

35   I feel sure that she does not regard me with absolute
indifference, for she could never look at me without

having to go to bed with a sick headache. *Utopia Limited*

36   Whether you're an honest man or whether you're a thief
Depends on whose solicitor has given me my brief. *Ib.*

37   For ten years past I've ruled a theatrical company. A man
who can do that can rule anything! *The Grand Duke*

38   When a man maintains a bachelor establishment he has the
best of reasons to decline to take his wife there. *The Palace
of Truth*

39   My cook gets eighty pounds a year and gives me a kipper.
Sullivan's cook gets five hundred pounds a year and gives
him the same thing in French.
(Quoted in Hesketh Pearson's *Gilbert and Sullivan*)

40   Old age is the happiest time in a man's life. The worst of it is,
there's so little of it. *Ib.*

OLIVER GOLDSMITH

Oliver Goldsmith (1728–1774), poet, essayist, novelist, and
dramatist, was the son of an Irish clergyman. His literary fame
now rests chiefly on his novel *The Vicar of Wakefield* (1766) and
his stage comedy *She Stoops to Conquer* (1773).

1   Those who lack money when they come to borrow, will also
lack money when they should come to pay. *A Citizen of the
World*

2   In reading the newspapers I have reckoned up not less than
twenty-five great men, seventeen very great men, and nine
very extraordinary men in less than half a year. *Ib.*

3   The true use of speech is not so much to express our wants as
to conceal them. *Ib.*

4   (At the theatre)

Those who sat in the boxes came to furnish part of the entertainment themselves – not a curtsey or a nod that was not the result of art. *Ib.*

5   "Wanted – an usher to an academy. N.B. He must be able to read." *Ib.*

6   I am told he makes a very handsome corpse, and becomes his coffin prodigiously. *The Good-Natured Man*

7   Silence has become his mother tongue. *Ib.*

8   There are some faults so nearly allied to excellence that we can scarce weed out the fault without eradicating the virtue. *Ib.*

9   (David Garrick)

On the stage he was natural, simple, affecting:
'Twas only that when he was off he was acting.
Retaliation

10   Logicians have but ill defined
As rational the human mind:
Reason, they say, belongs to man,
But let them prove it if they can.
Logicians Refuted

11   She freely lent to all the poor –
     Who left a pledge behind.
Elegy on Mrs Blaize

12   Her doctors found, when she was dead,
     Her last disorder mortal. *Ib.*

13   The dog, to gain some private ends,
     Went mad and bit the man.
Death of a Mad Dog

14   The man recovered of the bite –
     The dog it was that died. *Ib.*

15   Here lies poor Ned Purdon, from misery freed,
        Who long was a bookseller's hack.
     He led such a damnable life in this world
        I don't think he'll wish to come back.
     Epitaph

16   In my time, the follies of the town crept slowly among us in
     the country, but now they travel faster than a stage-coach.
     She Stoops to Conquer

17   MRS HARDCASTLE. I'm not so old as you'd make me. Add
     twenty to twenty, and make money of that.
     MR HARDCASTLE. Let me see – twenty added to twenty
     makes just fifty-seven. *Ib.*

18   MRS HARDCASTLE. Anybody who looks in his face can see
     he's consumptive. He coughs sometimes.
     MR HARDCASTLE. Yes, when his liquor goes the wrong
     way. *Ib.*

19   MR HARDCASTLE. He's very generous.
     MISS HARDCASTLE. I believe I shall like him.
     MR HARDCASTLE. Young and brave.
     MISS HARDCASTLE. I'm sure I shall like him.
     MR HARDCASTLE. And very handsome.
     MISS HARDCASTLE. My dear papa, say no more; he's
     mine. *Ib.*

20   When a girl finds a fellow's outside to her taste, she then sets
     about guessing the rest of his furniture. *Ib.*

21   If you know neither the road you are going, nor where you
     are, nor the road you came, the first thing I have to
     inform you is – you have lost your way. *Ib.*

22   In good inns you pay dearly for luxuries, in bad inns you are
     fleeced and starved. *Ib.*

23   There was a time when I fretted myself about the mistakes of
     the government; but finding myself every day grow more
     angry, and the government no better, I left it to mend
     itself. *Ib.*

24 They fall in and out ten times a day, just as though they were man and wife. *Ib.*

25 Let schoolmasters puzzle their brain
   With grammar, and nonsense, and learning;
Good liquor, I stoutly maintain,
   Gives genius a better discerning. *Ib.*

26 A book may be amusing with numerous errors, or it may be very dull without a single absurdity. *The Vicar of Wakefield*

27 There is no arguing with Johnson. When his pistol misses fire, he knocks you down with the butt end of it. (Quoted in Boswell's *Life of Johnson*)

RICHARD GORDON

Richard Gordon (1921–) qualified as a doctor at St Bartholomew's Hospital, and was a specialist in anaesthetics before his retirement in 1952, when he published his now famous humorous novel, *Doctor in the House.* Over a dozen 'Doctor' books came from his pen, as well as many others.

1 The brain of which man is so ridiculously proud is exposed in Gray's *Anatomy* as a huge, juicy walnut. *Bedside Manners*

2 A man's choice of doctor is second in importance only to his choice of wife, and is generally made as illogically. *Ib.*

3 To nab a nurse for a bedpan outside regulation hours is an art compared with which catching a waiter's eye in a busy restaurant is simple. *Ib.*

4 To lose two pounds of body fat you would have to walk from London to Dover and then swim the Channel. *Ib.*

5 A heart transplant operation is as simple as changing the wheel on your car. *Ib.*

6   After a kick on the head in a football match as a medical student, I woke up in my own hospital to find screens drawn round my bed, from which I concluded I was dead. *Ib.*

7   I don't believe the kindliest of men ever learned about the death of his doctor without a feeling of smugness. *Ib.*

8   There is as good a chance of your surviving a stay in hospital as any other disaster. Remember that every week people manage to get out of them alive. *Ib.*

9   In some South American hospitals patients must bring their own grub and a relative to cook it. *Ib.*

10 In a little while at St Swithin's you will learn enough bad habits to make life bearable. *Doctor in the House*

11 His low opinion of medical students sprang largely from the days when he had been reading Theology at Cambridge and, on his attempt to break up a noisy party of medicals late one night, he had been forcibly administered an enema of Guinness's stout. *Ib.*

12 On Christmas Day the patients were woken up by the night nurses at 5 a.m. as usual, given a bowl of cold water, and wished a Merry Christmas. *Ib.*

13 I believed that examiners, like lightning, never strike twice in the same place. *Ib.*

14 There is nothing delights a policeman more than being thrown into a midwifery case. There is a chance he might have to assist in the performance, which means a picture in the evening papers. *Ib.*

15 She clapped me to her bosom like a belladonna plaster and pushed me on to the dance floor...It was like being lashed to an upholstered pneumatic drill. *Doctor at Sea*

16 There is little wife-swapping in suburbia...It is unnecessary, the females all being so similar. *Good Neighbours*

17 My affair with Lucy, like some of the world's great passions, had blossomed delicately on a patch of prickly dislike. I happened to pinch her bucket, so she hit me over the ear with her spade. *Doctor in the Swim*

18 A doctor who isn't a hypochondriac is as rare as a teetotal pub-keeper. *Ib.*

19 He had been taken on the household strength of some frightfully rich American woman in the capacity of a husband, for which there happened to be a vacancy at the time. *Ib.*

20 It is remarkably easy to confuse the diagnosis of a broken heart with a scratch from a playful kitten. *Ib.*

21 All adolescents should be given a thoroughly beastly time of it, in order to leave them something to look forward to when they grow up. *Ib.*

22 Everyone goes into an aeroplane or a hospital wondering if they'll ever get out of either again alive. *Ib.*

23 Nothing is so uninteresting to look at as clouds from the inside. *Ib.*

HARRY GRAHAM

Harry Jocelyn Clive Graham (1874–1936) was an old Etonian soldier who combined a distinguished career with a prolific literary output. He was an officer in the Coldstream Guards and a Trustee of the British Museum, but he also wrote much humorous verse and prose, with a leaning towards black comedy.

1 Some people prefer children to dogs because a licence is not necessary for the former. *The Bolster Book*

2 To watch a little child drowning within a few yards of me has a dispiriting effect upon my appetite. *Ib.*

3   There are a large number of excellent restaurants in London.
     There is a particularly good one on the right-hand side. *Ib.*

4   When a burglar enters your flat and attempts to make away
     with the silver spoons which it has taken you years to
     collect from various restaurants, children (unlike dogs) do
     not rush out and hold him firmly by the trousers until you
     feel in a sufficiently heroic mood to emerge from under
     the bed and telephone for the police. *Ib.*

5   People used to ask me, "What do you call your dog?" and I
     always replied truthfully that I did not call it anything at
     all. I had tried calling it, but it never paid the slightest
     attention. *Ib.*

6   I am altogether averse to a dog being taught tricks. How
     would you like to sit up, with a lump of sugar balanced on
     the end of your nose, until some idiot said "Paid for"? *Ib.*

7   Whoever heard of a serious crime being committed by a
     gardener? *Ib.*

8   His house is Liberty Hall; and if his guests want to smoke they
     can go out into the greenhouse. *Ib.*

9   "Learn to take things easily," said a great Roman
     philosopher. "Especially other people's things." *Ib.*

10   The beach at Southsea bristles with those banana skins with
     which civilized man attempts to relieve the dull monotony
     of Nature's handiwork. *Ib.*

11   Late last night I killed my wife,
     Stretched her on the parquet flooring;
     I was loath to take her life
     But I *had* to stop her snoring.
     Ruthless Rhymes

12   Making toast at the fireside,
     Nurse fell in the grate and died;
     And what makes it ten times worse
     All the toast was burnt with nurse. *Ib.*

13   O'er the rugged mountain's brow
       Clara threw the twins she nursed,
   And remarked, "I wonder now
       Which will reach the bottom first?" *Ib.*

14   Father heard his children scream,
   So he threw them in the stream,
   Saying, as he drowned the third,
   "Children should be seen, *not* heard!" *Ib.*

15   You know "Lord's"? Well, once I played there,
       And a ball I hit to leg –
   Struck the umpire's head and stayed there,
       As a nest retains an egg. *Ib.*

16   Procure a grievance and a gun
   And you can have no end of fun.
   Verse and Worse

17   Corruption is not nice at all,
   Unless the bribe be far from small. *Ib.*

18   Don't be an anarchist, but if you must
   Don't let your bombshell prematurely bust. *Ib.*

19   He has the reputation, too,
       Of being what is known as "slim",
   Which merely means he does to you
       What you had hoped to do to him. *Ib.*

20   The righteous man has much to bear:
   The bad becomes a billionaire. *Ib.*

21   Be patient with your elders, babe, I pray...
   Each moonlike face that causes you to scream so
   Is really human, though it may not seem so. *Ib.*

22   Always assume an obsequious figure
   To all who are richer than you are – or bigger. *Ib*

23   A witty tongue may be within
   The contours of a feeble chin. *Ib.*

24   The thoughtful babe invariably takes
      The very greatest pains about his birth...
Doesn't arrive too early in the morning,
      Nor yet omit to give sufficient warning.
Deportmental Ditties

25   I gladly publish to the pop.
      A scheme of which I make no myst.,
And beg my fellow scribes to cop.
      This labour-saving syst.
I offer it to the consid.
Of every thoughtful individ. *Ib.*

26   Augustus was a sober child:
For eighteen months he never smiled...
Still, I was thankful when at three
He grew as bright as bright could be.
At six he was so sharp and quick
When shown a dog he'd say "Tick, tick!"
When birds across his vision flew
He'd point and say "Bow-wow!" or "Moo!"
Strained Relations

27   He over-ate at times, perhaps,
And after ev'ry meal would lapse
Into a kind of torpid doze,
Replete and almost comatose –
To wake refreshed and full of zeal
In time for the ensuing meal. *Ib.*

28   To Percival, my youngest son,
Who cut his sister's throat for fun,
I said: "Now, Percy! Manners, please!
You really mustn't be a tease!
I shall refuse, another time,
To take you to the Pantomime!"
More Ruthless Rhymes

29 I never shall forget the shame
To find my son had forged my name.
If he'd had any thought for others
He might at least have forged his mother's. *Ib.*

30 Grandpapa fell down a drain:
Couldn't scramble out again.
Now he's floating down the sewer –
That's one grandpapa the fewer. *Ib.*

31 When ski-ing in the Engadine
My hat blew off down a ravine.
My son, who went to fetch it back,
Slipped through an icy glacier's crack
And then got permanently stuck.
It really was infernal luck. *Ib.*

32 My son Augustus, in the street one day,
    Was feeling quite exceptionally merry.
A stranger asked him: "Can you tell me, pray,
    The quickest way to Brompton Cemetery?"
"The quickest way? You bet I can," said Gus,
    And pushed the fellow underneath a bus. *Ib.*

33 Oh, gloomy, gloomy was the day
When poor Aunt Bertha ran away!
But uncle finds today more black:
Aunt Bertha's threatening to run back! *Ib.*

34 My publisher is most anxious that I should state that all the
characters mentioned in these pages are entirely
imaginary; no reference is made to any living person. I
am, indeed, very glad to hear this. *Ib.*

VIRGINIA GRAHAM

Virginia Graham (1910–), daughter of Harry Graham, was
educated at Notting Hill High School. She has been film critic
of the *Spectator*, a contributor to *Punch*, and a writer of regular

humorous articles in *Homes and Gardens.*

1   No woman should know more than a man. If she wants to be loved, that's to say. *Everything's Too Something*

2   Everybody knows that everybody gives everybody else bath essence, or bath salts, or bath powder for Christmas. *Ib.*

3   The terrible question which confronts all brides on their honeymoon is whether to pin up their curls and cream their faces before going to bed. *Ib.*

4   (House painting)

     "I'd better do the narrow bits, my hand is steadier," said boastfully, is enough to wreck any marriage. *Ib.*

5   I'm fairly nonchalant about the poor. *Ib.*

6   Go to any bazaar and you will find dozens of kind-hearted women in varying stages of muddle...selling identical pots of honey at different prices, losing raffle tickets, leaning against meringues, struggling with paper and string, and sticking chutney labels on to pots of marmalade. *Ib.*

7   I was tidying out a cupboard the other day, by which I mean I was picking up all the polythene bags, looking at them and putting them down again. *Ib.*

8   Now that we all travel abroad so much, there comes a dreadful moment in our lives when our foreign friends, whom we strongly urged to visit us, actually do so. *Ib.*

9   It's difficult not to feel sorry for derelict cars... abandoned in the streets.... Sometimes when nobody, absolutely nobody, is looking, I go quietly up and pat one, and say, "Poor old thing". *Ib.*

10   Plumbers, as you know, have to go back to fetch their tools, and what is so fascinating is that in spite of thousands and thousands of jokes about them having to go back and fetch their tools, they still have to go back and fetch their tools. *Ib.*

11   My house is far, far uglier than sin,
Gamboge without and chocolate fudge within.
Punch (1941)

12   Oh, the men looked fine in their hunting pinks,
they upped their horses and downed their drinks,
but I still maintain that there's nothing stinks
    like a Meet of the Hounds in the Morning. *Ib.* (*1948*)

MICHAEL GREEN

Michael Frederick Green (1927–), English journalist and
humorous writer, has worked on the staff of several
newspapers. His books include *The Art of Coarse Rugby* (1960);
The Art of Coarse Drinking (1973); *Even Coarser Sport* (1978);
Tonight Josephine (1982).

1   A Coarse Golfer is one who has to shout "Fore" when he
putts. *The Art of Coarse Golf*

2   The most important part of a Coarse Golfer's equipment is
that which he keeps for lending to an opponent... with the
intention of sabotaging his game. *Ib.*

3   I have changed my grip, which had previously been based on
a diagram in a book on how to play cricket. *Ib.*

4   No new golf joke has been invented for forty years. *Ib.*

5   A golf magazine...recommends a golfer to visit his pro. once a
month to have his grip checked. Or perhaps it was to have
his cheque gripped. *Ib.*

6   What is needed instead of all these instructional books on how
to play golf is a walloping good book on how to give it up.
Ib.

7   Golf balls are attracted to water as unerringly as the eye of a
middle-aged man to a female bosom. *Ib.*

8   The secret of missing a tree is to aim straight at it. *Ib.*

9   Only the other day I actually saw someone *laugh* on a posh golf course in Surrey. *Even Coarser Sport*

10   I haven't been so scared since the TV licence-detector van stopped in our road. *Ib.*

11   The yacht sailed with all the speed and panache of a very fat old age pensioner shopping at Sainsbury's on Saturday morning. *Ib.*

12   When office management can think of nothing else to do, they issue a memo. As they can think of nothing else to do most of the time, memos have become debased coinage. *The Art of Coarse Office Life*

13   The advertisement referred to "an opportunity for a well-educated and motivated man to earn a fortune in the academic field." The job was selling encyclopedias on commission only. *Ib.*

14   To leave a message in a drawer marked private is the best way of spreading information round the office quickly. *Ib.*

15   If you wish to be a failure in life, offend the chief executive's secretary. *Ib.*

16   A business lunch has become an art form in its own right and any relation to business or lunch has long since disappeared. *Ib.*

17   Communication by phone between two British business people is almost impossible. There will never be a time when one of them is not in conference, at lunch, out of the office, away today, busy at the moment, seeing somebody, coming in late this morning, leaving early this afternoon. *Ib.*

18   A Coarse Drinker is a man who blames his hangover on the tonic water and not the gin. *The Art of Coarse Drinking*

19   A notice behind the reception desk announces that Consolidated Hotels Ltd. welcome you, and won't be responsible if they lose your baggage. *Ib.*

20   Hospitality after funerals is much more lavish than after weddings, and there are no speeches. *Ib.*

21   The greatest mistake made about parties is to think guests are going to be grateful to their hosts. *Ib.*

22   Coarse Rugby is played by those who are too old, too young, too light, too heavy, too weak, too lazy, too slow, too cowardly, or too unfit for ordinary rugger. *The Art of Coarse Rugby*

23   During a fog players have been known to touch down on a neighbouring hockey pitch. *Ib.*

24   The first half is invariably much longer than the second. This is partly because of the late kick-off, but is also caused by the unfitness of the average coarse referee. *Ib.*

25   It is always useful to have a first-aid expert in the team. Not to heal the injured, but to order the removal of hurt opponents, whether they need it or not. *Ib.*

JOYCE GRENFELL

Joyce Grenfell (1910–79), born Joyce Phipps, was partly American, and the niece of Lady Astor. Her particular talent was shown in humorous monologues revealing many different types of character, but she was also successful as a stage and film actress, e.g. *The Happiest Days of Your Life* (1947).

1   Thank you, Dicky, for closing the cupboard door for me...Dicky, is there someone *in* that cupboard? Well, let her out at once! *George – don't do that*

2   We're going to be lovely flowers growing in the grass... Geoffrey stand up – flowers don't look backward through their legs. *Ib.*

3   (Nativity play)
Stop hitting each other! Mary and Joseph were friends. *Ib.*

4   Of course, we know that by tradition the Wise Men and the Kings were one and the same, but we did want everyone in our Nursery School to have a chance. *Ib.*

5   I'm ashamed of you Sidney, a big boy of four to go around eating buttons off little girls' frocks. *Ib.*

6   My father was the only person I ever knew who addressed babies in their prams as if they were his contemporaries. He spoke as he would to a bank manager or a bishop; friendly but respectful. *Ib.*

7 No, Sidney, Mrs Hingle has *not* got a funny hat on, that's her hair. So sorry, Mrs Hingle. Sometimes we *are* just a trifle outspoken. *Ib.*

8 A Chinese man-cook was a decided novelty...Then one day we discovered he was mixing the soup in what used to be called a domestic article...He thought the pot was a very large cup. *Joyce Grenfell Requests the Pleasure*

9 Her parents were friends of my parents, and that is often reason enough for the children to shy away from each other. *Ib.*

10 The best shopping is done when it is unpremeditated. Virginia and Tony went out one Saturday morning to buy a reel of cotton and came back with a Bentley car. *Ib.*

11 (On a hospital tour in wartime)

Viola and I were a little surprised to hear ourselves announced as "two well-known artistes who have flown out from home to entertain men in bed." *Ib.*

12 I can imagine myself being happy as a choosy domestic servant...and I'd recommend myself for everything except cleaning of baths and ironing. *Ib.*

13 He was a pear-shaped man with ears that looked as if they had been taken off, ironed out, and put back like teapot handles. *Ib.*

ST JOHN HANKIN

St John E. C. Hankin (1869–1909), British playwright and humorist, was a regular contributor to *Punch*, and author of several comedies, e.g. *The Two Mr Wetherbys* (1903), *The Return of the Prodigal* (1905), notable for their lively cynical humour.

1 The Rector says a clergyman should have no politics, but I say a clergyman with no politics is never made a bishop. *The Return of the Prodigal*

2   My girls were allowed to begin French directly they went to school. But I'm bound to say they don't seem to have learnt any, so perhaps it did no harm. *Ib.*

3   When people have far more children than is either convenient or necessary, the babies always exhibit extraordinary vitality. Nothing seems to kill them. *Ib.*

4   People who go to the Colonies always write home for money. *Ib.*

5   If you marry a man you like, you may come to love him – in time. But if you marry a man you love, you may easily come to loathe him. *Ib.*

6   What clever beggars you doctors are! You feel a fellow's pulse and look at his tongue and you know all about him at once. *Ib.*

7   It was no use making a cloth that would last a lifetime if people only wanted it to last twelve months. So now we don't make any *good* cloth at all, and your father has trebled his income. *Ib.*

8   The lower classes are always sympathetic to intoxication. *Ib.*

9   I don't like this pernicious modern jargon about shopkeepers and gentlefolk being much the same. There's far too much truth in it to be agreeable. *Ib.*

10   The law won't even allow me to put an end to myself. I should be rescued, very wet and bedraggled, from the muddy waters of the river by the solitary local policeman. *Ib.*

MIKE HARDING

Mike Harding (1944–), was born and educated in Manchester. Despite holding an Education degree he has not taught, but he achieved success as an entertainer with songs and patter. He has written several books and plays, and is a keen rambler and cyclist.

1 Did you ever have nightmares about going to school dressed only in a vest that was too short anyway? *The Armchair Anarchist's Almanac*

2 The craziest war ever was the War of Jenkins's Ear since there was nobody else it would fit. *Ib.*

3 Most people are now of the opinion that Mr and Mrs Einstein should never have given little Albert that chemistry set. *Ib.*

4 Have you ever wished that God would come out into the open and own up? *Ib.*

5 The Do-It-Yourself fanatic's wife is usually a nervous wreck because everything in the house either falls on her, traps her, or gives her an electric shock. *Ib.*

6 (Houses)
"Needs some renovation" means that the woodworm holding hands is the only thing keeping the house standing. *Ib.*

7 Mechanical things are made, in the main, so that they will go wrong. *Ib.*

8 Cars are an inconvenience...They cannot get you from door to door because you are not allowed to park there. *Ib.*

9 He was sent to prison for stealing an elastic band. Unfortunately the elastic band was wrapped around 80,000,000 francs. *Ib.*

10 British Rail gravy is specially made to stay on your plate even if trains turn upside down. *Ib.*

11 She launched herself at him, her bosoms sailing before her like railway buffers. *Punch Goes Abroad*

12 A table of fair-haired people were shouting and bawling and banging the table. "Are they fighting?" I asked. "No, boss,

they're Germans saying hello to each other." *Ib.*

13   The first time I went to a posh kid's house I couldn't understand why his eiderdown didn't have pockets and sleeves. (Quoted in Michael Parkinson's *The Best of Parkinson*)

14   At school I used to get out of fights by making people laugh. *Ib.*

15   He once said he'd have his toes amputated so he could stand closer to the bar. *Not With a Bang*

16   Me going on strike against sex is like an Eskimo going on strike against snow. *Ib.*

17   Eve gives Adam the apple, and what happens? The landlord evicts them! *Ib.*

18   The drab khaki of former years used to make ramblers in the rain look like mobile giant cow-pats. *Rambling On*

19   Nature is red in tooth and claw and it smells and sticks to your boots. *Ib.*

20   He carries a rucksack with compass and whistle. The compass to find his way and the whistle to blow for help when he finds that he hasn't found his way. *Ib.*

21   Map reading is incredibly easy and can be learnt in a couple of centuries by anyone with a first-class degree in Geography or a doctorate in Mathematics. *Ib.*

22   The photographs seem to be of creases in a blanket taken on a grey day in a darkened room. *Ib.*

23   Bonaparte was an insignificant little horror who realized that a good way to make people notice him was to kill them. *Ib.*

24   God didn't drive Adam and Eve out of the Garden of Eden, the midges did. *Ib.*

IAN HAY

John Hay Beith (1876–1952), educated at Fettes and Cambridge, was a distinguished officer in the First World War. In addition to writing two notable war books he made a reputation as author of humorous novels, e.g. *A Safety Match* (1911) and stage comedies, e.g. *Housemaster* (1936).

1   In the Army, "crime" is capable of infinite shades of intensity...from making a frivolous complaint about potatoes at dinner to irrevocably perforating your rival in love with a bayonet. *The First Hundred Thousand*

2   "Avoid amateur ministering angels...For twenty-four hours they nurse you to death, and after that they leave you to perish of starvation." *Ib.*

3   Mimic warfare enjoys one enormous advantage over the genuine article: battles *must always* end in time for the men to get back to their dinners at five o'clock. *Ib.*

4   The further away you remove the English soldier from the risk of injury, the higher you pay him. *Ib.*

5   The faint-hearted report themselves sick; but the Medical Officer merely recommends them to get well as soon as possible. *Ib.*

6   In July 1914 a headmaster received a letter from a mother intimating that her son had obtained a commission in the army for the duration of the war. She asked the Head to keep his place open for him until he came back! *Ib.*

7   At a well-regulated British dinner-table, if you wish to offer a glass of port to your neighbour on your right, you hand the decanter to the neighbour on your left, so that the original object of your hospitality receives it, probably empty, after a complete circuit of the table. *Ib.*

8   We were separated by an abyss of years, so our stomachs told us, from our last square meal. *Carrying On*

9   (In the First World War)

In France we contented ourselves with devising a pronounceable variation of the existing name. If a road was called La Rue du Bois, we simply called it "Roodiboys". Etaples was modified to "Eatables", and Sailly-la-Bourse became "Sally Booze". *Ib.*

10   The chief penalty of doing a job well is that you are immediately put on to another. This is supposed to be a compliment. *Ib.*

11   The Practical Joke Department has plainly taken a hand in the issue of so-called fur jackets...Corporal Mucklewame's costume gives him the appearance of a St Bernard dog. Sergeant Carfrae is attired in what looks like the skin of Nana, the dog-nurse in *Peter Pan*. *Ib.*

12   Schoolmasters always shout at one another after half-term. It's a useful alternative to homicide. *Housemaster*

13   (On rowing)

I've never been interested in an institution which the ancients reserved for galley slaves and a later age for convicted felons. *Ib.*

14   Eight men in an insecure boat, all looking one way and progressing another! *Ib.*

15   Everyone is sorry for saxophone players. *Ib.*

16   If you were a woman you'd know that the most difficult five years in a woman's life are from twenty-nine to thirty. *Ib.*

17   She comes of a class whose sole criterion of respectability is represented by a laborious solvency during life and an extravagant funeral after death. *Tilly of Bloomsbury*

18   It's no compliment to be loved by a man who has had no experience. *Ib.*

19   The proper thing to do was to deliver my lecture first and treat myself to a magnum of champagne afterwards. Unfortunately I reversed the order. *Ib.*

20   His knowledge of the English language was limited apparently to a few expletives of the most blood-curdling type, such as could only have been acquired from a sailor's throat. *A Sporting College*

21   The Headmaster of Fiction is invariably called "The Doctor" and he wears a cap and gown even when birching malefactors...For all we know he wears them in bed. *The Lighter Side of School Life*

22   School inspectors...receive a princely salary for indulging in the easiest and most congenial of all human recreations – that of criticising the efforts of others. *Ib.*

23   What is an educational expert? The answer is simple. Practically everybody...The only section of humanity to whom the title is denied are the people who have to teach. *Ib.*

JOSEPH HELLER

Joseph Heller (1923–), is an American advertising writer and novelist. He achieved considerable notice with his first book, a war novel, *Catch-22* (1961), and has also written plays.

1   He was a self-made man who owed his lack of success to nobody. *Catch-22*

2   He had decided to live for ever or die in the attempt. *Ib.*

3   Doc Daneeka was his friend and would do just about nothing in his power to help him. *Ib.*

4   Colonel Cathcart had courage and never hesitated to

volunteer his men for any target available. No target was too dangerous. *Ib.*

5   He knew everything about literature except how to enjoy it. *Ib.*

6   He had observed that people who did lie were, on the whole, more resourceful and ambitious and successful than people who did not. *Ib.*

7   All he was expected to do in the hospital was to die or get better, and since he was perfectly all right to begin with, getting better was easy. *Ib.*

8   Hungry Joe collected lists of fatal diseases and arranged them in alphabetical order so that he could put his finger without delay on any one he wanted to worry about. *Ib.*

9   "Don't tell me God works in mysterious ways," Yossarian continued. "There's nothing mysterious about it. He's not working at all. He's playing. Or else He's forgotten all about us." *Ib.*

10   The diabolical old man reminded Nately of his father because the two were nothing at all alike. *Ib.*

11   "My only fault," he observed, "is that I have no faults." *Ib.*

12   There is record that Shakespeare lived but insufficient proof he could have written his plays. *Picture This*

13   People in the seventh century before Christ has no idea they were living in the seventh century B.C. *Ib.*

14   To know that you do not know is to know a great deal. *Ib.*

15   Peace on earth would mean the end of civilization as we know it. *Ib.*

16   At sea and abroad, there was no race more warlike than the peace-loving Dutch. *Ib.*

17   [Seventeenth-century] textile workers in Leiden dwelt in tiny huts with only a straw mat on the floor for furniture. Fortunately their workday was so long that they little time

to spend at home. *Ib.*

18 An expert in international relations is generally as useful to his country as an expert in palmistry or phrenology. *Ib.*

19 When I grow up I want to be a little boy. *Something Happened*

O. HENRY

William Sydney Porter (1862–1910) became a well-known American short-story writer under the name O. Henry, after earlier years as bank clerk and journalist. His first collection of stories was *Cabbages and Kings* (1904). Other collections followed, e.g. *Strictly Business* (1910).

1 A favourite dodge to get your story read by the public is to assert that it's true, and then add that Truth is stranger than Fiction. *Whirligigs*

2 The woman showered us with a quick rain of well-conceived adjectives that left us in no doubt as to our place in her opinion. *Ib.*

3 By his eloquent and moving appeals Lawyer Gooch often sent estranged husband and wife back into each other's arms...and received big fees from these reyoked clients. Prejudiced persons intimated that his fees were in due course doubled, because the couples always came back later, anyhow, for a divorce. *Ib.*

4 The lawyer never circumlocuted when dealing with a woman. Women do, and time is wasted when both parties in debate employ the same tactics. *Ib.*

5 A city editor knows something about everything. *Ib.*

6 If a justice of the peace can marry a couple, it's plain he's bound to be able to divorce 'em. *Ib.*

7 All sociologists are more or less bald and exactly thirty-two. *Ib.*

8   Smite the poet in the eye when he would sing to you praises of
     the month of May. It is a month presided over by the
     spirits of mischief and madness. *Ib.*

9   The burglar got into the house without much difficulty;
     because we must have action and not too much
     description in a 2,000-word story. *Ib.*

10   She plucked from my lapel the invisible strand of lint – the
     universal act of woman to proclaim ownership. *Strictly
     Business*

A. P. HERBERT

Sir Alan Herbert (1890–1971) was a very remarkable man, a
qualified barrister, for many years a leading *Punch* writer, and
author of many successful plays, e.g. *Bless the Bride* (1947),
novels, e.g. *The Water Gipsies* (1930), and revues. He was
Independent M.P. for Oxford University (1935–50), and
notable for his wit and reforming zeal.

1   In the statutory regulations of many railway companies, for
     the purpose of freight a typewriter is counted as a musical
     instrument. *Misleading Cases*

2   The Reasonable Man...is devoid of any human weakness, with
     not a single saving vice...This excellent but odious
     character stands like a monument in our Courts of Justice.
     Ib.

3   Among the numerous tributes (in judicial pronouncements)
     to the Reasonable Man we might expect at least some
     passing reference to a reasonable person of the opposite
     sex; no such reference is found. *Ib.*

4   There is no conduct in a public thoroughfare which cannot
     be brought into some unlawful category. *Uncommon Law*

5   The only legal right of a person in a public street is to pass at

an even pace from one end of if to the other, breathing unobtrusively through the nose. *Ib.*

6 Public speech should be classed among those dangerous instruments, such as motor-cars and fire-arms, which no man may employ without a special licence. *Ib.*

7 At the beginning of a Parliament the Government have no time to do anything: at the end of a Parliament they have no courage to do anything. *Look Back and Laugh*

8 A Government Department appointing a Royal Commission is like a dog burying a bone, except that the dog does eventually return to the bone. *Ib.*

9 Beer (unlike milk) does not have to be boiled before it is fit to drink. *Ib.*

10 Greenfly, it's difficult to see
Why God, who made the rose, made thee. *Ib.*

11 No feature of the female form
Should strikingly exceed the norm.
What famous beauty comes to mind
Who boasted an immense behind?

12 It is not in the village pub that slander flows most free,
But in the virtuous shop and club where women swill their
tea. *Ib.*

13 Nothing's been the same since I took up with orange juice.
Derby Day

14 TO-DAY I am MAKing aN inno6£vation. as you mayalready
have gessed, I am typlng this article myself to save time
and exvBKpense. *Light Articles Only*

15 Why is the wicket seven miles away?
And why have I to walk to it alone?
Mild and Bitter

16 I love the doctors – they are dears;
But must they spend such years and years

Investigating such a lot
Of illnesses which no one's got,
When everybody, young and old,
Is frantic with the common cold. *Ib.*

17   I have only to draw a horse in a sweepstake and it bursts out coughing or swells at the knees. *Riverside Nights*

18   There is more joy in Fleet Street over one sinner that cuts his sweetheart's throat than over the ninety and nine just men who marry and live happily ever after. *Ib.*

19   As soon as they start talking about hearing the cuckoo, it snows. *Mr Pewter*

20   Almost any Englishman can steal a day off for the Derby if he gives his mind to it. *The Water Gipsies*

21   She reflected curiously that all relations with men seemed to lead in the end to cramp and pins and needles. *Ib.*

22   Her conversation became very subtle...very difficult to follow, like Henry James read aloud on the Underground Railway. *Ib.*

23   Surprised in a bedroom at his quiet work, the redistribution of the national income, the burglar made off. *Bardot M.P.*

24   I don't like champagne – hardly anybody does if the truth were told. *Ib.*

25   Yes, Vicar, I *do* give this woman away, and I'm also giving the wedding-dress, and three at least of those horrible bridesmaid's dresses...What's more, I'm giving the party afterwards. *Ib.*

26   Cricket is a tough and terrible, rough, unscrupulous game. No wonder our American friends do not like it. *Speech at Surrey CCC dinner*

27   I wake at dawn each day and murmur "Drat 'em!"
Those careless Cambridge men who split the atom.
Speech at Oxford University (June 1958)

SEYMOUR HICKS

Sir Edward Seymour Hicks (1871–1949), famous light comedy star, was born in Jersey. He first became an actor in 1887, and subsequently acted in, wrote, and presented numerous plays, being particularly connected with the Gaiety Theatre. He was knighted in 1935.

1   Why any reader should be called gentle I have yet to discover, for those whom I've watched have usually been frowning. *Vintage Years*

2   Having written this book, I have read it with the greatest possible pleasure. *Ib.*

3   Had the critics not been so generous, how easily they could have taken the wind out of my sales! *Ib.*

4   The desires of men and women have always been alike, from the day that Eve opened a fruiterer's shop and persuaded Adam to become her first customer. *Ib.*

5   A famous soldier on whose breast a great Queen had pinned a much-coveted decoration observed that the bravest thing he had ever done was to cross Piccadilly Circus! *Ib.*

6   The waving plumes on the heads of Flemish geldings were so grotesque-looking that no corpse with a sense of humour could have helped laughing. *Ib.*

7   The line Mrs Langtry should have spoken was, "Come, my love, let us seek some cosy nook," – instead of which she whispered into her bridegroom's ear, "Come, my love, let us seek some nosey cook." *Ib.*

8   As a travelling companion a fire on board a ship is worse than taking your mother-in-law on a honeymoon. *Me and My Missus*

9 [J.M.] Barrie once mischievously instructed an actor to try and convey the idea, as he stood without speaking, "that he had a brother who drank port in Shropshire". *Ib.*

10 I have always been a magnificent dancer with one foot; the other one, I think, is better on the violin. *Ib.*

11 As Fred Leslie was leaving, the slovenly owner of the boarding-house said: "I don't know what you mean about the place not being clean. There isn't a single flea in the house." "No," replied Leslie, "I quite agree. They're all married with large families." *Ib.*

STANLEY HOLLOWAY

Stanley Holloway (1890–1982), British stage and film actor. His most famous part was probably Doolittle in *My Fair Lady* (1964). He was noted also for his humorous monologues about Sam Small, a northern soldier under Wellington, and Albert, the young son in a northern family, some of which were written by Marriott Edgar (1880–1951).

1 (Sam's musket has been accidentally knocked out of his hand by a sergeant.)
   "Sam, Sam, pick oop tha' musket,"
   The Sergeant exclaimed with a roar.
   Sam said "Tha' knocked it down, reet, then tha'll pick it oop,
   Or it stays where it is, on't floor."
   Old Sam

2 "Sam, Sam, pick oop tha' musket,"
   The Duke said as quiet as could be.
   "Sam, Sam, pick oop tha' musket,
   Come on, lad, just to please me." *Ib.*

3   So Sam picked it up. "Gradely, lad," said the Duke,
       "Righto, boys, let battle commence." *Ib.*

4   (On sentry duty at Buckingham Palace)
       Sam stood there cold and haughty-like
       With dignity sublime.
       Some asks "Were you at Waterloo?"
       And some asks "What's the time?"
      'Alt, Who Goes There?

5   So Sam started swimming to Blackpool;
         It took 'im best part of a week.
      'Is clothes were wet through when he got there,
         And 'is boots were beginning to leak.
      Three Ha'pence a Foot

6   So straightway the brave little feller,
         Not showing a morsel of fear,
      Took 'is stick with the 'orses 'ead 'andle
         And pushed it right in the lion's ear.
      The Lion and Albert

7   Pa said, "Yon lion's et Albert,
       And 'im in his Sunday clothes, too." *Ib.*

8   "Has your son been evacuated?"
      Said the ARP man at the door.
      "He'd all them things done as a baby," said Mother,
      "He's not being done any more!"
      Albert Evacuated

9   I hated cabaret work. It was what I called appearing before
      knives and forks. *The Stanley Holloway Monologues*

10   Said Jonah "I've eaten a kipper or two
         But I never thowt one would eat me."
      Jonah and the Grampus

11   In England today we can do what we like
      So long as we do what we're told.
      The Magna Charter

W. DOUGLAS HOME

Hon. William Douglas Home (1912–), was educated at Eton, Oxford, and RADA. After starting as an actor he became a dramatist, most of his plays being light comedies e.g. *The Chiltern Hundreds* (1947); *The Reluctant Debutante* (1955); *The Secretary Bird* (1968). *Half Term Report* (1954) is an autobiography.

1   What a waste of good food! His teeth don't fit, and she talks so much that she never has the faintest idea what she's eating. *The Reluctant Peer*

2   You're just like me, dear. Always with the Don't Knows. Someone ought to form a party around us. *Ib.*

3   Poor Mr Gallup. He must be so busy. Nipping in and out of people's houses, asking the most naive questions. *Ib.*

4   To think those flawless sounds[from the Cathedral] should be produced by twenty vicious, spotty little boys. *The Bad Samaritan*

5   There are only two kinds of people in this world: those who are good enough to think they're wicked, and those who are wicked enough to think they're good. *Ib.*

6   Lancelot was grand, because he had his Achilles' heel. But Galahad went rushing about behind the Holy Grail, and never had a single human weakness. *Ib.*

7   I sometimes wonder if there aren't advantages in missing some of the facts of life. *Ib.*

8   Facetiousness is not a quality that women find endurable for long. *Ib.*

9   It isn't decent for a chap to get religion till he's over thirty. *Ib.*

10   "He's had three wives."
     "His own, or other people's?" *The Secretary Bird*

11   I knew a don at Oxford who couldn't understand all the fuss
     about sex. He said it only took place about three times a
     year at the outside. *Ib.*

12   It's a mad world, isn't it? And I can never quite understand
     which side of the asylum wall is the inside. *Ib.*

13   Women like a bit of domination. Kick them in the teeth and
     you're in clover. *Ib.*

14   Nothing killed romance so much as men going to bed at the
     same time as women...Who wants some great purple-faced
     baboon lying in bed behind them when they're working
     on the Pond's Cold Cream! *Ib.*

15   They say that in America marriage counts as reasonable
     grounds for divorce. *The Manor of Northstead*

THOMAS HOOD

Thomas Hood (1799–1845), a Londoner, was editor of various
magazines and author of many poems, both serious and
humorous. A feature of the latter was the free use of punning.

1   Ben Battle was a soldier bold,
        And used to war's alarms;
     But a cannon-ball took off his legs,
        So he laid down his arms.
     Faithless Nelly Gray

2   "I will never have a man
     With both legs in the grave!" *Ib.*

3   Oh, false and fickle Nelly Gray;
    I know why you refuse:
   Though I've no feet – some other man
    Is standing in my shoes! *Ib*.

4   There he hung till he was dead
    As any nail in town –
   For though distress had cut him up,
    It could not cut him down! *Ib*.

5   The body-snatchers they have come
    And made a snatch at me;
   It's very hard them kind of men
    Won't let a body be!
   Mary's Ghost

6   You thought that I was buried deep,
    Quite decent-like and chary,
   But from her grave in Mary-bone
    They've come and boned your Mary. *Ib*.

7   A constant sprinkle patters from all leaves,
   The very Dryads are not dry, but soppers,
    And from the houses' eaves
    Tumble eaves-droppers.
   Ode to St Swithin

8   In the fullness of joy and hope
   He seemed washing his hands with invisible soap
    In imperceptible water.
   Miss Kilmansegg

9   He had rolled in money like pigs in mud,
   Till it seemed to have entered into his blood. *Ib*

10   Alas, to think how people's creeds
   Are contradicted by people's deeds!
   A Tale of a Trumpet

11   No warmth, no cheerfulness, no healthful ease,
    No comfortable feel to any member –

No shade, no shine, no butterflies, no bees...
November!
NO!

12   His death, which happened in his berth,
        At forty-odd befell:
    They went and told the sexton, and
        The sexton tolled the bell.
    Faithless Sally Brown

13   When dishes were ready with garnish
        My watch used to warn with a chime –
    But now my repeater must furnish
        The dinner in lieu of the time!
    Fugitive Lines on Pawning My Watch

14   O there's nothing is certain in life, as I cried
        When my turbot eloped with the cat.
    Epicurean Reminiscences

15   When Eve upon the first of men
    The apple pressed, with specious cant,
    O, what a thousand pities then
    That Adam was not adamant!

BOB HOPE

Lester Townsend (Bob) Hope (1904–), American comedian, was born and spent most of his early years in England. As well as vaudeville and nightclub entertaining, he made over seventy films, a good many with Bing Crosby. His humour featured the brisk wisecrack.

1   When my wallet stopped aching, I had to admit that my new home was quite something.
    (Quoted in Morella, Epstein and Clark's *The Amazing Career of Bob Hope*)

2   (Hope is a great golf enthusiast.)

I'll go on living as long as I can. I've got a few jokes for the box [coffin]. If they raise the lid I'll say a few words on the way to the last hole. *Ib.*

3   He's a Scotsman. He got married in the backyard so the chickens could get the rice. *Ib.*

4   The first radio programme I did was so bad I got an envelope from my sponsor. There was no letter in it. Just a handful of his hair. *Ib.*

5   I can't stand torture. It hurts. *Ib.*

6   A comedy should build up like a rolling snowball, not sag in the middle like an ageing mattress. *Ib.*

7   It seems only yesterday that people were saying Bob Hope was a no-good bum who'd never amount to anything. In fact, it *was* only yesterday. *Ib.*

8   I used to be a starving actor. Then one day I got a break. My landlady started putting real cheese in the traps. *Ib.*

9   (In Moscow)

I'm not having any trouble with the language. Nobody talks to me. *Ib.*

10   It was so cold last night one chap fell out of bed and broke his pyjamas. *Ib.*

11   It's rather chic in a nauseating sort of way. *Ib.*

12   (To airmen in Alaska)

You know what you are? God's frozen people!
(Quoted in Pamela Trescott's *Bob Hope*)

13   Some folks slept on the floor,
Some in the corridor;
But I was more exclusive for
My room had "Gentlemen" on the door. *Ib.*

14   I think the first time I made anybody laugh was when I was

born – my mother was hysterical! (Quoted in Michael Parkinson's *The Best of Parkinson*)

15   Middle age is when your age starts to show around your middle.

16   If they liked you, they didn't applaud. They just let you live.

17   I've always felt England was a great place to work in. It's an island and the audience can't run very far. *I Owe Russia 1200 Dollars*

18   I don't know how old the plane was, but Lindbergh's lunch was still on the seat. *Ib.*

E. W. HOWE

Edgar Watson Howe (1853–1937), American editor and novelist, a printer in his youth, was later founder of the *Daily Globe*. His books include *The Story of a Country Town* (1883); *Country Town Sayings* (1911); *Ventures in Common Sense* (1919).

1   No one thinks he looks as old as he is. *Country Town Sayings*

2   Every time a boy shows his hands, someone suggests he should wash them. *Ib.*

3   It is well-known that we should not expect something for nothing – but we all do, and call it Hope. *Ib.*

4   If there were no schools to take the children from home for part of the time, the lunatic asylums would be filled with mothers. *Ib.*

5   A good scare is worth more to a man than good advice. *Ib.*

6   When you're in trouble, people who call to sympathize are really looking for the particulars. *Ib.*

7   A really busy person never knows how much he weighs. *Ib.*

8 There is no such thing as a convincing argument, though every man thinks he has one. *Ib.*

9 A woman might as well propose; her husband will claim that she did, anyway. *Ib.*

10 It is a matter for regret that many mean, low suspicions turn out to be well founded. *Ventures in Common Sense*

11 A man has his clothes made to fit him; a woman makes herself fit her clothes. *Ib.*

12 A modest man is often admired – if people ever hear of him. *Ib.*

13 Instead of loving your enemy, treat your friend a little better. *Ib.*

14 If you think before you speak, the other fellow gets his joke in first.

15 No woman ever falls in love with a man unless she has a better opinion of him than he deserves.

FRANKIE HOWERD

Francis Alick Howard (1921–), British eccentric comedian, performer in music halls, clubs, pantomime, and on radio, later branched out into films, plays, e.g. *A Funny Thing Happened On the Way to the Forum* (1963), and TV series, e.g. *Up Pompeii* (1970). *On the Way I Lost It* (1976) is an autobiography.

1 Descriptions of my face have included comparisons with most root vegetables (usually in an advanced state of decomposition). *On the Way I Lost It*

2 Falling down the stairs and landing on my head (as an infant)...was to leave me with a permanent dread of heights: to this day I get vertigo when the heels of my shoes are repaired. *Ib.*

3   In February 1940 I passed my first audition. Despite vague hopes that I'd be rejected on the grounds of insanity, the Army signed me up. *Ib.*

4   They sent me on a driving course. After a few rudimentary lessons they put me behind the wheel of what seemed the world's largest lorry packed with the entire British Army...which I predictably drove straight into a hedge. *Ib.*

5   I was so thin that only the sergeant's stripes on my arm distinguished me from the barrel of the Bren gun. *Ib.*

6   TV make-up was then fairly primitive, so that I resembled a grey boiled pudding. *Ib.*

7   You can always tell when he's lying – his lips move. *Ib.*

8   Inspiration and I have long gone our separate ways, and it's not easy to effect a reconciliation. *Ib.*

9   There's one really big advantage in staying single: you're never likely to be faced with the misery of divorce. *Trumps – and How to Come Up*

10   Nowadays I'm half expected to make an idiot of myself. So when I do, even by mistake, it doesn't matter. *Ib.*

ELBERT HUBBARD

Elbert Hubbard (1859–1915) was an American business man who retired early to found a printing firm and to establish magazines (e.g. *The Philistine*) for which he himself wrote much of the material.

1   One machine can do the work of fifty ordinary men. No machine can do the work of one extraordinary man. *Book of Epigrams*

2   A lie goes by the Marconi route, while Truth goes by slow freight. *Epigrams*

3   Orthodoxy is a corpse that doesn't know it's dead. *Ib.*

4   To escape criticism – do nothing, say nothing, be nothing. *Ib.*

5   Man is Creation's masterpiece. But who says so? *Ib.*

6   A pessimist is a man who has been compelled to live with an optimist. *The Notebook*

7   The greatest mistake in life is to be continually fearing you will make one. *Ib.*

8   Genius is the capacity for evading hard work. *The Philistine*

9   The worst thing about medicine is that one kind makes another necessary. *Ib.*

10   We shall never have a civilized society until we spend more money on books than we do on chewing-gum. *Ib.*

11   A miracle is an event described by those to whom it was told by people who did not see it.

12   If you can't answer a man's argument, all is not lost – you can still call him names.

13   Prison is a Socialist paradise where equality prevails, everything is supplied, and competition is eliminated.

14   No sensible working bee listens to the advice of a bedbug on the subject of business.

15   The world is moving so fast these days that the man who says a thing can't be done is interrupted by someone doing it. *The Notebook*

KIN HUBBARD

Frank McKinney Hubbard (1868–1950), was an American humorist who worked as a newspaper cartoonist and columnist. He created the character Abe Martin, a rustic whose wisecracks and epigrams formed an important part of Hubbard's writing.

1   You've got to be fifty-nine to believe a fellow is at his best at sixty. *Abe Martin's Primer*

2   There's no secret about success. Did you ever meet a successful man that didn't tell you all about it? *Ib.*

3   The trouble with mixing business with pleasure is that pleasure always comes to the top. *Ib.*

4   It's no disgrace to be poor, but it might as well be. *Abe Martin's Sayings and Sketches*

5   Now and then an innocent man is sent to the legislature. *Ib.*

6   It's going to be fun to watch and see how long the meek can keep the earth when they inherit it. *Ib.*

7   In spite of all our speeding it's still the fashion to be late. *Abe Martin on Things in General*

8   There's plenty of peace in any home where the family don't make the mistake of trying to get together. *Abe Martin*

9   I'll say this for adversity – people seem to be able to stand it, and that's more than I kin say for prosperity. *Abe Martin's Broadcast*

10   Alcoholic psychosis is D.T.'s in a dinner suit. *Ib.*

11   If there's anything in a beauty nap, most of the flappers I see must suffer from insomnia. *Ib.*

12   It's hard to say what does bring happiness. Poverty and wealth have both failed. *Ib.*

13   Nobody ever forgets where he buried the hatchet. *Ib.*

14   The safest way to double your money is to fold it over and put in your pocket.

15   Lots of folks confuse bad management with destiny.

SPIKE HUGHES

Patrick Cairns Hughes (1908–), educated at Perse School and abroad, has been a music and radio critic, BBC producer, and author of several humorous books, e.g. *The Art of Coarse Travel*, and books on music, e.g. *The Toscanini Legacy*.

1   A vigorous thicket of brambles (was) apparently holding the house up. *The Art of Coarse Gardening*

2   The plants that thrive best in the district are plastic daffodils. *Ib.*

3   When I have to lend a hand with the roses I do so in an old thick rubber macintosh.... At other times the roses make a grab at me as I pass by. Perhaps this is a gesture of affection. *Ib.*

4   Secateurs give you a wonderful feeling of power; and you become a menace to all you survey. *Ib.*

5   Even cows lose their domestic cosiness when they escape from the farmer's yard and lean over the fence and prune the lilac, flowers and all. *Ib.*

6   While ladybirds go about their pest control in an inconspicuous way, wasps show little inclination to devour greenfly or anything else if there is a chance of joining you for luncheon in the garden. *Ib.*

7   How on earth can one tell a male melon flower from a female unless one is a melon? *Ib*

8   Daffodils and garlic are not botanically related, and although they share the same bed are no more than just friends. *Ib.*

9   In these days people discuss the food they eat as frankly as they discuss their sex life. *Ib.*

10   Modern Normans cross from Dieppe to the South Coast in their thousands every summer disguised as students, and carrying tape-recorders, guitars, transistor sets, and other traditional aids to learning. *Ib.*

11   All Guide Books are invariably out of date before they are published. *The Art of Coarse Travel*

12   The motorist in distress on the high roads of the Continent...can expect no help from his fellow-countrymen, who, seeing a G.B. car drawn up by the side of the road, will think you have drawn up for natural causes and tactfully avert their eyes. *Ib.*

13   It is precisely the ageing and unagile fielders who are most use in front of the wicket, for their reflexes are slow and they are no longer able to side-step with ease the hard drive coming straight towards them. *The Art of Coarse Cricket*

ALDOUS HUXLEY

Aldous Leonard Huxley (1894–1963), English novelist and essayist, grandson of the scientist T. H. Huxley, educated at Eton and Oxford, was one of the most significant writers of his time. His novels include *Chrome Yellow* (1921), *Point Counter Point* (1928), and the famous satirical *Brave New World* (1932).

1   "I must have read twenty or thirty tons of books in the last five years." *Chrome Yellow*

2   "Farming seems to be mostly indecency and cruelty," said Anne. *Ib.*

3   Ragtime came squirting out of the pianola in gushes of treacle and hot perfume. *Ib*

4   The necessities of nature are base and brutish...To counteract these degrading effects he advised that the privy in every house should be in the room nearest heaven. *Ib.*

5   He resembled Shakespeare in knowing little Latin and less Greek. *Ib.*

6   Henry Wimbush rubbed his chin thoughtfully. "I can only think of two suicides, one violent death, four or perhaps five broken hearts, and half a dozen little blots on the scutcheon...On the whole it's a placid and uneventful record." *Ib.*

7   Women are always wonderfully the same. Shapes vary a little, that's all. *Ib.*

8   "At the present time" (said Mr Scogan) "the Anglican clergy wear their collars the wrong way round. I would compel them to wear not only their collars but all their clothes turned back to front." *Ib.*

9   "Beetles, black beetles" – his father had a really passionate feeling about the clergy. *Antic Hay*

10   The polished oaken stalls were devilishly hard...The real remedy , it flashed across his mind, would be trousers with pneumatic seats. *Ib.*

11   How pleasant it was to waste time! *Ib.*

12   Everything tasted as though it had been kept soaking for a week in the river before being served up. *Ib.*

13   "You've made me look," said Mrs Viveash (to the artist), " as though I were being blown out of shape by the wind." *Ib.*

14   He pointed to a couple of green iron chairs, standing isolated in the middle of the grass close together and with their fronts slanting inwards a little towards one another in a position that suggested confidential intimacy. *Ib.*

15   "We must explain scientifically why these trousers will be good for their health...We can even show that the trousers will be good for their souls." *Ib.*

16   There are few who would not rather be taken in adultery than in provincialism. *Ib.*

17   Mr Mercaptan went on to preach a brilliant sermon on that melancholy sexual perversion known as continence. *Ib.*

18   Lady Capricorn, he understood, was still keeping open bed. *Ib.*

19   People feel superior if they possess something new which their neighbours haven't got. *Ib.*

20   It's a pity they should have chosen the day of the Eton and Harrow match for the funeral. *Mortal Coils*

21   It is very difficult to flagellate yourself with a cane in a room so small that any violent gesture imperils the bric-à-bac. *Limbo*

22   Several excuses are always less convincing than one. *Point Counter Point*

23   The umbrellas were like black mushrooms that had suddenly sprouted from the mud. *Ib.*

24   The news is always bad, even when it sounds good. *Time Must Have a Stop*

25   In a few years, no doubt, marriage licences will be sold like dog licences, good for a period of twelve months. *Brave New World*

26   It was decided to abolish the love of nature, at any rate among the lower classes. *Ib.*

EUGENE IONESCO

Eugène Ionesco (1912–), Romanian-born dramatist who lives in France. A leading figure in the Theatre of the Absurd. His first play was *The Bald Prima Donna* (1948); his later ones include *Rhinoceros* (1958) and *Exit the King* (1961).

1   Arithmetic never did anyone any good. *The Lesson*

2   Arithmetic leads to Philology, and Philology leads to Crime. *Ib.*

3   How would you say, in English, the roses of my grandmother are as yellow as my grandfather who was born in Asia? *Ib.*

4   My dear friends, I've caught a flea somewhere, and I've come to see you in the hope of losing it again. *The Chairs*

5   Yoghurt is very good for the stomach, the lumbar regions, appendicitis, and apotheosis. *The Bald Prima Donna*

6   All doctors are charlatans. And all their patients too. *Ib.*

7   A really conscientious doctor ought to die with his patient. The captain goes down with his ship. He doesn't survive the wreck! *Ib.*

8   In the newspaper, why do they always give you the age of someone who's died but never tell you how old the babies are. *Ib.*

9   His father asked me if he could marry my daughter if ever I should have one. *Ib.*

10 He walked off in two directions at once. *Ib.*

11 It's a useless but absolutely vital precaution. *Ib.*

12 Describe a circle, stroke its back, and it turns vicious. *Ib.*

13 Look at yourself with one eye, listen to yourself with the other. *Improvisation*

14 There are more dead people than living. And their numbers are increasing. *Rhinoceros*

15 You can only predict things after they've happened. *Ib.*

16 A civil servant doesn't make jokes. *Ib.*

17 Characters in a play don't have to be bigger fools than in everyday life. *Foursome*

18 A nose that can see is worth two that sniff. *The Motor Show*

19 Just because she's our only daughter it doesn't mean she's sterile. *The Future Is in Eggs*

CLIVE JAMES

Clive James (1939–) was born in Australia and educated at Sydney University and Cambridge. His TV criticisms, e.g. *The Crystal Bucket* (1981) were originally written for the *Observer* (1972–82), and he has frequently appeared on television himself. He has also published books of literary criticism, and his autobiography, *Unreliable Memoirs* (1980).

1 The greatest risk to the television critic is bedsores. *Glued to the Box*

2 Kenneth Griffith is incapable of just standing there. He drops into a crouch, feet splayed, arms loosely gesticulating, eyes popping, teeth bared in a vulpine snarl. *Ib.*

3 During Stalin's speeches to the Praesidium the first delegate to stop clapping was routinely hauled off to be shot. *Ib.*

4 The black male dancers in Hot Gossip...making movements with their hips which suggest a doomed no-hands attempt to scratch their groins against an invisible tree. *Ib.*

5 I have hung around television studios long enough to know that there are people perfectly ready to commit suicide in order to star in a show of their own, even when they have nothing to say. *Ib.*

6 *Grease* – a movie of such grubbiness that after seeing it I felt like washing my skull out with soap. *Ib.*

7 Nureyev and a drowsily sexy ballerina engaged in a long attempt to pull each other's tights off without using fingers. *Ib.*

8   McEnroe was as charming as always, which means that he was
    as charming as a dead mouse in a loaf of bread. *Ib.*

9   Rod Stewart has an attractive voice and a highly unattractive
    bottom...He now spends more time wagging the latter
    than exercising the former. *Ib.*

10 Even in moments of tranquillity Murray Walker sounds like a
    man whose trousers are on fire. *Ib.*

11 Reformed drunks who don't realise that sobriety isn't
    supposed to be exciting are usually doomed to become
    drunks again. *The Crystal Bucket*

12 (BBC's *The Flying Dutchman*)
    This was the second showing of a production I had been lucky
    enough to miss on the first occasion. *Ib.*

13 Philippe likes making love with the light on, a sure sign of
    Continental sophistication. *Ib.*

14 David Frost was in terrific form...cueing in savants from all
    over the world, cutting them off before they had said
    enough, switching to the studio audience whenever
    somebody sitting in it had something irrelevant he wanted
    to contribute. *Ib.*

15 Disco dancing is really dancing for people who hate
    dancing...There is no syncopation, just the steady thump
    of a giant moron knocking in an endless nail. *Ib.*

16 Connors has taken to grunting loudly at the instant of hitting
    the ball instead of just afterwards. Confused opponents try
    to hit the grunt instead of the ball. *Ib.*

17 Out of a nightmare by Bram Stoker came the incredible
    Magnus Pyke, coiling and uncoiling around the studio like
    one of those wire toys that walk downstairs. *Visions Before
    Midnight*

18 A Bunny girl needs more than just looks. She needs idiocy,
    too. *Ib.*

19 Too good an actress to invest such claptrap with a single atom of belief, Billie Whitelaw plays Josephine with the effortless desperation of Rubinstein playing "Chopsticks". *Ib.*

20 Kenneth Tynan read the autocue as if it contained a threatening letter from somebody else instead of a script written by himself. *Ib.*

21 Robin Day, looking as if he had been wrestling with a mattress full of treacle, retired defeated. *Ib.*

22 One man smashed a milk bottle and lay down on the pieces while they put a heavy roller over him...Then they drove a Mercedes truck over him. Plainly this skill would come in handy any time you fell asleep on a broken milk bottle in the middle of an autobahn. *Ib.*

23 Nothing I have said is factual except the bits that sound like fiction. *Unreliable Memoirs*

24 Out on safari I lit a fire by the primitive method of rubbing a match against the side of a box.

ANTONY JAY & JONATHAN LYNN

Sir Antony Rupert Jay (1930–), British author and broadcaster, was head of BBC Talks Features 1963–4. He achieved fame (with Jonathan Lynn) with TV series *Yes, Minister* (1980–82) and *Yes, Prime Minister* (1986–7). Jonathan Lynn (1943–), is author of a number of screen plays and TV series.

1 So long as there is anything to be gained by saying nothing, it is always better to say nothing than anything. *Yes, Prime Minister, Volume 1*

2 The first rule of politics is Never Believe Anything Until It's Been Officially Denied *Ib.*.

3   "The truth" in politics means any statement that cannot be proved false. *Ib.*

4   If he was the sole entrant in an intelligence contest, he'd come third. *Ib.*

5   We should always tell the Press, freely and frankly, *anything* that they can easily find out. *Ib.*

6   "Statesmen" – the word politicians use to describe themselves. *Ib.*

7   "Surely we should use the United Nations debate to create peace, harmony, and goodwill?"
     "That would be most unusual," replied Humphrey, eyebrows raised. "The UN is the accepted forum for the expression of international hatred." *Ib.*

8   Bishops tend to live long lives – apparently the Lord is not all that keen for them to join Him. *Ib.*

9   It's an awful country. Women get stoned when they commit adultery. Unlike Britain, where women commit adultery when they get stoned. *Ib.*

10   Diplomacy is about surviving till the next century. Politics is about surviving till Friday afternoon. *Ib.*

11   I've often thought we should breathalyse M.P.s not when they're driving but when they're legislating. *Yes, Prime Minister, Volume 2*

12   Hacker devoted a great deal of his time to talking into his cassette recorder...It was the only thing in the world that was willing to listen to him uncritically. *Ib.*

13   Members of the Civil Service preserved a cloak of anonymity...which concealed from the rest of the country the fact that they were running it. *Ib.*

14   If he can't ignore facts, he's no business to be a politician. *Ib.*

15   Being a journalist, Hacker had no particular talent for

reporting facts. *Yes, Minister*

16   No potential Cabinet Minister ever moves more than twenty feet from a telephone in the twenty-four hours following the appointment of a new Prime Minister. *Ib.*

17   They have two types of chair to go with two kinds of Minister – one sort folds up instantly and the other sort goes round in circles. *Ib.*

PAUL JENNINGS

Paul Francis Jennings (1918–) for many years contributed an 'Oddly Enough' column to the *Observer*, and has published several 'Oddly' books, e.g. *Model Oddlies* (1956); *Next to Oddliness* (1955).

1   I once heard a lady, discussing who should be invited to a party, say, "Oh, don't let's have him. He's always the Life and Soul." *Model Oddlies*

2   No matter how many chairs you provide, they always sit on the edge of a little table and knock sherry on to the carpet. *Ib.*

3   I am, as far as I know, the only writer who has been presented with a ball of string by the National Federation of Ironmongers. *Ib.*

4   (Giving up smoking)

The Green Tablets (one after every meal) are supposed to make cigarettes taste awful. But they make everything else, including my tongue, nay, my very soul, taste awful as well. *Ib.*

5   The chemist's shop is filled with the most terrible, silent, beaten-looking people, all waiting for prescriptions, like a dumb chorus in some anguished play. *Ib.*

6   It is obvious that the Post Office does not really want to sell stamps from machines.... They are forever running out. I put my last coin in, a little flap comes down saying EMPTY, and my coin stays inside. *Ib.*

7   It's a curious thing, but I was never worried by moths while driving until I got a new car. *Ib.*

8   I once played the harmonium at a wedding, and on one of the bellows was affixed a stapled metal plate saying MOUSE-PROOF PEDAL. *Ib.*

9   Insurance is a cross between betting and philosophy. *Ib.*

10   If cats were in the police they'd never come below the rank of detective. *Ib.*

11   An intense French actor, beginning Hamlet's speech to Gertrude with "mère, mère", sounds exactly like a sheep. *Next to Oddliness*

12   Economics...always talks about the "flow" of money as though it were a sort of tide, with people carried helplessly on it like chicken-coops or dead trees. *Ib.*

13   A balance-sheet always reminds me of a dead butterfly, pinned out with the dead, beautiful wings in perfect symmetry. *Ib.*

14   Whenever I see a green car I know, sluggishly, that it's going to do something eccentric. *Ib.*

15   "Come along, darling, we must get back in case the plumber comes," I heard a lady say to her dog. *Ib.*

16   The *Radio Times* is the most losable of all papers, in spite of those tooled-leather covers for it that people give each other at Christmas. *Ib.*

17   I can't waltz very well; I gabble meaningless conversation with my partner while in my head I mutter *LONG short short LONG short short. Ib.*

18 Whichever way you tear up a shirt, it always makes seven long, thin pieces, a yard long by four inches; one of the pieces has a collar. *Ib.*

19 My car is frightened of thunder; it always does something odd. *Ib.*

20 It is only possible to operate my motor-mower at a steady trot.... The instant you engage the clutch the machine will rush away, with or without you. *Ib.*

21 How curious England will be in fifty years' time, when every fair-sized town has a university, doubtless interconnected by motorways. *Ib.*

22 It is time enough for football, prosaic and sober
In October...
Why should the time of mists and mellow fruitfulness
Succumb so soon to this dreary bootfulness?

JEROME K. JEROME

Jerome Klapka Jerome (1859–1927), English humorist, was at different times railway clerk, reporter, schoolmaster, actor, and editor. He is now best known for his humorous *Three Men in a Boat* (1889) and a play, *The Passing of the Third Floor Back* (1908).

1 If you desire to drain to the dregs the fullest cup of scorn and hatred that a fellow human creature can pour out for you, let a young mother hear you call her baby "it". *Idle Thoughts of an Idle Fellow*

2 Whatever you do, don't forget to say that the child has got its father's nose...You need have no conscientious scruples on the subject, because the thing's nose really does resemble its father's – at all events, as much as it does anything else. *Ib.*

3   It is impossible to enjoy idling thoroughly unless one has plenty of work to do. *Ib.*

4   Idling has always been my strong point. I take no credit to myself – it is a gift. *Ib.*

5   Love is like the measles; we all have to go through it. *Ib.*

6   It is easy enough to say that poverty is no crime. If it were, men wouldn't be ashamed of it. *Ib.*

7   I want a house that has got over all its troubles. I don't want to spend the rest of my life bringing up a young and inexperienced house. *They and I*

8   Veronica would find something to tumble over in the Sahara desert. *Ib.*

9   He was a powerfully built young man, and he didn't seem able to get it into his head that he was playing billiards, not cricket.... The balls flew before him, panic-stricken. *Ib.*

10   I like work; it fascinates me. I can sit and look at it for hours. *Three Men in a Boat*

11   I can't sit still and see another man working. I want to get up and superintend, and walk round with my hands in my pockets, and tell him what to do. It's my energetic nature. *Ib.*

12   George goes to sleep at a bank from ten to four each day, except Saturdays, when they wake him up and put him outside at two. *Ib.*

13   (Hanging a picture)

     When half an hour had been spent in tying up Uncle Podger's finger, he would have another go...Two people would have to hold the chair, and a third would help him up on it, and hold him there, and a fourth would hand him a nail, and a fifth would pass him a hammer, and he would take hold of the nail, and drop it. *Ib.*

14   I never read a patent medicine advertisement without being

impelled to the conclusion that I am suffering from the particular disease in its most virulent form. *Ib.*

15   There never was such a boy for getting ill. If there was any known disease going within ten miles of him, he had it...He would go out in a November fog and come back with sunstroke. *Ib.*

16   All that is required to make a good fisherman (some people say) is the ability to tell lies easily and without blushing. *Ib.*

17   You can see the fish in shoals when you are out for a walk along the banks; they come and stand half out of the water with their mouths open for biscuits...But they are not to be "had" by a bit of worm on the end of a hook. *Ib.*

18   Who wants to be foretold the weather? It is bad enough when it comes, without our having the misery of knowing about it beforehand. *Ib.*

19   Montmorency [the dog] came and sat on things just when they were wanted to be packed. He put his leg into the jam, and he worried the teaspoons, and he pretended that the lemons were rats, and got into the hamper and killed three of them. *Ib.*

20   It is a curious fact, but nobody is ever sea-sick – on land. *Ib.*

21   If a woman wanted a diamond tiara, she would explain that it was to save the expense of a bonnet. *Three Men on the Bummel*

22   It is the theory of the man in front [on a tandem] that the man behind does nothing; it is equally the theory of the man behind that the man in front merely does the puffing. *Ib.*

23   Every time you went over a stone or a rut the saddle nipped you. It was like riding on an irritable lobster. *Ib.*

24   When you are wearing a pair of stout boots, furniture gets out of your way; when you venture among things in

woolwork slippers and no socks, they come at you and kick you. *Ib.*

25 If you see a dog scampering across the grass in Germany, you may know for certain that it is the dog of some unholy foreigner. *Ib.*

26 A German plants seven rose-trees on the north side and seven on the south, and if they do not grow up all the same size and shape it worries him so that he cannot sleep. *Ib.*

27 In Germany you must not wear fancy dress in the streets. A Highlander of my acquaintance spent the first few days of his residence in Dresden arguing this question with the Government. *Ib.*

28 English spelling would seem to have been designed chiefly as a disguise for pronunciation. It is a clever idea, calculated to check presumption on the part of the foreigner. *Ib.*

29 Whatever he touched he upset; whatever he came near he knocked over. If it was a fixture, it knocked *him* over. *Novel Notes*

30 I'm looking forward to a future when travel will be done away with altogether. We shall be sewn up in a sack and shot there. *Tea Table Talk*

31 You can generally make people ridiculous by taking them at their word. *Ib.*

32 A lover and a husband are not the same. You run after somebody you want to overtake; but when you have caught him up you settle down quietly beside him. You don't continue shouting and waving. *Ib.*

DOUGLAS JERROLD

Douglas William Jerrold (1803–1857), was an English humorist,

dramatist, editor, and novelist. He was a leading contributor to
Punch, notably with *Mrs Caudle's Curtain Lectures*, and had a
great reputation as a wit.

1   He is one of those wise philanthropists who in a time of
     famine would vote for nothing but a supply of toothpicks.
     Wit and Opinions of Douglas Jerrold

2   The surest way to hit a woman's heart is to take aim kneeling.
     Ib.

3   That fellow would vulgarize the Day of Judgement. *Ib.*

4   Love's like the measles – all the worse when it comes late in
     life. *Ib.*

5   If I were a grave-digger, or even a hangman, there are some
     people I could work for with a great deal of enjoyment. *Ib.*

6   He was so good he would put rose-water on a toad. *Ib.*

7   Religion's in the heart, not in the knees. *The Devil's Ducat*

8   The only athletic sport I ever mastered was backgammon.
     (Quoted in W. Jerrold's *Douglas Jerrold*)

BRIAN JOHNSTON

Brian Johnston (1912–), British radio and TV commentator,
educated Eton and Oxford, was one of the earliest BBC cricket
commentators and has continued to act in this capacity. He
also successfully presented the radio programme *Down Your
Way* for many years.

1   I asked the old lady whether she had received a telegram from
     the Queen on her hundredth birthday. "Oh yes," she
     said, "I did, but I was very disappointed. It wasn't in her
     own handwriting." *It's a Funny Game*

2   Stuart Hibbert admitted that when introducing a programme

of American music he announced that the next piece would be The Star Bangled Spanner! *Ib.*

3   The day before I saw him [Air Marshal Sir Arthur Harris] he had judged the local Baby Competition in the town – and that *does* take courage. *Ib.*

4   An Irishman was told to take his car for a service, but he got it stuck in the church door. *Ib.*

5   He wore an earring on his left ear. I asked him why not one on the other ear. "Well," he replied, "I'd look an awful fool if I wore two, wouldn't I?" *Ib.*

6   A Round Table chairman announced after the loyal toast: "You may smoke now the Queen's drunk!" *Ib.*

7   I evidently greeted listeners with the words: "You join us at an interesting time. Ray Illingworth has just relieved himself at the pavilion end." *Ib.*

8   When I said that Peter May was lucky to have made a century as he was dropped when he was two, back came a listener's letter bemoaning the carelessness of mothers with their young children. *Ib.*

9   John Snagge was once reading the latest cricket scores. He said: "Yorkshire 232 all out – Hutton ill. No, I'm sorry – Hutton 111." *Rain Stops Play*

10   I was once doing a commentary on a match between Middlesex and Sussex when John Warr was captain of Middlesex. After a while I began: "Well, the latest news here is that Warr's declared." *Ib.*

11   Once when I said that "Ray Illingworth has two short legs, one of them rather square," a lady wrote and told me not to be so personal. *Armchair Cricket*

12   Everyone has an aunt in Tunbridge Wells. *Down Your Way*

PHILIP KING

Philip King (1904–79), was a prolific British playwright, with several years' acting experience. Many of his plays were produced in the West End, e.g. *See How They Run* (1944); *Sailor Beware* (co-author, 1955), and some were filmed.

1   You can't reason with men. You've just to train 'em. *Sailor Beware*

2   (After a fall)
     Every bone that isn't broken is bent. *Pools Paradise*

3   "What's this – coffee or Oxo?"
     "Coffee. I mean, it must be – I've put sugar in it" *Ib.*

4   VICAR. I want new bells in the belfry. I started a fund. I told my congregation "Stop at nothing" – and they did! *Ib.*

5   If I was caught in Blandford in uniform I should be shot at dawn – *and* they'd cancel my next leave. *See How They Run*

6   In the army there is never any reason for anything. *Ib.*

MILES KINGTON

There is nothing conventional about Miles Kington (1941–). An Englishman born in Ireland and educated in Scotland, he plays double-bass with the humorous singing group Instant Sunshine, and is a staff member of *Punch* and a *Times* columnist. He revels in mixing French and English.

1   The only Oxford and Cambridge Boat Races ever remembered are those in which one side has gratifyingly sunk. *Miles and Miles*

2   After taking a bath, however hard you dry yourself, you are still wet when you put your clothes on. *Ib.*

3   Just because 6 times 9 has always equalled 54 never seems to me quite good enough a reason for supposing it will do so next week. *Ib.*

4   The only talk I've had on sex was from an embarrassed headmaster about the reproduction of lupins. I'm as ready as can be if ever I fall in love with a lupin. *Ib.*

5   The Spaniards were a fierce but well organized people who tricked the Incas into believing that they had come as tourists. *Ib.*

6   Flushing a lavatory is always described as pulling a chain, though I daresay nine times out of ten we push a knob or depress a handle. *Ib.*

7   The three wise men...probably thought at the time, well, nice to give the baby a little start in life with a few gifts: myrrh and frankincense to enjoy now, and some gold to put in the Roman Post Office savings account for later on. *Ib.*

8   There is no climate in Lima, only a sort of light drizzle. *Ib.*

9   When birds sing and hop around, they are not being merry and affectionate, of course; they are being aggressive and demanding the price of a cup of coffee. *Nature Made Ridiculously Simple*

10   The exclamation mark is the literary equivalent of a man holding up a card reading LAUGHTER to a studio audience. *Punch*

11   Before I went to Moscow I knew two things about Lenin. One, it wasn't his real name. Two, he couldn't possibly be forty feet high, as his pictures and statues tended to suggest. *Punch Goes Abroad*

12   ADAM. Je ne suis pas anti-God. Il a fait un job terrifique. Mais pourquoi les slugs? Et pourquoi surtout, les greenfly?

Il a inventé le greenfly, mais il a oublié le garden spray.
The Franglais Lieutenant's Woman

13   Je ramblais, lonely comme un cloud,
    Qui flotte en haut sur dale et hill,
    Quand tout à coup je vis un crowd
    De touristes dans le Lakeland Grill. *Ib.*

14   Opinion Poll: a survey which claims to show what voters are thinking but which only succeeds in changing their minds. *The Times (10 May 1983)*

15   Holiday: a period of activity so intense that it can only be undertaken three or four weeks in the year. *The Times*

16   Alderney – a great spinach omelette off the coast of France. *On BBC2 (16 November 1988)*

E. V. KNOX

Edmund George Valpy Knox (1881–1971), educated at Rugby and Oxford, was for many years editor of *Punch*, to which he usually contributed under the pen-name Evoe.

1   One should bathe about noon. But when you look out of the window you find that the sea has gone about half-way across the Channel...One cannot help looking a fool as one pursues a reluctant sea half-way to France. *It Occurs To Me*

2   What I have never been able to discover is whether the fellows who swim the Channel are obliged to keep their feet off the ground all the way. *Ib.*

3   It has never been found possible to put the whole of one's life in an autobiography. The first few hours have to be taken on hearsay, and the last few added by a later hand. *Ib.*

4   There were no clues at all. The utmost efforts of Scotland

Yard failed to shed any light on the mystery. Even the newspapers were baffled. *Ib.*

5   I cannot weave or spin. The number of wheels and spindles confuses my mind...When I contemplate ridiculous machinery of this kind I can only marvel that men, and quite frequently women, wear clothes. *Ib.*

6   There is a kind of person who will sit down and compose an answer to a family letter directly it has been received. *Ib.*

7   There is no more popular exhibition in London than the smashing up of a road, especially when it is done by a forty-thousand horsepower dentist's drill. *Ib.*

8   Of the simple truth that Mary Queen of Scots wrote the so-called works of Shakespeare I have long been earnestly convinced...note the intimate knowledge of court procedure in Scotland (*Macbeth*), the close familiarity with the French tongue (*Henry V*), and the ample leisure for playwrighting afforded by long imprisonment. *Ib.*

9   How relieved we all were when the Einstein trouble blew over and it was no longer necessary to go about wondering whether there was a kink in space or time! *Ib.*

10   I used to be a fearful lad,
The things I did were downright bad...
At Bickershaw and Strood and Staines
I've often got on moving trains,
And once alit at Norwood West
Before my coach had come to rest.
The Everlasting Percy

CHARLES LAMB

The writings of Charles Lamb (1775–1834), one of the great English essayists, are marked by gentle humour, despite sadness and tragedy in his personal life. Most of his essays were originally written for the *London Magazine* under the pseudonym Elia.

1 The human species...is composed of two distinct races, those who borrow and those who lend. *Essays of Elia*

2 *Borrowers of books* – those mutilators of collections, spoilers of the symmetry of shelves, and creators of odd volumes...That foul gap in the bottom shelf, like a great eye-tooth knocked out, once held the tallest of my folios. *Ib.*

3 They affirm that they have no pleasure in winning; that they can while away an hour very agreeably at a card-table, but are indifferent whether they play or no...These insufferable triflers are the curse of a table. *Ib.*

4 The modern schoolmaster is expected to know a little of everything, because his pupil is required not to be entirely ignorant of anything. *Ib.*

5 I have been trying all my life to like Scotchmen, and am obliged to desist from the experiment in despair. *Ib.*

6 When I consider how little of a rarity children are...I cannot for my life tell what cause for pride there can possibly be in having them. *Ib.*

7 Coleridge holds that a man cannot have a pure mind who refuses apple dumplings. *Ib.*

8 The author of the *Rambler* [Dr Johnson] used to make inarticulate animal noises over a favourite food. *Ib.*

9 When I am not walking, I am reading; I cannot sit and think. Books think for me. *Last Essays of Elia*

10 A pun is a pistol let off at the ear; not a feather to tickle the intellect. *Ib.*

11 A presentation copy of a book is a copy of a book which does not sell, sent by the author, with his foolish autograph at

the beginning of it. *Ib.*

12 My grandmother had never-failing pretexts for tormenting children for their own good. *Saturday Night*

13 (To his friend Martin Burney)

If dirt was trumps, what hands you would hold!

14 (To Wordsworth)

Separate from the pleasure of your company, I don't much care if I never see another mountain in my life. *Letters*

15 Nothing puzzles me more than time and space, and yet nothing troubles me less, as I never think about them. *Ib.*

16 I have made a little scale, supposing myself to receive various accessions of dignity: 1, Mr C. Lamb; 2, C. Lamb, Esq.; 3, Sir C. Lamb; 4, Baron Lamb of Stamford; 5, Viscount Lamb; 6, Earl Lamb...9th, King Lamb; 10th, Emperor Lamb; 11th. Pope Innocent; higher than which is nothing but the Lamb of God. *Ib.*

17 Some cry up Haydn, some Mozart,
Just as the whim bites. For my part,
I do not care a farthing candle
For either of them, or for Handel.
Free Thoughts on Some Eminent Composers

18 The devil, with his foot so cloven,
For aught I care may take Beethoven;
And, if the bargain does not suit,
I'll throw him Weber in to boot! *Ib.*

19 I would not go four miles to visit
Sebastian Bach – or Batch – which is it? *Ib.*

20 The greatest pleasure I know is to do a good deed by stealth, and have it found out by accident. *Table Talk*

21 We are ashamed at the sight of a monkey as we are shy of poor relations. *Ib.*

HARRY LAUDER

Sir Harry Lauder (1870–1950) worked in the mines as a lad, but lived to become a famous music-hall singer and comedian, knighted in 1919. He wrote his own songs, one of them, *Roamin' in the Gloamin'*, being used as the title of his autobiography (1926).

1 I pictured my ancestors as bold buccaneers setting forth from their caves on the rock to harry and rob the English...still popularly supposed to be one of Scotland's principal occupations. *Roamin' in the Gloamin'*

2 The chief qualification for the job of strawberry picking was the ability to whistle. The young pickers were supposed to whistle all the time to prove they were not eating the strawberries. *Ib.*

3 His song began with the assertion that he was a soldier and a man. As he was a weedy individual...wearing steel-framed spectacles, the audience refused to accept his statement. *Ib.*

4 Sandy had an extraordinary big nose, and when he sang he had a habit of shaking his head, which made his nose wobble. *Ib.*

5 (A music-hall in Glasgow)
The trial turns preceding mine had all got short shrift...Those that didn't retire of their own accord were hauled off by the stage manager with the aid of a long crooked stick hooked round their necks. *Ib.*

6 They used to say that Sir Henry Irving's manner of nodding his head while declaiming his part was actually his method of counting the people in the house. *Ib.*

7 The audience took me and my songs to their hearts. I was as

happy as a king – indeed a lot happier than most kings I have met. *Ib.*

8   The only trouble the officers of the Highland division had to face was to prevent the men fighting among themselves when they were not fighting the Germans. *Ib.*

9   How did I feel under shell fire? Horrible! I knew I had legs and a head, but there was nothing in between. *Ib.*

STEPHEN LEACOCK

Stephen Butler Leacock (1869–1944), born in England, was Professor of Economics at McGill University in Canada for many years, but is best remembered for his humorous writings, e.g. *Nonsense Novels* (1911); *Frenzied Fiction* (1917).

1   At the moment when Annerly spoke of the supernatural I had been thinking of something entirely different. The fact that he should speak of it at the very instant when I was thinking of something else struck me as a very singular coincidence. *Nonsense Novels*

2   He flung himself upon his horse and rode off madly in all directions. *Ib.*

3   His long aristocratic face proclaimed his birth, and he was mounted on a horse with a face even longer than his own. *Ib.*

4   A keen sportsman, he excelled in fox-hunting, dog-hunting, pig-killing, bat-catching, and the pastimes of his class. *Ib.*

5   It was a wild and stormy night on the west coast of Scotland. This, however, is immaterial to the present story, as the scene is not laid in the west of Scotland. *Ib.*

6   It was a gloriously beautiful Scotch morning. The rain fell softly and quietly. *Ib.*

7   I was a tall, handsome young fellow...with a face in which honesty, intelligence, and exceptional brain power were combined with simplicity and modesty. *Ib.*

8   I eked out a miserable existence on the island...Eating sand and mud undermined my robust constitution. I fell ill. I died. I buried myself. *Ib.*

9   Captain Bilge, with a megaphone to his lips, kept calling out to the men in his rough sailor fashion: "Now then, don't over-exert yourselves, gentlemen. Remember, we've plenty of time. And keep out of the sun as much as you can." *Ib.*

10 Think how it must feel to be alone in New York, without a friend or relation at hand, with no one to know or care what you do. It must be great! *Ib.*

11 Take the question of germs and bacilli. Don't be scared of them...If you see a bacilli, walk right up to it and look it in the eye. *Literary Lapses*

12 The progress of science is a wonderful thing...A hundred years ago there was no bacilli, no ptomaine poisoning, no diphtheria, no appendicitis. All these we owe to medical science. *Ib.*

13 The rich jewels that he wore, the vast fortune that rumour ascribed to him, appealed to something romantic in Gwendoline's nature. *Ib.*

14 The barber gets his customer pinned in the chair with his head well back, covers the customer's face with soap, and then, holding his hand firmly across the customer's mouth, to prevent all utterance and force him to swallow the soap, he asks: "What did you think of the game yesterday?" *Ib.*

15 I detest life-insurance agents; they always argue that I shall some day die, which is not so. *Ib.*

16 I cannot honestly deny that it takes a good deal of physical courage to ride a horse. This, however, I have. I get it at about forty cents a flask. *Ib.*

17 The true botanist knows a tree as soon as he sees it. He learns to distinguish it from a vegetable by merely putting his ear to it. *Ib.*

18 (Boarding-house Geometry)

Boarders in the same boarding-house and on the same floor are equal to one another. *Punch*

19 All the other rooms being taken, a single room is said to be a double room. *Ib.*

20 A pie may be produced any number of times. *Ib.*

21 The clothes of a boarding-house bed, though produced ever so far both ways, will not meet. *Ib.*

EDWARD LEAR

Edward Lear (1812–88), artist and traveller, wrote nonsense verses intended for children, and he is now best known for these, e.g. *The Owl and the Pussy-Cat* (1871) and for his rather primitive limericks.

1   Thank the Lord you are not a Centipede! Every Sunday morning...happens the weekly cutting of toenails and general arrangement of toes. And if that is a bore with ten toes, what would it have been if the will of Heaven had made us with a hundred feet! *Letters* (in *A Book of Learned Nonsense*)

2   I think of marrying some domestic henbird and then of building a nest in one of my olive trees. *Ib.*

3   These muttering, miserable, mutton-hating, man-avoiding, misogynic, morose and merriment-marring, mocking, mournful, minced-fish and marmalade masticating Monx. [monks]. *Ib.*

4   I was never in so dry a place as this in all my life! When the children cry, they cry dust and not tears. *Ib.*

5   He wove him a wondrous Nose –
     A Nose as strange as a Nose could be!
     Of vast proportions and painted red,
     And tied with cords to the back of the head.
     In a hollow rounded space it ended,
     With a luminous lamp within suspended.
     The Dong with the Luminous Nose

6   The Pobble who has no toes
         Swam across the Bristol Channel;
     But before he set out he wrapped his nose
         In a piece of scarlet flannel.
     The Pobble Who Has No Toes

7   It's perfectly known that a Pobble's toes
    Are safe – provided he minds his nose. *Ib.*

8   She made him a feast at his earnest wish
    Of eggs and buttercups fried with fish. *Ib.*

9   The Owl and the Pussy-Cat went to sea
        In a beautiful pea-green boat.
    The Owl and the Pussy-Cat

10 They dined on mince, and slices of quince,
        Which they ate with a runcible spoon. *Ib.*

11 Our mother was the Pussy-Cat, our father was the Owl,
    And so we're partly little beasts and partly little fowl.
    Children of the Owl and the Pussy-Cat

12 There was an old person of Dean,
    Who dined on one pea and one bean;
        For he said, "More than that
        Would make me too fat,"
    That cautious old person of Dean.
    One Hundred Nonsense Pictures and Rhymes

ERIC LINKLATER

Eric Linklater (1889–1974), Scottish author, educated at
Aberdeen University, is best known for his humorous, satirical
novels, such as *Poet's Pub* (1929), *Juan in America* (1931), and
Private Angelo (1946).

1   It has taken us [Italy] a long time to lose the war, but thank
    heaven we have lost it at last. *Private Angelo*

2   You are still a soldier, and you have no right to talk common
    sense. *Ib.*

3   "You are old enough to realise," said the Count, "that a statement of fact is nearly always damaging to someone."
     Ib.

4   He had long since recognized that promotion in war-time was like a greasy pole, or a game of snakes and ladders. *Ib.*

5   The English all regarded football as a more exacting and therefore more praiseworthy art than making love. *Ib.*

6   We English have been in a muddle for so long that most of us now regard it as our normal environment. *Ib.*

7   The table delicacies of Tibet would nauseate a French epicure. *Ib.*

8   The British War Office has always set its face against militarism. *Ib.*

9   A bomb has no political opinions. *Ib.*

10   Whenever there's a war the first casualties are the Ten Commandments. *Ib.*

11   She asked me to come and see her at once; and when I got there she was in the bathroom feeding an alligator with sardines. *Love in Albania*

12   All married women should make a habit of saying, "In spite of everything, dear, I'm still devoted to you." *Ib.*

13   If everyone could choose where he was going to be born, some countries would be left quite empty. *Ib.*

14   I've never heard anything that so clearly suggests the agony of primitive man as your attempt to play the cello. *Ib.*

15   To stay married should clearly be recognized as one of the fine arts. *Ib.*

16   His two years in the city had seemed like two years among white mice in a revolving cage. *Poet's Pub*

17   Poets are really the most practical people on earth so long as they are allowed to do what they like. *Ib.*

18 It's time that acrimony and bad taste came back to enliven our criticism. *Ib.*

19 Many women looked more virginal after they were married than they did before – just to make it more difficult. *Ib.*

20 First novels are generally indigestible, like a steak-and-kidney pie that has been baking ever since adolescence. *Ib.*

21 "I've touched my toes twenty times every morning for the last twelve years," said Van Buren, "but I don't like the look of them any better."

22 [One theory] was that Bacon cribbed his essays from a notebook of Shakespeare's that he had picked up in a tavern. *Ib.*

23 I dislike reading unpublished poetry as much as I dislike seeing a newly-born baby. *Ib.*

24 Nearly all educated people lose their temper when they read the paper. *Ib.*

MAUREEN LIPMAN

Maureen Lipman (1946–), lively Yorkshire-born Jewish actress, has successfully played many parts, especially in comedy. In 1988 she re-created some of Joyce Grenfell's sketches in a solo performance.

1 I've never seen a horse in real life except under a policeman. *How Was it For You?*

2 The plans of mice, men, and Maureen gang aft a cock-up. *Ib.*

3 *Don't* buy an automatically igniting gas hob. They automatically don't ignite for several days if you've had the temerity to wash them. *Ib.*

4   The car wouldn't reverse. It would do everything else it had done before – like start, stall, and attack old ladies at pelican crossings. But it just wouldn't retreat. *Ib.*

5   She taught us Hygiene. And you know what that meant: s-x, pr-cr-ation, and p-r–ds. *Ib.*

7   I can't face my face first thing in the morning – so in order to avoid the confrontation I stagger out of the house looking like the Ghost of Christmas Past. *Ib*

8   No more holidays abroad. "Jack," I swore, "if I ever mention going abroad again I want you to hit me on the head with a rolled-up travel agent." *Ib.*

9   We watched Ryan O'Neal in *Irreconcilable Differences,* which should have won an award – for us, I mean, for sitting through it. *Ib.*

10   (At the dentist's)

     For some unaccountable reason I have always disliked having a big, hairy hand in my mouth, hurting me like hell. *Ib.*

11   I'm a games player by nature. Don't get me wrong. Nothing that involves movement. Like leaving my chair. *Ib*

12   Are you sitting comfortably? Then get up. This is no time for sloth. *Something to Fall Back on*

13   Every plant entering our portals appears to see a sign reading, "Abandon Hope All Ye Who Enter Here". *Ib.*

14   The make-up sat on the surface of my skin like scrambled egg. *Ib*

FREDERICK LONSDALE

Frederick Leonard (1881–1954), English dramatist born in Jersey, wrote (under the name Lonsdale) several witty comedies of upper class life, cleverly constructed, e.g. *The Last of Mrs*

Cheney (1925), *On Approval* (1927), and collaborated in musical comedies, e.g. *The Maid of the Mountains* (1916).

1   Rumour has it she has remained faithful to him, one of the most stupid of God's creatures. She is either a very good woman or very nervous. *The Last of Mrs Cheney*

2   He has a reputation with women that is extremely bad... Women ask him everywhere. *Ib.*

3   She's a woman who calls a spade a bloody spade and means it! *Ib.*

4   "Who the devil told those women that they could sing?" "Their music teacher, when she found they had the money to pay for lessons." *Ib.*

5   By marrying I could only make one woman happy: by remaining single I can make so many! *Ib.*

6   If there are to be insults, let's get them in first. *Ib.*

7   It's the first thrill I've had since that horrid man tried to be familiar with me in a railway carriage. *Ib.*

8   Never kill an ass who may have to lay a golden egg. *Ib.*

9   The only nice women are the ones who have had no opportunities. *Ib.*

10   "You become younger every day." "I'm glad, because it takes most of the day to become it." *Aren't We All?*

11   Many a woman has carried on a long conversation with me without opening her mouth. *Ib.*

12   "I only want you to tell her the truth." "There are more men separated from their wives for doing that than you or I could ever count." *Ib.*

13   How many women of your acquaintance have had the privilege of catching their husbands in the arms of another woman? *Ib.*

14   All my life I've found it difficult to refuse a woman anything – except marriage. *Ib.*

15   There are many more unhealthy places than the British Museum. *Ib.*

E. V. LUCAS

Edward Verrall Lucas (1868–1938), versatile English writer, was at one time assistant editor of *Punch*. He was also a reader for the publishers Methuen, and later became Chairman. In addition to numerous light essays and articles, he wrote novels, travel books, and an authoritative biography of Charles Lamb.

1   No baby is admired sufficiently to please the mother. *One Day and Another*

2   It is the fashion for husbands to say sarcastic things about their babies and pretend to be bored by the whole business. *Ib.*

3   The kind of view of human life a dog acquires I have sometimes tried to imagine by kneeling or lying full length on the ground and looking up. *Ib*

4   A horse's eye disquiets me. It has an expression of alarm that may at any moment be translated into action. *Charade and Comedy*

5   Like all great men when one comes closely in touch with them, the conjurer was quite human, quite like ourselves; so much so that in addition to his fee he wanted his taxi fare both ways. *Ib.*

6   I know a dozen boys at least whom I would willingly exchange for the intimacy of a pair of long-tailed tits. *Fireside and Sunshine*

7   The two landladies took the demise of Mr Carstairs as a personal affront...To die under their roof they held to be not only ungentlemanly but dishonest. *London Lavender*

8   An ugly man was promised by a photographer that he would have justice done to him. "Justice!" he exclaimed. "I don't want justice – I want mercy!" *A Boswell of Baghdad*

9   The mushroom meadow next to my home, although I don't happen to rent it, is obviously more mine by sheer right of proximity than anyone else's. *Mixed Vintages*

10   People who mean well – always a poisonous class. *Ib.*

11   One of the first things children should be taught, in addition to those in the curriculum, is not to hang about seeing people off by train. *Ib.*

12   I dislike...people who take one of your own pet stories, begin to tell it to you, and won't stop even when you say you know it. *Ib*

13   The local gentleman who introduces a visiting speaker must be short. He cannot, indeed, be too short, and he never is. *Ib.*

14   The phrase "I'll think it over" is the one most dreaded by sellers of White Elephants. Their one mastering desire is to prevent people from thinking anything over. *Ib.*

15   Strange as it may sound, among all the millions of countenances with two eyes, a nose in the middle, and a mouth below it, no two precisely resemble each other. *'Twixt Eagle and Dove*

16   One of the odd things about loss of memory is that it is catching. How often when one person forgets a name well known to him, his companion forgets it too. *Ib.*

17   What is literature compared with cooking?. One is shadow and the other is substance. *Rose and Rose*

18   "If the good God had asked me to help Him in making the world, which I'd take shame to put my signature to as it is, I'd have left uric acid out of it." *Ib.*

19   By always telling the truth one saves oneself from a multitude of fatiguing cares. *Ib.*

20   He reminded me of a well-bound book in a gentleman's library. *Ib.*

21   Americans are people who prefer the Continent to their own country but refuse to learn the language. *Wanderings and Diversions*

22   Readers of novels are strange folk on whose probable or even possible tastes no wise book-maker would venture to bet. *Reading, Writing, and Remembering*

23   Oatmeal is not only the child's breakfast; it is the favourite food of the Edinburgh reviewers. Thus do extremes meet. *Domesticities*

24   The art of life is to keep down acquaintances. *Over Bemerton's*

ROBERT LYND

Robert Lynd (1879–1949) was born in Ireland but worked in London as journalist, essayist, and literary editor, contributing a regular column to the *New Statesman* under the initials "Y.Y.". His work was marked by a pleasant, easy humour.

1   Let a thousand men set up their houses in a wood, and the wood becomes a hideous small town. Let a thousand birds settle in the same wood, and it will take a skilled eye to find even twenty of them. *The Blue Lion*

2   Good conversation is a poor substitute for good food. *Ib.*

3   A cat is only technically an animal, being divine. *Ib.*

4   We rightly speak of a storm in a teacup as the tiniest
     disturbance, but out of a coffee-cup come hurricanes. *Ib.*

5   There is no tribe of human being more pestiferous than the
     people who insist on lending you books whether you wish
     to borrow them or not. *Ib.*

6   The act of chewing makes a man look like a sulky cow. *Ib.*

7   Man is so ashamed of his appetite that he would blush to be
     caught abstracting delicacies from his neighbour's plate,
     as a chicken would do. *Ib.*

8   People who had never visited the Louvre to see the "Mona
     Lisa" came to see the space on the wall from which it had
     been stolen. *Ib.*

9   In a controversy it is safest to assume that both sides are lying.
     Ib.

10   Never speak when you are angry. If you do you'll make the
     best speech you'll ever regret. *Ib.*

11   In the bedroom the hum of insects seems to belong to the
     same school of music as the buzz of the dentist's drill.
     Selected Essays

12   Some houses were built at a time when there was rivalry as to
     who could invent a brick of the most repulsive colour. *Ib.*

13   The bee is morally far superior to the mosquito. Not only
     does he give you honey instead of malaria, but he aims at
     living a quiet inoffensive life, at peace with everybody. *Ib.*

14   It was through the Germans that soap reached the Romans.
     We all know what happened after that – the decline and
     fall of the Roman Empire. *News Chronicle*

15   We cannot go about, unfortunately, telling everybody about
     the temptations we have resisted. As a result, people judge
     us exclusively by the temptations to which we yield. *The
     Peal of Bells*

16 Knowing myself intimately, I am able to take a more sympathetic view of myself than other people do. *Ib.*

17 He is so conceited that he will not even guess that we are saying how conceited he is. *Ib.*

18 It is an engaging problem in ethics whether, if you have been lent a cottage, you have the right to feed the mice. *Ib.*

19 Coleridge says in a letter that to bait a mouse-trap is as much as to say to the mouse, "Come and have a piece of cheese," and that, when it accepts the invitation, to do it to death is a betrayal of the laws of hospitality. *Ib.*

20 Almost any game with almost any ball is a good game. *Ib.*

21 If you speak in praise of a patent medicine in company, you will only invite ridicule...yet fifty people buy patent medicines for one who buys books. *Ib.*

22 Friendship will not stand the strain of very much good advice for very long. *Ib.*

23 Most human beings are quite likeable if you do not see too much of them. *Ib.*

24 No human being believes that any other human being has a right to be in bed when he himself is up. *Rain, Rain Go To Spain*

25 Every artist has his own distorting mirror. *John O'London's Weekly*

A. G. MACDONNELL

Archibald Gordon MacDonnell (1895–1941), born in Aberdeen, educated at Winchester, at one time on the staff of the League of Nations, wrote several novels, the best-known of which was the satirical *England, Their England* (1933).

1   Donald Cameron had no qualification for any profession...so
     he resolved to try his fortune as a journalist. *England, Their
     England*

2   She was so proud of her beautiful voice that she always used to
     go to Mass late so that the congregation could notice the
     difference in the singing before and after her arrival. *Ib.*

3   Letters of introduction are always silly and usually lies. *Ib.*

4   Irresistible is the flattery of a beautiful woman to every man
     who ever lived except that superlative boob, St Anthony. *Ib.*

5   The [cricket] ball went up and up...and then at the top
     seemed to hang motionless in the air, fighting, as it were,
     a heroic but forlorn battle against the chief invention of
     Sir Isaac Newton. *Ib.*

6   No one can appreciate the finer points of cricket if they allow
     their minds to wander. *Ib.*

7   Mr Harcourt had had a fit of artistic tantrums and had thrown
     a raw tomato at the editor and, being a poet, had
     fortunately missed. *Ib.*

8   A guest in the country who cannot amuse himself is a
     nuisance to busy people. *Ib.*

9   The girl persuaded her horse to stand still for a moment and
     looked at Donald as if he was some kind of slug. *Ib.*

10   The English are the kindliest souls in the world, but if they
     see anything beautiful flying in the air or running along
     the ground, they rush for a gun and kill it. *Ib.*

11   The fox had dived into a hole from which not even the
     terriers could extract him. He was, as *The Times* said, "a
     bad fox". *Ib.*

LORD MANCROFT

Stormount Samuel Mancroft (1917–87), was a barrister, business man, politician, columnist, and after-dinner speaker. At one time he was Director of Great Universal Stores, Deputy Chairman of Cunard Line, and Chairman of the Horse-race Totalisator. His writings include *Booking the Cooks* (1969) and *A Chinaman in My Bath (1974).*

1   My first car was painted red down one side and blue down the other to confuse witnesses in case of an accident. *A Chinaman in My Bath*

2   Nobody ever seemed quite clear whether the expression "drunk as a lord" should be taken as a compliment or an insult. *Ib.*

3   It is better to travel hopefully, Robert Louis Stevenson assures us, than to arrive...He lived before the age of the Jumbo-jet, the Inter-City express, and the T. and G.W.U. *Ib.*

4   To a background of gin and Musak you are given far tee many Martoonis. *Ib.*

5   Tourists from a Cunard vessel were once held up for three hours because mice had been discovered in the dockers' canteen and the staff were out on strike, presumably for danger money. *Ib.*

6   The only exercise I ever take is walking up hospital stairs to visit friends who've damaged themselves by taking exercise. *Ib.*

7   Before the war you took your secretary to Paris and called her your wife. Now, in order to wriggle through the tax-gatherer's net, you take your wife to Paris and call her your secretary. *Ib.*

8   There are really only three things to lean in ski-ing: how to put on your skis, how to slide downhill, and how to walk along the hospital corridor. *Ib.*

9 At two o'clock in the morning the noise sounded like a cross between the Battle of Alamein and the House of Commons at Question Time. *Ib.*

10 Cricket is a game which the English, not being a spiritual people, have invented in order to give themselves some conception of Eternity. *Ib.*

11 They way in which Father Christmas's sack is overloaded clearly contravenes all the safety regulations for the carriage of goods by air. *Ib.*

12 All men are born equal, but quite a few get over it. *Observer (1967)*

13 Happy is the man with a wife to tell him what to do and a secretary to do it. *Ib. (1966).*

DON MARQUIS

Donald Robert Perry Marquis (1878–1937), American
journalist and humorist, regularly contributed a column to the
New York Sun. Much of his humorous satire was ostensibly typed
by a cockroach (a free verse poet) who could not manage
capitals. (mehitabel is a friendly cat.)

1   i was once a vers libre bard
     but i died and my soul went into the body of a cockroach
     it has given me a new outlook on life
     archy and mehitabel

2   the high cost of
     living isnt so bad if you
     dont have to pay for it *Ib.*

3   live so that you
     can stick out your tongue
     at the insurance
     doctor *Ib.*

4   an optimist is a guy
     that has never had
     much experience *Ib.*

5   to a flea or a
     mosquito a
     human being is
     merely something
     good to eat *Ib.*

6   the bees got their
     governmental system settled
     millions of years ago
     but the human race is still
     groping *Ib.*

7   you want to know
    whether i believe in ghosts
    of course i do not believe in them
    if you had known
    as many of them as i have
    you would not
    believe in them either. *Ib.*

8   the octopus' secret wish
    is not to be a formal fish
    he dreams that some time he may grow
    another set of legs or so
    and be a broadway music show *Ib.*

9   when you see a seagull sitting
    on a bald man's dome
    she likely thinks she's nesting
    on her rocky island home *Ib.*

10 roses are more handsome
    than insects
    beauty gets the best of it
    in this world *Ib.*

11 should i kick the woolworth tower
    so hard i laid it low
    it probably might injure me if it fell on my toe *Ib.*

12 (The spider's complaint)

    curses on these here swatters
    what kills off all the flies
    me and my poor little daughters
    unless we eats we dies *Ib.*

13 the quite irrational ichneumon
    is such a fool it's almost human *Ib.*

14 procrastination is the
    art of keeping
    up with yesterday *Ib.*

15 Alas, the hours we waste in work
    And similar inconsequence.
    Friends, I beg you do not shirk
    Your daily task of indolence.
    The Almost Perfect State

16 The art of newspaper paragraphing is to stroke a platitude
    till it purrs like an epigram. *New York Sun*

17 An idea isn't responsible for the people who believe in it. *Ib.*

18 Middle age is the time when a man is always thinking that in
    a week or two he will feel just as good as ever. *Ib.*

19 We pay for the mistakes of our ancestors and it seems only
    fair they should leave us the money to pay with.

20 Pity the meek, for they shall inherit the earth.

ARTHUR MARSHALL

Arthur Marshall (1910–89), was at various times a master at
Oundle School, a humorous Nurse Dugdale on radio, secretary
to Lord Rothschild, TV script writer, freelance journalist, and
regular performer for the TV series *Call My Bluff*. His sunny
nature was shown both on TV and in his writings.

1   In early January friendly Christmas cards continue to arrive,
    struggling gamely home like the last few stragglers on a
    London Marathon. *Sunny Side Up*

2   Alfred Krupp forced workmen in his enormous factories to
    get *written* permission from the foreman to go to the
    lavatory. *Ib.*

3   Queen Victoria economised on lavatory paper and substituted
    back numbers of *The Times*. *Ib.*

4   Feminists will regret to hear that there was a time in history
    when the birth of a princess was on a par with defeat in
    the World Cup. *Ib.*

5   Particularly pleasing is the story of Queen Alexandra muddling golf with croquet and, when on the green, gaily hitting her husband's golf-ball away from the hole and then pushing her own in. *Ib.*

6   Red Indians keen on peace smoked in a very chummy manner, sharing both the communal pipe and, I fear, communal dribble. *Ib*

7   It would be hard to beat the record of the hijacker who, during a flight across America, took the stewardess hostage, waving a gun. "Take me to Detroit!" he demanded. "We're already going to Detroit," she replied. *Ib.*

8   (On Carmen)

A chance meeting outside a cigarette factory is no proper commencement for a Life Partnership. *Ib.*

9   When I am in the Wash area I shall keep my eyes peeled for King John's carrier-bag labelled with what was the 1215 equivalent of Sainsbury's and stuffed with the more portable of the crown jewels. *Ib.*

10   Can you picture Joan of Arc in see-through pyjamas? *Ib.*

11   The French are tremendous snobs, despite that rather showy and ostentatious Revolution. *I'll Let You Know*

12   The school authorities deceived nobody when they blandly announced that joining the Officers Training Corps was "entirely voluntary". In actual fact it was about as voluntary as being born. *Ib.*

13   The only possible message to be extracted from *Hamlet* is that it doesn't pay to take an after-lunch nap in an orchard. *Ib.*

14   Enormous commercial success consorts ill with the Order of Merit. Those aiming at this distinction must be careful not to bring too much enjoyment to too many people. *Ib.*

15   The croupiers looked like eminent French cabinet ministers who had decided to retire and go into the undertaking business. *I Say!*

16   The buzz-bombs had started flying over us, and some of them had decided not to go on but to stop and rest awhile. *Ib.*

17   I bought an account book. I have it still. It contains just one entry: "Account book – 1s.6d." *Ib.*

18   My wardrobe has the ignominious and unusual record of containing items that have ben refused, if politely, for a parish jumble sale. *Ib.*

19   Pageants invariably require horses, and horses have little or no idea of what constitutes appropriate public behaviour. *Ib.*

20   In the 13th century...the Bishop of Winchester had an interesting lay sideline – eighteen brothels, jammed to the doors. *Ib.*

21   In 1851, in the world's richest capital city (London), there was not a single public lavatory, and the mind boggles as to how they all *managed. Ib.*

22   When Lord Berners returned, many years later, to visit his old school, he was astonished to observe nothing but smiling faces...only to learn that it was a school no more and that the building was a lunatic asylum. *Ib*

23   Peter Townsend once had, as in some frightful nightmare, to teach Queen Mary how to dance the Hokey Cokey. *Sunday Telegraph (15 October 1986)*

24   Nowadays the only serious aquatic sport that I indulge in is the occasional game of Pooh-sticks. *Ib.*

25   It has always seemed to me hard luck on the very best ice-dancing skaters that they have to spend so much of their time whizzing along backwards, with their bottoms sticking rather undecoratively out. *Ib.*

26   Is it at all widely known that the shooting of the Korda film about Nelson was held up because nobody could remember which arm it was he lost? *Ib.*

GROUCHO MARX

Julius Henry Marx (1890–1977), American film comedian, was by far the most articulate and prominent of the four Marx Brothers, whose zany humour was seen in many films, e.g. *Monkey Business* (1931); *Duck Soup* (1933).

1   I've worked myself up from nothing to a state of extreme poverty. *Monkey Business*

2   A child of five would understand this. Somebody fetch a child of five! *Duck Soup*

3   Go and never darken my towels again! *Ib.*

4   This would be a better world for children if parents had to eat the spinach. *Animal Crackers*

5   One day I shot an elephant in my pyjamas. How it got into my pyjamas I'll never know. *Ib.*

6   (Feeling pulse)
Either he's dead or my watch has stopped. *Ib.*

7   The way his horses ran could be summed up in a word. Last. *Esquire.*

8   (On dust jacket of book by S.J.Perelman)
From the moment I picked up your book until I laid it down I was convulsed with laughter. Some day I intend reading it.

9   My mother loved children. She would have given anything if I had been one.

10   Anybody can get old. All you have to do is to go on living.

11   I never forget a face, but I'll make an exception in your case.

12   I resign. I wouldn't want to belong to any club that would have me as a member.

13   Whoever called it necking was a poor judge of anatomy.

14   You've got the brain of a four-year-old-boy – and I bet he was glad to get rid of it. *Horse Feathers*

15   To be forewarned is to be forearmed – but who wants to walk around with four arms. (Quoted in Kenneth Williams' *Just Williams*)

16   BANK MANAGER. Can I be of service to you?
      GROUCHO. Yes – steal some money from one of your rich clients and credit it to my account.

W. SOMERSET MAUGHAM

William Somerset Maugham (1874–1965), British novelist, playwright, and short-story writer, was educated at King's School, Canterbury. He drew on his experience as a physician in such novels as *Liza of Lambeth* (1897) and *Of Human Bondage* (1915). Some of his best plays are sophisticated, satirical comedies, e.g. *Lady Frederick (1907); The Circle* (1921); *Our Betters* (1923).

1   Only the aristocracy can afford to drop aitches. *Jack Straw*

2   When I make a joke I always laugh quickly, so that there's no doubt about it. *Ib.*

3   My idea of going for a walk is sitting on a gate. *Ib.*

4   Your husband was a strictly religious man, and made a point of believing the worst about his neighbours. *Lady Frederick*

5   You have a magnificent chance, with all the advantages of wealth and position. Don't throw it away by any exhibition of talent. *Ib.*

6   You're never so dangerous as when you pretend to be frank. *Ib.*

7   Thank God I'm a bachelor, and no ministering angel ever smoothes my pillow when I want to be left alone. *Ib.*

8   Protestations of undying affection are never ridiculous when they are accompanied by emeralds. *Ib.*

9   Dullness is the first requisite of a good husband. *Ib.*

10   I often wonder why gambling debts are known as debts of honour. *Ib.*

11   I confess I prefer people to say horrid things about me only behind my back. Especially if they're true. *Ib.*

12   A good hairdresser can express every mood and every passion of the human heart. *Ib.*

13   If people waited to know one another before they married, the world wouldn't be so grossly over-populated. *Mrs Dot*

14   I never mind what a man says to me when I know I could knock him down if I wanted to. *Smith*

15   I much prefer new acquaintances to old friends. *Ib.*

16   I'm not crying. It's only tears running out of me eyes. *Sheppey*

17   No married man's ever made up his mind till he's heard what his wife has got to say about it. *Ib.*

18   I hate giving a straight answer to a straight question. *The Constant Wife*

19   The sort of woman who wants to be made love to in a consulting-room...is the sort who wears horrid undies. *Ib.*

20   It's not the seven deadly virtues that make a man a good husband. *Ib.*

21 Why didn't you tell me you were going to propose? I'd have had my hair waved. *Our Betters*

22 I tried to be pleasant and chatty. It was like engaging the pyramids in small talk. *Ib.*

23 She's been my greatest friend for fifteen years...and I tell you she hasn't a single redeeming quality. *Ib.*

24 It was like a gathering of relations who hate one another, after the funeral of a rich aunt who's left all her money to charity. *Ib.*

25 If one felt about things at night as one does next morning, life would be a lot easier. *Ib.*

26 It's not an unpleasant death to have a stroke while you're eating your favourite dish. *Ib.*

27 Why should you lie on the bed you've made if you don't want to? There's always the floor. *The Circle*

28 You always get the best food if you come in unexpectedly and have the same as they're having in the servants' hall. *Ib.*

29 I hate people who play bridge as if they were at a funeral and knew their feet were getting wet. *Ib.*

30 Hypocrisy is the most difficult and nerve-racking vice that any man can pursue. *Cakes and Ale*

PHYLLIS McGINLEY

American teacher, copy-writer, and humorous poet (1905–), has been a contributor to *The New Yorker* and *Saturday Evening Post*. She has been called a feminine counterpart of Ogden Nash (q.v.), though her humour is quieter.

1 This is the gist of what I know:
Give advice and buy a foe.
The Love Letters of Phyllis McGinley

2   Perhaps the literary man
       I most admire among my betters
    Is Richard Brinsley Sheridan,
       Who, viewing life as more than letters,
    Persisted, like a stubborn Gael,
    In not acknowledging his mail. *Ib.*

3   Few friends he kept that pleased his mind.
       His marriage failed when it began,
    Who worked unceasing for mankind
       But loathed his fellow-man
    Ib. (The Old Reformer)

4   I wish I didn't talk so much at parties.
    When hotly boil the arguments
    Ah! would I had the common sense
    To sit demurely on a fence.
    Ib. (Reflections at Dawn)

5   Buffet, ball, banquet, quilting bee,
       Whenever conversation's flowing,
    Why must I feel it falls on me
       To keep things going? *Ib.*

6   Sand on the beaches;
       Sand at the door,
    Sand that screeches
       On the new-swept floor;
    In the shower, sand for the foot to crunch on;
    Sand in the sandwiches spread for luncheon.
    Ib. (Season at the Shore)

7   How pure, how beautiful, how fine
    Do teeth on television shine!
    Ib. (Reflections Dental)

8   Of the small gifts of heaven,
    It seems to me that more than equal share
    At birth was given
    To girls with curly hair.
    Ib. (Meditations during a Permanent Wave)

9   Who are the friends of Dr Gallup? Who,
Ah, who are they
Incessantly he puts inquiries to?...
All I can vouch for is the fact I see:
Nobody quizzes me.
Ib. (The Forgotten Woman)

10   By all the published facts in the case
Children belong to the human race.
Times Three

11   What in me is pure Conviction
Is simple Prejudice in you. *Ib.*

ALAN MELVILLE

Alan Melville (1910–), is a British dramatist, lyric writer, and BBC script writer, educated at Edinburgh Academy. He is the author of sketches and lyrics for revues, e.g. *Sweet and Low* (1943) and of several plays, e.g *Simon and Laura* (1954) and novels.

1   A piddling little embezzlement here, a trifling spot of arson there...nowadays it's all put down to juvenile delinquency or unsettled home conditions. *Devil May Care*

2   They were joined together in what is satirically referred to as holy matrimony. *Ib*

3   You assume that Goodness, like Guinness, is good for people. That's never been proved. *Ib..*

4   Whoever is responsible for the running of the Universe is sadly in need of a refresher course in business management. *Ib.*

5   You're right about there being some good in me. That's what's been holding me back for years. *Ib.*

6   "The most satisfying gesture in the world is turning the other cheek."
"Of course...to the bloke who's going to slosh the other cheek the same as he sloshed the first one." *Ib.*

7   "An English tourist was arrested for throwing flowers during the Fête des Fleurs."
"But that's what the festival is for – throwing flowers."
"The flowers were in their pots." *Ib.*

8   You were educated at Fettes and sent down from Edinburgh University. What could be more English than that? *Mrs Willie*

9   There is already enough potential trouble in a garden without having one of those smug, self-satisfied, rosy-cheeked little bastards squatting year after year at the edge of the goldfish pond pretending he's fishing. *Gnomes and Gardens*

10   Each fairy and each elf
Says quite firmly to itself,
"I shall not go *near* that ghastly garden's bottom." *Ib*

11   Ladybirds did their level best to destroy pretty well every known garden pest except perhaps the next-door neighbour's children. *Ib*

12   "Mary, Mary, cautious, chary,
How does your garden grow?"
"Through a permanent haze of aerosol sprays...
And pesticides all in a row." *Ib.*

13   "Your hair looked so nice when you came off the train I hardly recognized you." *Ib.*

GEORGE MIKES

George Mikes (1912–) was born in Hungary and educated at Budapest University. He emigrated to England, and has written many humorous books in English, e.g. *How to Be an Alien* (1946); *Humour in Memoriam* (1970).

1   There is a constant danger of my losing my poverty. Any book of mine could become a runaway bestseller. *How to be Poor*

2   Switzerland, though lovely, is very full of the Swiss. *Ib.*

3   I have seen often that you do not own a country house; a country house owns you. *Ib.*

4   Many people cannot resist bargains and sales. Provided they think they are getting a bargain... old ladies will buy roller-skates and non-smokers will buy pipe-cleaners. *Ib.*

5   To be extravagant you need money. True. But you do not need your own money. *Ib.*

6   Capitalism, they say, is the exploitation of one man by another; Communism is the other way round. *Ib.*

7   If everybody becomes middle-class, the middle-class will automatically be abolished. If everybody is in the middle, there is no middle. *Ib.*

9   I would sooner be seen in medieval knightly armour than in a morning coat and top hat. *Ib.*

10   All the ills of history are always blamed on poor old God, who is unable to defend Himself. *Ib.*

11   An Englishman, even if he is alone, forms an orderly queue of one. *How to Be an Alien*

12   Many continentals think that life is a game; the English think that cricket is a game. *Ib.*

13   The aim of introductions [at parties] is to conceal the persons' identities. *Ib*

14   In Budapest, when a rather ugly actress joined a nudist club, her younger and prettier colleagues spread the story that she had been accepted only on condition that she wore a fig leaf over her face. *Ib.*

15   A fishmonger is a man who mongs fish; an ironmonger...does the same with iron. *Ib.*

16   Some people drive out to Hampstead Heath or Richmond Park, pull up all the windows, and go to sleep...The procedure is called "spending a lovely afternoon in the open". *Ib.*

17   (Game for bus drivers)
     Whenever you approach a request stop hide behind a large lorry or another bus. *Ib.*

18   "Travel" is the name of a modern disease... The patient grows restless in the early spring and starts rushing from one travel agent to another, collecting useless information. *How to Be Inimitable*

19   If you win £250,000 on the football pools, it is *de rigueur* to declare that your win will not make the slightest difference to your way of life. *Ib.*

20   The most heinous offence known to the police is officially called "obstructing the Queen's highway". The Queen is brought into it to underline the close connection between a parking offence and high treason. *Ib.*

21   Whenever I call an Englishman rude he takes it as a compliment. *Ib.*

22   Cricket is the only game where the major part of a team can just idle around and watch a few of their number do the work. *Down With Everybody*

23   Baseball is cricket played with a strong American accent. *Ib.*

24   I love to go on a journey with two shirts and a toothbrush, but I consider myself lucky if I can persuade my wife to leave the refrigerator and the piano behind. *Ib.*

SPIKE MILLIGAN

Terence Alan Milligan (1918–) was born in India, where his father was a soldier. After various jobs, from factory work to trumpet playing, he achieved fame as chief writer for the anarchic radio *Goon Show* (1951–1960). His other writings include the novel *Puckoon*.

1   People only get cold if they walk like cripples. I walk very fast; as a result I arrive at work warm as toast and exhausted for the day. *Indefinite Articles*

2   The English Dog Cult now vies with Christianity in the top ten religions. *Ib.*

3   A bundle of yapping nerves with hair on called a poodle has become a status symbol. *Ib.*

4   The public of dear old England had been coaxed into giving £350,000 towards buying a Leonardo cartoon which was in "danger" of being bought abroad (up till then it had been kept in a cellar). *Ib.*

5   I contact Alun Owen in Eire and ask him what the tax advantages would be if I became domiciled in Dublin. "None," he says. "What you save on tax you spend on drink." *Ib.*

6   Bentine is confined to bed with a severe overdraft. *Ib.*

7   She was growing up, and that was the direction I wanted her to take. Who wants a daughter that grows sideways? *Ib.*

8   Just by throwing his kit down he can make the room look untidy. *Goodbye, Soldier*

9   He had a brain that would have fitted into a thimble with room to spare. *Ib.*

10 I smoke sixty a day and am as fit as a fiddle, I said, coughing. *Ib.*

11 Toni was a practising Catholic. Why are they always practising? When do they become good enough not to? *Ib.*

12 The most dreaded meal in the English culinary calendar: the dead chicken, the dead lettuce, the watery mayonnaise, the lone tomato ring. *Ib.*

13 There was the Fifty Shilling Tailors, where I had ordered a dreadful suit that made me look deformed. *Ib.*

14 Naked, I had a body that invited burial. *Ib.*

15 Harry Lauder always drank from a bottle in a paper bag; it gave him an air of respectability. *Ib.*

16 I had travelled extensively in Catford, Lewisham and Brockley SE26, but somehow never in Austria. *Ib.*

17 Unlocking his wallet, he pays with money that hasn't seen the light of day for months. *Ib.*

18 The doctor's fee is two thousand lire. I feel worse. I'm sickening for bankruptcy. *Ib.*

19 The ship is sinking. We must try and save it. Help me get it into the lifeboat. *Goon Show*

20 Listen. Someone's screaming in agony. Fortunately I speak it fluently. *Ib.*

21 Are you going to come quietly or do I have to use ear-plugs? *Ib.*

22 Sit down and warm yourself by the candle. *Ib.*

23 BLOODNOK. Now to divide up the money.
    MORIARTY. Yes, I have it here in this sack.
    BLOODNOK. Good. We'll split it evenly. I'll take the money and you take the sack. *Ib.*

24 Contraceptives should be used on every conceivable occasion. *Ib.*

25 He opened his eyes with a sound like the tearing apart of fly-papers. *Monty – His Part in My Victory*

26 We were issued with seasick pills. I never suffer from this so I threw them over the side, where fish ate them and were immediately sick. *Ib.*

27 By midday the heat is so unbearable that the streets are empty but for thousands of Englishmen taking mad dogs for walks. *A Dustbin of Milligan*

28 Personally, I think all modern architects should be pulled down and redeveloped as car parks. *Daily Telegraph (4 November 1988)*

29 My father had a profound influence on me – he was a lunatic. (Quoted in Michael Parkinson's *The Best of Parkinson*)

A. A. MILNE

Alan Alexander Milne (1882–1957), born in Scotland, educated at Westminster School and Cambridge, wrote regularly for *Punch*, among other journals. Though best known now for his delightful children's stories and verse, e.g. *Winnie the Pooh* (1926), he also wrote many successful stage comedies and several novels.

1 A quotation is a handy thing to have about, saving one from the trouble of thinking for oneself. *If I May*

2 Getting an elephant into a play is merely a question of stage-craft. *Ib.*

3 A wedding always finds me melancholy next morning. "She has married the wrong man," I tell myself. "I wonder if it is too late to tell her." *Ib.*

4 The Countess (wisely, I think) was dieting herself. *Ib.*

5   My trouble is that I look guilty so easily...If I walk through any of the big stores with a parcel in my hand I expect to hear a voice whispering in my ear, "The manager would like to see you quietly in his office." *Ib.*

6   Middle age – by which I mean anything over twenty and under ninety. *Ib.*

7   For one person who dreams of making fifty thousand pounds, a hundred people dream of being left fifty thousand pounds. *Ib.*

8   Golf is the best game in the world at which to be bad...It is the bad player who gets the most strokes. *Not That It Matters*

9   You cannot tell a man by the lobster he eats, but you can tell something about him by the literature he reads. *Ib.*

10   The seats at Lords are uncommonly hard, and a *Daily Telegraph*, folded twice and placed beneath one, brings something of the solace which good literature will always bring. *Ib.*

11   My most frequent dream...is that I am back at school, trying to construe difficult passages from Greek authors unknown to me. *Ib.*

12   The fable of the boy who cried "Wolf"...is (usually) used to point a moral directed against the boy...But the moral might equally be directed against the villagers. Silly villagers! See what happened to *them*! The boy may have been no great loss, but they also lost their flocks. *War With Honour*

13   Has the fact that the finest qualities of man came out in the Great Plague ever been advanced as an apology for bad sanitation? *Ib.*

14   The owner of a dog which snapped at a little girl who teased it said apologetically to the mother: "After all, the dog's only human." *Ib.*

15   The modern Englishman can show his courage every day by
     crossing Piccadilly Circus. *Peace With Honour*

16   Although he provided the opinions himself, he always
     depended on his secretary for the arguments with which
     to support them. *Stories of Successful Lives*

17   In this country immoral plays are only allowed on Sundays.
     To Have the Honour

18   "There's not one person in the world who could give you a
     complete list of the Nobel prize-winners. My own theory is
     that every other year they invent the name and stick to the
     money." *Ib.*

19   She has to her credit the achievements of wifehood and
     motherhood, and can therefore speak with authority on
     all subjects. *Ib.*

20   There's a small boy whose duty it is to forget to bring the
     newspaper every day. He's amazingly reliable, so I
     generally go to fetch it myself. *Ib.*

21 Really, darling, you forget that I'm old enough to be – in fact, am – your mother. *Belinda*

22 Not domesticated? Why, didn't I hear her say she had arranged all the flowers? *Ib.*

23 Why do kippers *want* all these bones? Other fish manage without them. *The Dover Road*

24 Had he been only a trifle more incompetent, he might have been assisted out of the House of Commons altogether with a peerage. *Mr Pim*

25 No doubt the weather of the British Isles is detestable at times, but Lady Marsden always seemed to have been out in the worst of it. *Ib.*

26 We cannot get rid of the idea that there is a special Providence looking after us, a Providence much more interested, much more careful, than the one looking after our neighbour. *Ib.*

27 She had done her duty by her husband. Three daughters she had given him, in spite of the inevitable interference on each occasion with the hunting season. *Ib.*

28 The only reason for making a buzzing noise that I know of is because you're a bee. *Winnie the Pooh*

29 It was just as if somebody inside him were saying, "Now then, Pooh, time for a little something." *Ib.*

30 The cuckoo was trying over his voice carefully and listening to see if he liked it. *Ib.*

NANCY MITFORD

Nancy Freeman Mitford (1904–73), was an English novelist and biographer. Her novels, mainly ironical comedies of manners, include *The Pursuit of Love* (1945), *The Blessing* (1951); her biographies include *The Sun King* (1966), a study of Louis XIV.

1   They passed by a hideous late-Victorian church... a church so ugly that it might have been made to be bombed. *Pigeon Pie*

2   Her ideal hero was a suave, perhaps slightly bald, enormously cultivated diplomat. *Ib.*

3   She loved England, and never thought abroad was worth the trouble it took getting there. *Ib.*

4   Sophia was never able to get it out of her head that the City was a large room in which a lot of men sat all day doing sums. *Ib.*

5   Sophia feared that divorce, re-marriage, and subsequent poverty would not bring out the best in her character. *Ib.*

6   "The only people I care to be very intimate with are the ones you feel would make a good third if God asked you out to dinner." *Ib.*

7   You want to go to the loo and it is miles away down a freezing cold passage and yet you know you have to go down that passage before you can be happy and sleep again. *Ib.*

8   Although she always looked like an elderly negress in them, she liked to see photographs of herself in the papers. *Ib.*

9   At school and at Oxford they had been clever boys with literary gifts and a passion for the humanities; it was only their too early excursion into politics which had reduced their intellectual capacity. *Ib.*

10   I've yet to hear of anybody refusing a dukedom. *Ib.*

11   In New York...the authorities have issued a very comprehensive little pamphlet entitled "The Bomb and You" designed to bring the nuclear bomb into every home and invest it with a certain cosiness. *The Blessing*

12   "What makes you think Americans are so good?"
     "You can see it, shining in their eyes."
     "That's not goodness, it's contact lenses." *Ib.*

13 I often wonder how social life – or life at all – can be much pleasure to people who don't care about dress. *Ib.*

14 Having a baby is not a sovereign cure for everything, although most men, I know, think it is. *Ib.*

15 Paris brothels, having been lately driven underground by the ill-considered action of a woman Deputy, had become rather difficult for a foreigner to find. *Ib.*

16 In France you are always in a witness-box...You must sharpen your wits if you want a favourable verdict. *Ib.*

17 They crossed the Place de la Concorde as only Frenchmen can; that is to say they sauntered through the traffic chatting away, looking neither to right nor to left. *Ib.*

18 One never hears of a French politician dying – they live for ever. *Don't Tell Alfred*

19 All French politicians love each other, or so they say. They never know when they may want to join each other's governments. *Ib.*

20 In small countries like the Channel Islands practically all the male adults are ambassadors. *Ib.*

21 Eccentric old men are still sailing boats on the Round Pond, Kensington Gardens, which has not, as yet, been dried and levelled and turned into a car park. *Ib.*

22 The privileged being of the future is the travel agent. He lives free, travels soft – don't imagine he shares the sufferings of his people. He has a first-class sleeper and the best room in the hotel. *Ib.*

23 I hate health. The more over-populated the world becomes, the more people bother about health. *Ib.*

24 Americans are fighting to express themselves in a language they've never properly learnt. *Ib.*

MORECAMBE & WISE

Eric Bartholomew (1926–84) took the name Morecambe from his home town. He began his career in a youth show, where he met Ernie Wise. They formed a long-lived comic partnership, particularly notable on TV. Ernest Wiseman (1925–), born in Yorkshire, performed in working men's clubs before joining Eric.

1   ERIC. Horses are temperamental. Look – you read something in the paper which upsets you, and you're off colour for the rest of the day. Horses are just the same.
ERNIE. Well, we'll pick a horse that can't read. *Bring Me Sunshine*

MORECAMBE

2   It may surprise you to learn that Ernie Wise is part Italian. His wig comes from Venice.. *Bring Me Sunshine*

3   I always wore my football shirt the wrong way round. The opposition never knew if I was coming or going. *Ib.*

4   I couldn't referee a football match and please everybody. I'd demand a crash helmet, police protection, and danger money. *Ib.*

5   That Japanese chap gets up really high when he's vaulting. It's what is known as a Nip in the air. *Ib.*

6   The dialogue was always the same, whether the pantomime setting was Hardup Hall in *Cinderella* or Widow Twankey's laundry in *Aladdin*. *Ib.*

7   I learnt the art of driving on one of the trickiest and most competitive tracks in the country... Luton High Street. *Ib.*

8   Lew Grade wasn't a Lord then – just "Your Majesty". *There's No Answer to That*

9   My watch has stopped. But it's still right twice a day. *Ib.*

241

10 Ladies and gentlemen, welcome to the show. We want you to relax and enjoy yourselves... and if you don't laugh there's a spike that comes up out of the seat. *Ib.*

WISE

11 I'm not interested in the Noble Art – only in winning the Nobel Prize. *Bring Mw Sunshine*

12 One of my boyhood ambitions was to become a doctor. The headmaster supported the idea. At least, he said I had the handwriting for it. *Ib.*

13 When I was a child I used to sing and dance and do jokes. They were very good jokes – the ones I do now. *Ib.*

14 As we came off Eric said, "This must be the worst bloody act we've ever done." The trouble was we still had our throat mikes on. *There's No Answer to That*

15 Diana Rigg played Nell Gwynn, a superb sight that made the oranges blush. But when she took a look in the mirror... all she could say was, "Good Lord, I'm Danny La Rue!" *Ib.*

16 She was wearing a going-away dress. It looked like part of it had already left. *Ib.*

17 The first Royal Command performance we performed in, we chased a girl wearing a grass skirt across the stage with a lawn-mower. *Ib.*

18 We wouldn't go on the stage to perform to half-empty houses. Half-full ones, yes, perhaps. *Ib.*

CHRISTOPHER MORLEY

Christopher Darlington Morley (1890–1957), American novelist, essayist, and poet, attended Oxford as a Rhodes Scholar. His novels include *Thunder on the Left* (1925). *John Mistletoe* (1931) is an early autobiography.

1   He is too experienced a parent ever to make positive
    promises. *Thunder on the Left*

2   New York – the nation's thyroid gland. *Shore Leave*

3   Prophets were twice stoned. First in anger, then, after their
    death, with a handsome slab in the graveyard. *Where the
    Blue Begins*

4   When someone tries to argue with you say, "You are nothing
    if not accurate, and you are not accurate." Then escape
    from the room. *Mince Pie*

5   Loafing needs no explanation and is its own excuse. *Ib.*

6   The censure of a dog is something no man can stand. *The
    Haunted Bookshop*

7   A human being is an ingenious assembly of portable
    plumbing. *Human Being*

8   April prepares her green traffic light and the world thinks Go.
    John Mistletoe

9   You are the first You that ever was. *Inward Ho*

10 What makes the cider blow its cork
        With such a merry din?...
    It is the fatal apple, boys,
        The fruit of human sin.
    A Glee upon Cider

11 Being in a hurry seems so fiercely important when you
    yourself are the hurrier and so comically ludicrous when it
    is someone else. *Pipefuls*

12 We've had bad luck with our children – they've all grown up.

ROBERT MORLEY

Robert Morley (1908–), English actor and author, made his
first appearance on the stage in 1928, and has achieved a great

reputation, particularly in comedy. He has also written plays, and numerous articles for such magazines as *Punch, Tatler,* and *Playboy.*

1   There is something about a buttered egg that sustains and fortifies me in my darkest hour. *Book of Worries*

2   Suspension bridges don't look safe; there is something unnatural about defying gravity for such a span. *Ib.*

3   A good deal of thought and worry can go into planning your own burial service. *Ib.*

4   It takes enormous courage to dislike members of your own family. *Ib.*

5   Feet are incorrigible trouble makers. *Ib.*

6   Is there something wrong with me because I cannot take an interest in medieval Byzantine frescos partially restored? *Ib.*

7   Most dog owners are at length able to teach themselves to obey their dog. *Ib.*

8   The lift doors may imprison you within their grasp if you are foolish enough to allow others to enter before you. *Ib.*

9   Up to the time of going to press there is no final solution as to which religion the Almighty himself prefers. *Ib.*

10   I have no affinity with big cats and I fear the feeling is mutual. Exploring safari parks...I am quite frankly terrified. *Ib.*

11   I have little patience with anyone who is not self-satisfied...The high spot of every day is when I first catch a glimpse of myself in the shaving mirror. *Playboy*

12   I was invited to taste crocodile. I resisted the offer. Tough as old boots, I imagine, which indeed they are often made into. *Punch*

13 I once asked a circus proprietor her opinion of lion tamers. "Any fool can do it," she told me. "And only a fool does." *Ib.*

14 At school Divinity was my best subject. It usually is with backward pupils. *Ib.*

15 I am not a man who has read widely, preferring to keep my mind relatively uncluttered with the ideas of others. *Ib.*

16 In my youth, when I was overdrawn at the bank, I was admonished in the tone of voice usually used to those whose flies are undone. *Tatler*

17 When I asked my accountant if anything could get me out of the mess I am in now, he thought for a long time..."Yes," he said. "Death would help." *Ib.*

18 The show which, alas, every actor has to miss is his own memorial service. *Ib.*

19 People who lie for hours face down on the sand dunes should be removed by mechanical scoops. *A Musing Morley*

20 Most airports, certainly all European ones, have been built and are still operated as cattle markets. How long will it be before mankind is actually marshalled to the plane by dogs? *Ib.*

21 In Istanbul I found a bear trained as a masseur. *Ib.*

22 I genuinely like myself, and have no reason to believe that the feeling is not reciprocated. *Ib.*

23 My attitude to France was, I suppose, inherited from my father, who always felt perfectly at home there because he never attempted to talk or make friends with the natives. *Ib.*

24 To watch a Frenchman pay for something is to watch him die a slow death. *Observer*

25 How important bread is to a nation and how utterly we are betrayed in this country! If Mother's proud, she must be the only one. *Morley Marvels*

J. B. MORTON

J. B. Morton (1893–1979), British journalist, was educated at
Harrow School. In 1924 he took over the "Beachcomber"
humorous column in the *Daily Express* and retained the post for
nearly forty years.

1   Marriage is a vulgar effort on the part of dull people to bring
     boredom to a fine art. *Beachcomber: the Works of J.B.Morton*

2   Autobiography: a book of gossip about other people. *Ib.*

3   Library: room where the murders take place. *Ib.*

4   At 6.30 a.m., when I was asked to play billiards with a broken
     umbrella handle and three boiled eggs, I realized that I
     am too old for the modern night life. *Ib.*

5   She said the stars made her sick because they were so putridly
     smug. *Ib.*

6   Picnic: a meal of tinned food eaten in a motor-car by the
     roadside. *Ib.*

7   As I passed down the street the mellow tones of the electric
     drills blended soothingly with the machine that was
     blaring swamp-music from the open door of a shop. *Ib.*

8   If thou wouldst know Melrose aright,
     Go visit it by pale moonlight.
     If thou wouldst view Melrose awrong,
     Go visit it by sharrabong. *Ib.*

9   When Hadrian built the Roman Wall
         To keep the horrid Scots away,
     He didn't build it long enough
     Or high enough or strong enough,
         And look at us today! *Ib.*

10   Let me protest against recent attacks on the fagging system at
      school. In all my four years I can recall only eleven deaths
      from fagging. *Ib.*

11   The score picks up – somebody's slammed a one
      And run it out.
      Ballade of the Rodmell Cricket Match

12   Lift her up tenderly,
          Raise her with care,
      Catch hold of one leg
          And a handful of hair;
      Swing her round savagely,
          And when this palls,
      Heave-ho! Away with her
          Into the stalls.
      The Song of the Ballet

13   It is being said of a certain poet that though he tortures the
      English language, he has never yet succeeded in forcing it
      to reveal his meaning. *The Best of Beachcomber*

FRANK MUIR

This lanky humorist (1920–), familiar to TV viewers in *Call My
Bluff* and *My Music*, first came to notice when, with Denis
Norden, he wrote the scripts for the radio series *Take It From
Here* (1948–60). He has edited several humorous books, often
with Simon Brett.

1   The word ''loch'' is pronounced like the word ''lock'' except
      that you clear your throat rather noisily at the end. *Oh, My
      Word*

2   It was a shock to the system, like suddenly coming face to face with a policeman in a ballet skirt, or Miss Barbara Cartland in jeans and a T-shirt. *Ib.*

3   Confectioners caught on that customers would buy a hole if it had a bit of mint round it. *Ib.*

4   A food which is called "instant" superficially resembles the original, but has been dealt with chemically so that it takes slightly less time to prepare in return for losing ninety per cent of its flavour and all its nourishment. *Ib.*

5   Most of the geography of Scotland consists of mountains, grass, heather, and Edinburgh. *Ib.*

6   They all lived in houses backing on to golf-courses and all boasted..."There are fairways at the bottom of our garden." *Ib.*

7   It looks, and I must say tastes, like roughly chopped-up corrugated cardboard, but the blurb on the packet says that it is made from cereal husks. *Ib.*

8   Are you all sitting comfortably? If you are, shuffle about a bit, otherwise you might go to sleep. *Ib.*

9   Knowing that my old friend Sherlock Holmes was partial to a newly-baked loaf, I stopped off at his bakers in Chamber Street before going on to his chambers in Baker Stret. *Ib.*

10   There was something almost feminine in his grace of movement as he folded the banknote and put it in his handbag. *You Can't Have Your Kayak and Heat It*

11   In no time we had the place shipshape: fresh newspaper on the table, and a packing-case lined with straw for the children to sleep in. *Ib.*

12   He used the old-fashioned wooden mangle for getting the last scrap of toothpaste out of the tube. *Ib.*

13   I arrived an hour and a half late for my appointment with the manager of the Post Office Tower restaurant.... I have since learnt that it is possible to get to the top by lift. *Ib.*

14 All Russian lavatory cisterns are made by the same firm and none of them works. *Ib.*

15 I am in my fifties, and looking forward to the first glimmerings of the approach to the beginning of the first foothills of early middle-age. *Ib*

16 [At fourteen] I was overcome with shyness if anybody even looked in my direction, let alone spoke to me. *Ib*

17 I was interested in moths and butterflies at school, and when my friend slipped the book to me in class and whispered its name I accepted it gratefully: I thought he had whispered "Lady Chatterley's Larva". *Ib.*

19 John Aubrey was against flogging, though for serious naughtiness he recommended the use of thumb-screws. *Frank Muir on Children*

19 Any parent who really wants to confuse himself should try helping his offspring with mathematics homework. *The Second Frank Muir Goes Into...*

20 If you decline the verb "to be a bore", it goes: "you are a bore" – "he is a bore" – "they are bores". You very rarely hear "I am a bore". *Ib.*

21 The modern superstition is that we're free of superstition. *Ib.*

22 Some late-night chat-shows are so infantile it seems criminal to keep them up so late. *The Third Frank Muir Goes Into...*

OGDEN NASH

Ogden Nash (1902–71), American writer, mainly of light verse, was a frequent contributor to *The New Yorker*. His sophisticated humour was marked by deliberately rambling couplets and unconventional rhyming.

1   Home is heaven, and orgies are vile,
But I like an orgy once in a while.
The Face is Familiar

2   Some people suffer weeks of remorse after having
committed the slightest peccadillo.
And other people feel perfectly all right after
feeding their husbands arsenic or smothering
their grandmother with a pillow. *Ib.*

3   You never get any fun
Out of the things you haven't done. *Ib*

4   Experience! Wise men do not need it!
Experience! Idiots do not heed it! *Ib.*

5   I'd rather have a rude word from someone who has done me
no harm
Than a graceful letter from the Prince of Wales saying he's
sorry he broke my arm. *Ib.*

6   Everybody in the car can drive better than the chauffeur. *Ib.*

7   I recommend to you this moral:
In real life it takes only one to make a quarrel. *Ib.*

8   You can stand on a corner and a hundred taxis will go by
when you don't want them, but there isn't one in sight
when you do. *Ib.*

9   I am constantly in
The mood
For food. *Ib.*

10   He who attempts to tease the cobra
Is soon a sadder he, and sobra. *Ib.*

12   Every Englishman is convinced of one thing, viz:
That to be an Englishman is to belong to the most
exclusive club there is.
I'm a Stranger Here Myself

13 Behold the hippopotamus!
We laugh at how he looks to us;
And yet in moments dank and grim
I wonder how we look to him. *Ib.*

14 I think it's very nice for ladies to be lithe and lissome,
But not so much that you cut yourself if you happen to
    embrace or kissome. *Ib.*

15 One would be in less danger
From the wiles of the stranger
If one's own kin and kith
Were more fun to be with.
Hard Lines

16 My fellow man I do not care for.
I often ask me, What's he there for?
The only answer I can find
Is, Reproduction of his kind. *Ib.*

17 What is life? Life is stepping down a step or sitting in a chair,
And it isn't there.
Good Intentions

18 It is a fact that a lady wants to be dressed exactly like
everybody else but she gets pretty upset if she sees anybody
else dressed exactly like her. *Ib.*

19 Some people call the parsnip edible;
Myself, I find this claim incredible. *Ib.*

20 Tell me, O Octopus, I begs,
Is those things arms, or is they legs? *Ib.*

21 Should you ask me when Chicago was founded,
I could only reply I didn't even know it was losted. *Ib.*

22 Forty-five isn't really old, it's right on the border,
At least, unless the elevator's out of order.
Versus

23   The people upstairs all practise ballet.
      Their living-room is a bowling alley...
      I might love the people upstairs wondrous
      If instead of above us, they lived just under us. *Ib.*

24   The best way to give a party
      Is leave town the night before.
      You Can't Get There From Here

25   Progress may have been all right once, but it went on too
      long. *Everyone but Thee and Me*

DENIS NORDEN

Denis Norden (1922–), humorous script writer, born in
London, has his own brand of dry wit. He achieved success on
radio, with Frank Muir, with *Take It From Here* (1948–60), and
has since presented many series on radio and TV both with
Muir and solo.

1   He had the kind of handshake that ought never to be used
     except as a tourniquet. *Your Can't Have Your Kayak and
     Heat It*

2   Some time ago Frank Muir and I wrote a television series so
     dire that one newspaper considered reviewing it in the
     obituary column. *Ib.*

3   What is a harp but an over-sized cheese-slicer with cultural
     pretensions. *Ib.*

4   I am allergic to cheese. It dates back to an incident in my
     boyhood when I pulled on a pair of swimming trunks,
     inside which someone had left a loaded mouse-trap. *Ib.*

5   Immigration is the sincerest form of flattery. *Ib.*

6   As the film camera moves in on his face, into his eyes comes
     that look that tells us he's going to have a flashback. *Ib.*

7   When giving children's parties, never serve eight jugs of orangeade in a house which has only one bathroom. *Ib.*

8   My small nephew got his head jammed in the hole of a Henry Moore statue. *Ib.*

9   One of the bodyguards was a great bearded fellow who looked as if he could open parking-meters with his teeth. *Oh, My Word*

10   (Duke of Wellington)

       The tent they have given me is very nice, if a bit on the small side, especially when I am on my horse. *Ib.*

11   Contrary to popular opinion, the most uncomfortable aspect of dieting is not the continual need to watch what you eat. The really difficult part is having to watch what other people are eating. *Ib.*

12   If I were asked to enumerate the Seven Deadly Virtues, the one I'd put right at the top of my list is Female Tidiness. *Ib.*

13   She had him standing for two hours trying to straighten a watercolour of the Leaning Tower of Pisa. *Ib.*

14   They found a will stipulating that he be cremated and his ashes scattered all over her best dining-room rug. *Ib.*

15   When it comes to mechanical assemblies, anything more complex than a door-knocker and I'm banjaxed. *Ib.*

16   The last time I took the car for an MOT test, they warned me that the only parts of it which could be considered roadworthy were the sun-visor and one ashtray. *Ib.*

17   There is an unseen force which lets birds know when you've just washed your car. *Ib.*

18   The girl was built in the way they used to build cars – all the weight at the back. *Ib.*

19   "We have a special room for anyone who wants to smoke," was her smiling reply as she led me out to the toolshed. *Ib.*

20   A counter tenor is anyone who can count to ten.
      (Quoted in Steve Race's *My Music*)

21   Smetana certainly knew which side his bride was Bartered. *Ib.*

22   An Idiophone is the work of the man who designed
      telephone boxes in such a way that however you approach
      them the door is always on the other side. *Ib.*
      (Actually a musical instrument to be struck or shaken)

23   A Bergamasque is what you put over your face when you're
      eating a Wimpey. *Ib.*

24   It's like throwing a drowning man both ends of the rope. *Ib.*

BARRY NORMAN

Barry Norman (1933–) began his career as reporter on a local
newspaper, and graduated to the *Daily Mail* and the *Guardian*.
He later became well known as a film critic for BBC television.

1   David Niven was taken on and registered as "Anglo-Saxon
      type No. 2008". Having thus pigeon-holed him to its own
      satisfaction, the agency promptly cast him as a Mexican.
      The Film Greats

2   Enough women must have shared his bed in those carefree
      bachelor days to have worn a groove in his mattress. *Ib.*

3   Niven once found a job as salesman for a wine company,
      which later showed appreciation of his services by
      displaying a photograph of him with the slogan, "Our first
      and worst salesman". *Ib.*

4   He formed his own ski-ing club, its emblem a ham on skis, of
      which he was the only member. *Ib.*

5   The upper levels of Hollywood society consist of a
      comparatively small number of people. Everyone knows
      everyone else, and sometimes it's possible to imagine that,
      sooner or later, everyone marries everyone else. *Ib.*

6   Hollywood...a place where it is firmly believed that God's final word of advice to Moses as He handed over the tablets was, "And remember, you're only as good as your last picture". *Ib.*

7   In Hollywood every waiter, waitress, or car-park attendant is not really a waiter or waitress or car-park attendant at all but an actor or actress waiting for the big break. *Ib.*

8   Failure is regarded in Hollywood as practically a contagious disease; people will literally cross the road to avoid someone who is tainted with it. *Ib.*

9   The main story in the *Los Angeles Times* claimed that the cops in the Hollywood Division of the LA Police Department were the best organized and most successful burglars in the whole city. *Ib.*

10   MGM came very close to cutting the song "Somewhere Over the Rainbow" out of *The Wizard of Oz* on the grounds that it wasn't much of a song and didn't do a lot for anybody. *Ib.*

11   In that peculiar way Americans have, the Crosbys claimed to be Irish. It's very difficult to find any American who admits simply to being American. *Ib.*

P. J. O'ROURKE

P. J. O'Rourke is an American humorist and journalist, and foreign correspondent to several American journals. *Holiday in Hell* (1988) is a record of his journeys to various trouble spots, mainly in the Third World, written in lively style.

1   Earnestness is just stupidity sent to college. *Holidays in Hell*

2   Once you've been on a plane full of drunken Australians doing wallaby imitations up and down the aisles, you'll never make fun of Americans again. *Ib.*

3   The larger the German body, the smaller the German bathing-suit and the louder the German voice issuing German demands. *Ib.*

4   Modern air travel means less time spent in transit. That time is now spent in transit lounges. *Ib.*

5   No present-day traveller...can say he's done it all if he hasn't been on a smell tour of Asia. *Ib.*

6   In Lebanon you'd be crazy not to have a gun. Though, I assure you, all the crazy people have guns too. *Ib.*

7   In Beirut...all driving is at top speed, much of it on the sidewalks since most parking is done in the middle of the streets. *Ib.*

8   The Korean voting was just what every journalist dreads, quiet and well organized. *Ib.*

9   In the Third World...honk your horn only under the following circumstances: 1. When anything blocks the road. 2. When anything doesn't. 3. When anything might. 4. At red lights. 5. At green lights. 6. At all other times. *Ib.*

10   Old Jerusalem is a medieval city...a real one where you can smell the medieval sanitation and smack your head on the dirty, low medieval ceilings. *Ib.*

11   Cats cannot be made to do anything useful. *Modern Manners*

12   In the past a man was expected to give up his seat on a bus to a woman. Today it would be much more courteous for that man to give her his job. *Ib.*

13   Don't send funny greetings cards at birthdays or at Christmas. Save them for funerals, when their cheery effect is needed. *Ib.*

14   A hat should be taken off when you meet a lady – and left off for the rest of your life. *Ib.*

DOROTHY PARKER

Dorothy Parker (1893–1967), was an American journalist, short story writer, and author of light verse. Much of her work was contributed to *The New Yorker,* and is noted for its wit and malice.

1   The one dependable law of life – everything is always worse than you thought it was going to be. *The Waltz*

2   George Jean Nathan said that the lovely rhythms of the waltz should be listened to in stillness and not accompanied by strange gyrations of the body. *Ib.*

3   I've been locked in his noxious embrace for the thirty-five years this waltz has lasted. *Ib.*

4   Scratch a lover and find a foe. *Enough Rope*

5   My own dear love, he is all my heart –
     And I wish somebody'd shoot him. *Ib.*

6   Men seldom make passes
     At girls wearing glasses. *Ib.*

7   Some men break your heart in two,
         Some men fawn and flatter,
     Some men never look at you,
         And that cleans up the matter.
     Experience

8   His voice was as intimate as the rustle of sheets. *Dusk Before Fireworks*

9   Every time I took my head off the pillow, it would roll under the bed. *You Were Perfectly Fine*

10   When I start getting tender about Our Dumb Friends...three highballs and I think I'm St Francis of Assisi. *Just a Little One*

11   Early to bed, and you'll wish you were dead. *The Little Hours*

12 My soul is crushed, my spirit sore;
    I do not love me any more.
    Sympton Recital

13 The only thing I didn't like about *The Barretts of Wimpole Street*
    was the play. *The New Yorker*

14 The affair between Margot Asquith and Margot Asquith will
    live as one of the prettiest love stories in all literature. *Ib.*

15 I invariably miss most of the last act of an Ibsen play; I have
    my fingers in my ears, waiting for the loud report that
    means the heroine has Passed On. *Vanity Fair*

16 (At a party)
    One more drink and I'll be under the host.

C. NORTHCOTE PARKINSON

Cyril Northcote Parkinson (1909–) was educated at York, Cambridge, and London. He has been a history master (Blundell's) and lecturer (Liverpool and abroad) and has written serious books. But he is best known for his famous Parkinson's Law (No. 1 below) and his satirical books on bureaucracy, e.g. *Parkinson's Law* (1958).

1   Work expands to meet the time available for its completion. *Parkinson's Law*

2   Heaven forbid that we should cease to read books on the science of public or business administration – provided only that these works are classified as fiction *Ib.*

3   The defect in intelligence tests is that high marks are gained by those who subsequently prove to be almost illiterate. *Ib.*

4   Choosing between two candidates, a member of the Admiralty Board would ask suddenly, "What was the number of the taxi you came in?" A candidate who said, truthfully, "I don't know" was rejected, and the candidate who said (lying) "Number 2351" was promptly admitted as a boy with initiative. *Ib.*

5   We all know how an estate agent will wander round a vacant house when acting for the purchaser. It is only a matter of time before he throws open a cupboard or kicks a skirting and exclaims, "Dry rot!" *Ib.*

6   It is now known that men enter local politics solely as a result of being unhappily married. *Ib.*

7   We know how to make our predecessors retire. When it comes to forcing *us* to retire, our successors must find some method of their own. *Ib.*

8   Until a fairly recent period...the man who deserted his wife, eloping with another woman...might find himself denied the Sacrament, refused an overdraft, blackballed at the Country Club, and deliberately cut by the Master of Foxhounds. *Mrs Parkinson's Law*

9   In the USA this is the age of the henpecked husband and the age, in consequence, of the deserted wife. *Ib.*

10 In the garden of Eden...the serpent is, of course, a piece of poetic symbolism representing the automobile. *Ib.*

11 Few moods of panic will survive a bucket of cold water emptied over the head. *Ib.*

12 The perambulator has existed for years...but no architect or builder has ever heard of it. It either blocks the passage to the kitchen or is wheeled into the garage where it prevents the car door from opening. *Ib.*

13 Today it is the children who talk and the parents who listen. *Ib.*

14 Legend would have it that we, the elderly, are deaf...but nothing could be further from the truth. What we do find is that few people speak up as they used to. *IB.*

15 When spectacles are mislaid we are left without means of seeing where they are. *Ib.*

16 Whereas Shakespeare told his audience to picture the battlefield for themselves, the modern producer has to show us the bloodshed in technicolour. *Ib.*

17 An advertisement for a Slimming Treatment says, "How to overeat without being overweight". It is obvious nonsense, but we mop our foreheads with relief. Now we can have our cake and eat it. *Ib.*

18 Expenditure rises to meet income. Individual expenditure not only rises to meet income but tends to surpass it. *The Law and the Profits*

19 Few people would admit to being quarrelsome, unpopular, idle, and dirty. It just so happens (they would explain) that all their neighbours are hostile, their colleagues unfriendly, their employers unreasonable, and the water too cold to wash in. *Ib.*

MICHAEL PARKINSON

Michael Parkinson (1933–), journalist (*Sunday Times, Punch*), TV talk show compère, and humorous writer on sport, has written several books including *Football Daft* (1968), *Cricket Mad* (1969), *Bats in the Pavilion* (1977), *Parkinson's Lore* (1981).

1 I am not saying it is necessary for a fast bowler to be a homicidal maniac, but it certainly helps. *Bats in the Pavilion*

2 The team had a fast bowler who wore a monocle and ran to the wicket with a ball in either hand. He was completely ambidextrous, so the batsman had no idea which hand the ball was coming from. *Ib.*

3 My old team knew that [against fast bowling] to follow the classic dictum of getting the nose over the ball simply meant a two-ounce missile up the left nostril. *Ib.*

4 I have never been injured, which probably argues much for my technique against pace bowling, consisting as it does of playing from a position somewhat adjacent to the square leg umpire. *Ib.*

5 Many's the time my old man (acting as umpire) leapt in the air and joined with the bowler in an ear-splitting appeal for lbw. *Ib.*

6 Nothing yet devised by man is worse for a sick hangover than a day's cricket in the summer sun. *Ib.*

7   It is easier to choose a cricket bat than pick a wife...A bat has a watermark of quality – the grain...The one basic flaw in the otherwise perfect construction of women is that you can't detect the knots in the grain until it's too late. *Ib.*

8   Women playing cricket should treat it as a matter between consenting females in private. *Ib.*

9   Soccer is a simple-minded game for simple people, golf merely an expensive way of leaving home. *Ib.*

10   The most offensive weapon I ever handled in the army was an ancient Imperial typewriter which occasionally shed one of its parts when in action. *Ib.*

11   My old man had only two ambitions in life. One was that I should never follow him down the mines, and the other that I should play cricket for Yorkshire. *The Best of Parkinson*

12   A talk show is an unnatural act between consenting adults in public. *Ib.*

13   It was my first encounter with the interviewer's nightmare, the unco-operative victim.... Nowadays, bearing the scars of many encounters, I have learned the art of talking to brick walls. *Ib.*

THOMAS LOVE PEACOCK

Thomas Love Peacock (1785–1866), English novelist, self-educated but a learned scholar, was employed in the East India Company. His unusual novels are often in dialogue form. The first was *Headlong Hall* (1816), the last *Gryll Grange* (1860).

1   There is nothing too monstrous for human credulity. *Gryll Grange*

2   The world will never suppose a good motive where it can suppose a bad one. *Ib.*

3   Mountebank advertisements promise the beauty of Helen in a bottle of cosmetic. *Ib.*

4   Marriage is at best a dangerous experiment. *Ib.*

5   I saw the other day some examination papers which would have excluded Marlborough from the army and Nelson from the navy. *Ib.*

6   Most singers are reluctant to comply when asked to sing, but never leave off once they have begun. *Ib.*

7   Lord Curryfin invented a sail of infallible safety which capsized its inventor on its first trial. *Ib.*

8   The man was the bore of all bores. His subject had no beginning, middle, nor end. It was Education. *Ib.*

9   The more his mind was troubled, the more Madeira he could drink without disordering his head. *Ib.*

10   (Song for the Stock Exchange)
     We've small taste for championing maids in distress;
     For State we care little; for Church we care less:
     To Premiums and Bonus our homage we plight:
     "Percentage!" we cry: and "A fig for the right!" *Ib.*

11   Respectable means rich, and decent means poor. I should die if I heard my family called decent. *Crotchet Castle*

12   A book that furnishes no quotations is no book – it is a plaything. *Ib.*

13   I have quarrelled with my wife, and a man who has quarrelled with his wife is absolved from all duty to his country. *Nightmare Abbey*

14   Marriage may often be a stormy lake, but celibacy is almost always a muddy horse-pond. *Melincourt*

S. J. PERELMAN

Sidney Joseph Perelman (1904–79), American humorist, was a frequent contributor to *The New Yorker*, and writer of many film scripts, including some for the Marx Brothers. His many books include *Crazy Like a Fox* (1944) and *Chicken Inspector No. 23* (1952).

1   The classical Tom Sawyer tooth extraction – the silk thread tied to the bedstead, the hot coal brandished in the patient's face – remains unsurpassed in home dentistry. *The Last Laugh*

2   The little match girl in the fairy tale of Hans Christian Anderson is rarely depicted with a moustache. *Ib.*

3   Far from being a member of any gymnastic team, I could not jump over a sawhorse without sustaining multiple fractures. *Ib.*

4   As the Lord Krishna says, cow dung cannot be gathered where no cow has been. *Ib.*

5   When that loveliest of actresses, Rachel Gurney, of *Upstairs, Downstairs*, perished on the *Titanic*, I wept so convulsively that I had to be force-fed. *Ib.*

6   I twice urged my colleague to leave by the fire escape, but his dentures were chattering so loudly that he did not hear me. *Ib.*

7   I tried to resist his overtures, but he plied me with symphonies, quartettes, chamber music, and cantatas. *Crazy Like a Fox*

8   He bit his lip in a manner which immediately awakened my maternal sympathy, and I helped him bite it. *Ib.*

9   The violent hush of twilight was descending over Los Angeles...How good it was to be alive, I thought, inhaling deep lungfuls of carbon monoxide. *Strictly From Hunger*

10   The whistle shrilled, and in a moment I was chugging out of
      Grand Central Station...I had chugged only a few feet
      when I realized I had left without the train, so I had to run
      back and wait for it to start. *Ib.*

11   The cigar stump you chewed throughout lunch did nothing
      to help your diction. *Chicken Inspector No.23*

12   The lady on my left...ignored me altogether, even when I
      politely inquired whether her diamonds were genuine or
      paste. *Ib.*

13   The critics must have decided to let you down easy, because
      not one of them reviewed your book. How's that for
      professional courtesy? *Ib.*

14   Ultimately the pandemonium simmered down to chaos. *Ib.*

JON PERTWEE

Jon Pertwee (1919–), British actor educated at Sherborne and
RADA, made his first stage appearance in 1936. He was best
known in films, e.g. the *Carry On* series, and particularly on TV
as Dr Who.

1   For some months after my birth I led a happy, useful, and
      productive life, lying nude on an astrakhan rug, eating
      coal. *Moon Boots*

2   My mother, having taken a good look at me and presumably
      not liking what she saw, divorced my father for his best
      friend. *Ib.*

3   My uncle never had a day's illness in his life. I only once knew
      him to take an aspirin, and this nearly did him in. *Ib.*

4   My uncle swayed back and forth in his driving-seat as if the
      additional momentum of his shifting weight would assist
      the ancient motor more easily up the hill. In retrospect I
      am of the opinion that the occasional change of gear
      might have helped. *Ib.*

5   Henry [the butler] would wear a white tie with his tail suit at
     Christmas, instead of the Major-Domo's traditional black.
     Because of this, Aunt Decima annually kissed him fondly
     on both cheeks, under the impression that he was a
     smartly dressed member of the family. *Ib.*

6   Few sights are more ludicrous than two grown men locked in
     verbal combat, completely unaware that they are sporting
     silly paper hats. *Ib.*

7   (The morning cold bath at school)
     I have never been given a lucid reason for this pagan ceremony
     apart from "It's good for you".

8   The only time I ever heard a bigger laugh in a classroom was
     when a master announced, "I want to see Jon P. in my
     study immediately after lunch." *Ib.*

9   One morning, having ridden my motor-cycle to the station, I
     left it padlocked to a lamp-post. Imagine my chagrin when
     I returned to discover that not only had my motor-cycle
     gone but so had the lamp-post! *Ib.*

EDEN PHILLPOTTS

Eden Phillpotts (1862–1960), British novelist and playwright,
was born in India but brought up in England. He settled in
Devonshire, the setting for many of his numerous novels, e.g.
Widecombe Fair (1913), and his famous play *The Farmer's Wife*
(1916).

1   Father kicked me out for trying to show him how to manage
     mother. *The Farmer's Wife*

2   Love ought to be got over early in life. To see an old man in
     love be worse than seeing him with the whooping-cough.
     Ib.

3   Marriage don't alter women. They change their clothes – not their claws. *Ib.*

4   Beer-drinking don't do half the harm of love-making. *Ib.*

5   Them what skim the cream off women keep bachelors. To marry be like jumping into a river because you're thirsty. *Ib.*

6   The very last speech she made, half a minute before she died, was "See master's under-pants be put to the fire". She perished with them beautiful words on her lips. *Ib.*

7   Sense in a girl be as rare as white feathers on a blackbird. *Ib.*

8   The rising generation only plays for its own hand, and its own hand don't pat Daddy's whiskers no more – 'tis busy in Daddy's pocket. *Ib.*

9   Most men take a woman – like a girl takes a box of chocolates – for the picture on the lid. *Ib.*

10   Lawyers and jackdaws be birds of a feather, come to think of it. *Devonshire Cream*

11   Have you ever thought what a fine world this would be if it weren't for the people in it? *Ib.*

12   She's one of they greedy females – can't see a worm without wishing she was a bird. *Ib.*

13   We struggled on for ten full year, and I prayed the Lord, night and day, to take one of us...I didn't care which went. Then in His mercy He fetched Eliza. *Ib.*

14   Lawyers pick the plums out of too many puddings. *Ib.*

15   In my young days a lot of marriages were made in Heaven; but 'tis the other place looks after most of 'em now. *Ib.*

16   I was in London myself once – for three days. A fussy place and not enough air to go around. *Ib.*

17   I've seen him let a black beetle run by into his wife's parlour, because he said 'twas doing its Maker's will. *Ib.*

18   I want for everybody to be as content as myself. If all the other fools would only listen to me, no doubt they might be. *Ib.*

19   Nothing breeds sound politics like a bit in the Savings Bank. *Yellow Sands*

20   If the New Jerusalem's like the Midlands, then there's a lot of people will be cruel disappointed. *Ib.*

21   I was wondering last night if the heavenly mansions would have bathrooms in 'em. *Ib.*

22   The woman who gets her own way never respects the man that lets her. *Ib.*

23   I've never been able to feel champagne's a respectable wine. *Ib.*

24   When a man or woman's making their will, they'll be independent for once in their lives...Many a hen-pecked man has pecked back on his death-bed. *Ib.*

25   Whenever he gets a cold on the chest he thinks he's going to die. *The Human Boy*

26   You look as if you'd been buried and dug up again. I don't say it unkindly. *Ib.*

27   With fathers or women the headmaster had a playful mood and an expression known as the "parent-smile". *Ib.*

28   A girl hates a joke something frightful. *Ib.*

PETER POOK

Peter Pook (d. 1979) wrote many popular humorous novels based on his own supposed experiences, e.g. *Banker Pook Confesses*; *Pook's Tours* (1974); *Pook's Love Nest* (1976). The author was himself widely experienced, having been (among other things) teacher, bank clerk, Royal Marine, antique dealer, estate agent, and lecturer.

1   It has been said that behind every successful man there stands a woman, but it does not specify if she carries a child or a gun. *Pook's Love Nest*

2   Remember the old saying, a friend in need is a damned nuisance. *Ib.*

3   She had learnt from her mother that, contrary to British common law, men are guilty until they can prove their innocence. *Ib.*

4   He inspected the premises with the eye of an expert but with the expression of a mourner. *Ib.*

5   The microphone whined in protest at being used. *Ib.*

6   Have you ever been suddenly confronted with an earring in your bed and come up with a perfectly logical explanation? *Ib.*

7   He hurried by with that furtive expression of the public when flag-sellers are abroad in the streets. *Ib.*

8   Nothing slows a boat so much as gradually sinking. *Ib.*

9   "Rugby is a game for the mentally defective," he agreed. "That is why it was invented by the British. Who else but an Englishman could invent an oval ball?" *Ib.*

10 They were remembering, perhaps, the boxer who told the referee he wore the horseshoe in his glove just for luck. *Ib.*

11 She is one of the few drivers in Britain who have managed to cross an intersection with a traffic policeman on the bonnet. *Ib.*

12 He said he hoped we had left enough room for tonight's evening meal. I told him I had left enough room for the evening meals of the next fortnight. *Pook's Viking Virgins*

13 Apparently nurses are taught to strip patients on the same principle as peeling a banana. *Ib.*

14 I felt too hungry to end it all. One requires strength to leap
    in the lake and drown so I decided to lunch first, then
    return and do myself in during the afternoon. *Ib.*

15 Once in the National Gallery I was seasick viewing
    Gainsborough's painting of a millpond. *Ib.*

16 Your last story-script was so bad it was rejected by a vanity
    publisher. *Ib.*

STEPHEN POTTER

Stephen Potter (1900–70), educated at Westminster School
and Oxford, was a British university lecturer, BBC producer,
and journalist. He published some literary criticism, but
achieved fame through his tongue-in-cheek books on how to
outwit other people by unsporting subtlety.

1 There is no finer spectacle than the sight of a good Lifeman,
   so ignorant that he can scarcely spell the simplest word,
   making an expert look like a fool on his own subject.
   Lifemanship

2 Sooner or later an expert will say, "But I'm talking too much"
   – always a prelude to talking still more. *Ib.*

3 In conversation play, the important thing is to get there early
   and stay there. *Ib.*

4 The general aim in music is to make other people feel
   outsiders. *Ib.*

5 In lawn tennis mixed, the basic chivalry move is to pretend to
   serve less fiercely to the woman than to the man. This is
   particularly useful if your first service tends to be out in
   any case. *Ib.*

6 Good gamesmanship which is also good sportsmanship can be
   practised in golf if the gamesman makes a great and
   irritatingly prolonged parade of spending time looking for
   his *opponent's* ball. *Gamesmanship*

7 Advice *must be vague*, to make certain it is not helpful. *Ib.*

8 He spent an entire season acquiring absolute ambidexterity as a batsman. Coming in eighth wicket down, he was able to irritate an already wearied field by playing alternate balls left- and right-handed, forcing the fielders to change position after each delivery. *Ib.*

9 Doctorship – the art of getting one up on the patient without actually killing him. *One-Upmanship*

10 Basic Doctorship is to suggest that Patient is worrying either (*a*) too little, but (*b*) far more generally, too much. *Ib.*

11 When answering Patient's telephone call he can, and generally does say, "Dr Meadows speaking" in a frightfully hollow and echoing voice, as if expecting to sign a death certificate. *Ib.*

12 A good general rule [with wine] is to state that the bouquet is better than the taste, and vice versa. *Ib.*

13 Babies are by nature one-up. Whatever they do it is your fault. *Supermanship*

14 The definition of reviewmanship is...to show that it is really you yourself who should have written the book, if you had had the time.

OLIVER PRITCHETT

Oliver Pritchett (1939–), educated at Bryanston and Magdalen College, Oxford, has written humorous articles for the *Sunday Telegraph* and *Daily Telegraph* since 1978. Previously he worked for the *Evening Standard*, the *Observer* and the *Guardian*. He has also written a novel, *A Prize Paradise* (1979).

1   I am a fully qualified hazardologist. I am acutely aware of the
     perils that lie in wait for us in life. To me, a drawing-pin is
     a sword of Damocles. *Sunday Telegraph*

2   The main hazard for the holidaymaker abroad is other
     holidaymakers abroad. *Ib.*

3   When I read that a certain place is 3,000 feet above sea level I
     have to imagine five hundred friends who are six feet tall,
     assemble them on a beach, and mentally stack them one
     on top of the other. At this point I realise that I don't have
     five hundred friends. *Ib.*

4   Red sky at night –
     You've left on the bathroom light. *Ib.*

5   I have always had some difficulty in distinguishing between
     charisma and after-shave. *Ib.*

6   The friendly rivalry between the Houses of York and Lancaster
     has been dubbed the "Wars of the Roses" simply because
     it made a catchy headline. *Ib.*

7   When people start talking to me about "an exciting
     challenge" I tend to get a pain behind my left knee. *Ib.*

8   Long before the present fuss [about salmonella] started I was
     warning about the hidden menace of eggs. In the
     frying-pan they spit in your face. *Ib.*

9   The frozen pea was a landmark in the development of
     convenience food. It is important to remember that word
     "convenience" as you wrestle the strong plastic packet
     with numb fingers before finally tearing it open with your
     teeth. *Ib.*

10   Two safety tips for anybody attempting to read this article. It
     would be wise not to do so while operating heavy
     machinery or riding a bicycle. *Ib.*

11   Certain people in this life are natural lift-button pressers.
     Should you presume to take on the function yourself, they
     will press the button anyway, after you have done so. *Ib.*

12 We do not suffer from ordinary colds any more. They are all uncommon and they are usually upgraded to the rank of flu. *Daily Telegraph*

13 As conversation stoppers, proverbs are ideal. They seem to contain meaning, but nobody can be quite sure what it is. *Ib.*

BRIAN RIX

Sir Brian Rix (1924–) trained as an actor under Sir Donald Wolfit, and made his first West End appearance in 1943. His reputation rests mainly on the successful farces which he regularly presented, particularly at the Whitehall Theatre. *My Farce From My Elbow* is his autobiography (1975).

1 If you decide against [buying this book]...please close it very gently and replace it on the bookshop shelf as unostentatiously as you can. *My Farce From My Elbow*

2 *The Stage* said I gave "able support". I felt like a jock-strap. *Ib.*

3 *Twelfth Night*...is a pot-boiler, and Belch and Feste have always reminded me of school pranksters and bullies. *Ib.*

4 You were confronted by a chipped, stained bath and a geyser which could have doubled for a Wurlitzer Organ. You turned on an assortment of taps, the mighty machine groaned and wheezed into life, and out came a trickle of tepid, rusty water. *Ib.*

5 Actor to landlady: "What are your lowest terms for actors? Landlady: "A thieving bunch of bastards!"

6 Many critics are actors manqué – some more manqué than others. *Ib.*

7 He offered her the lead in his first film, *Halfpenny Breeze*. The budget was practically a halfpenny, too. *Ib.*

8   To be enjoyed, overwork must be *seen* to be done. *Ib.*

9   Our production included the line Hattie Jacques hates so much: "Pull up a couple of chairs and sit down." *Ib.*

WILL ROGERS

William Penn Adair Rogers (1879–1935), was an American vaudeville performer and humorist. He began with a rope-spinning act spiced with humour but later developed into a film actor and comedian.

1   I was born because it was a habit in those days, people didn't know any different. *Autobiography*

2   Half our life is spent trying to find something to do with the time we rushed through life trying to save. *Ib.*

3   When you put down the good things you ought to have done, and leave out the bad ones you did do – that's Memoirs. *Ib.*

4   The only thing that can stop hair falling is the floor. *Ib.*

5   The movies is the only business where you can go out front and applaud yourself. *Ib.*

6   Being a hero is about the shortest-lived profession on earth. *Saturday Review (August 1962)*

7   Income Tax has made more liars out of the American people than Golf. *Ib.*

8   We don't know what we want, but we're ready to bite somebody to get it. *Ib.*

9   Everything is funny, as long as it's happening to somebody else. *The Illiterate Digest*

10   One-third of the people in the United States promote, while the other two-thirds provide. *Ib.*

11 With Congress, every time they make a joke it's a law, and every time they make a law it's a joke.

12 Live so that you wouldn't be ashamed to sell the family parrot to the town gossip.

13 My forefathers didn't come over on the *Mayflower*, but they met the boat.

14 Even if you're on the right track, you'll get run over if you just sit there.

15 A comedian can only last till either he takes himself serious or his audience takes him serious.

16 A diplomat and a stage magician are the two professions that have to have a high silk hat. *Autobiography*

LEONARD ROSSITER

Leonard Rossiter (1927–84), born in Liverpool, made many stage appearances, and was well known as a TV performer, particularly in *The Rise and Fall of Reginald Perrin* and *Rising Damp*. In 1980 he added some further devilish maxims and definitions to those of Ambrose Bierce (q.v.).

1 No doubt the real agony of Hell won't be burning fires but having all the secret humiliations of your life played back to you in perpetuity and in stereo. *The Devil's Bedside Book*

2 God moves in very mysterious ways. He never leaves any fingerprints. *Ib.*

3 Important dates are always remembered – the day after they happened. *Ib.*

4 If a nail is hit with exactly the right amount of force from exactly the right angle, it will bend over. *Ib.*

5 You will always find what you are looking for in the last place you look. *Ib.*

6   It always pours with rain the day after you've broken your umbrella, washed the car, cleaned the windows, or painted the gutters. *Ib.*

7   If ignorance is bliss, why aren't more people happy? *Ib.*

8   Once something is fouled up, anything done to improve it will only make it worse. *Ib.*

9   Anyone who says four times he isn't going to resign definitely will. *Ib.*

10   The behaviour of many children suggests that their parents embarked on the sea of matrimony without a paddle. *Ib.*

11   A consultant is a person called in when nobody wants to take the blame for what's going wrong. *Ib.*

DAMON RUNYON

Alfred Damon Runyon (1884–1946) made a name for himself as a sports writer before writing stories of the New York underworld in an informal style, usually in the historic present. One of his books, *Guys and Dolls* (1932), was later made into a musical.

1   Always try and rub up against money, for if you rub up against money long enough, some of it may rub off on you. *Furthermore*

2   The Lemon Drop Kid cannot even spell arthritis, let alone have it. *Ib.*

3   Any time you see him he is usually by himself because being by himself is not apt to cost him anything. *Ib.*

4   Even Mr Justice Veezee is not so old-fashioned as to believe any doll will go to his apartment just to look at etchings. *Ib.*

5   I judge from the sounds that he gets his kiss, and it is a very large kiss indeed, with the cut-out open. *Ib.*

6   These citizens are always willing to bet that what Nicely-Nicely
dies of will be over-feeding and never anything small like
pneumonia. *Take It Easy*

7   My wife does not allow me to go around marrying people.
More Than Somewhat

8   "In fact," Sam the Gonolph says, "I long ago came to the
conclusion that all life is six to five against." *Ib.*

9   She dances with all her clothes on which is considered a very
big novelty indeed. *Ib.*

10 He is a very hard guy indeed. In fact the softest thing about
him is his front teeth. *Ib.*

11 I go around to see Doc Brennan about my stomach, and he
puts a gag on my arm and tells me that my blood pressure
is higher than a cat's back. *Ib.*

12 "It is against the law to commit suicide in this town," I say,
"though what the law can do to a guy who commits
suicide I am never able to figure out." *Ib.*

13   I can see that it is a very homely baby indeed. Still I never see
      many babies that I consider rose geraniums for looks,
      anyway. *Guys and Dolls*

14   I once knew a chap who had a system of just hanging the
      baby on the line to dry...a wonderful innovation on
      changing a diaper. *Short Takes*

15   The race is not always to the swift nor the battle to the
      strong, but that's the way to bet.

WILLIAM RUSHTON

William Rushton (1937–), English humorist, who after
experience as a solicitor's clerk, helped to found *Private Eye*. He
has often appeared on TV, including the satirical programme
That Was the Week That Was. He is also a talented cartoonist and
book illustrator.

1   German is the most extravagantly ugly language... like
     someone using a sick-bag on a 747. *Holiday Inn, Ghent*

2   This is the sort of dish that has made the German what he is
     today. Industrious and fat. *Super Pig*

3   Take the giblets out of a chicken before insertion in a fridge.
     If you're squeamish, put on a rubber glove and pretend
     you're a best-selling vet. *Ib.*

4   If God had believed in love, he'd have thought of better
     rhymes than glove, turtle-dove, above, and shove. *Ib.*

5   "*Don't* Do-It-Yourself" is my battle-cry, you've probably heard
     it before, You have no redress against anybody if it goes
     wrong. *Ib.*

6   If the Devil is interested in some sort of barter, then my soul is
     his for good syrup puddings. *Ib.*

7   However carefully you phrase the history of your sex-life,
     you're bound to emerge as a boaster, a braggart, a liar, or
     a laughing-stock. *Ib.*

8   It's part of our British heritage that we need never say any
    more to anyone than a civil "good day". *Ib.*

9   Flies have unattractive personal habits...They come striding in,
    fresh from a tiny glut on some unedifying object best left
    to the darker reaches of your imagination, and pace
    nervously about on your meat or bread, leaving
    dysentry-footprints. *Ib.*

10 *How to give up smoking.* Stop putting cigarettes in your mouth
    and lighting them. *Ib.*

11 I've inclined to stoutness all my days...and studiously ignored
    the fact that I was pouring beer, bread, and potatoes down
    me like some giant waste-disposal unit. *Ib.*

12 Joggers do nothing but clog up the roads and have no saving
    grace except that they are easy to run down. *Daily Express*
    (*1989*)

13 Television is totally in the hands of semi-articulate barbarians
    who can barely read an autocue. *Ib.*

14 Do not confuse tubes of travelling detergent with toothpaste.
    I think the reason I grew a beard was that I was constantly
    cleaning my teeth with shaving cream. *Ib.*

15 My permanent hatred is for cordless telephones...those
    people who phone you from a train, just to say that they're
    phoning you from a train. *Ib.*

'SAKI'

Hector Hugh Munro (1870–1916), a Scot born in Burma, was
educated at Bedford Grammar School. He spent two years in
police service in India and then became a journalist. His
humorous short stories, novels, and a play, *The Watched Pot,*
(1924) were written under the pen-name 'Saki'.

1   I'm living so far beyond my income that we might almost be
    said to be living apart. *The Unbearable Bassington*

2   Once you've seen your features hurriedly reproduced in the newspaper you feel you'd like to be a veiled Turkish woman for the rest of your life. *Ib.*

3   If one hides one's talent under a bushel, one must careful to point out the exact bushel under which it is hidden. *Ib.*

4   If pressed in an unguarded moment to describe her soul, she would probably have described her drawing-room. *Ib.*

5   Constance is one of those strapping florid girls that go so well with autumn scenery or Christmas decorations. *The Chronicles of Clovis*

6   When one lives among greyhounds one should avoid giving life-like imitations of a rabbit. *Ib.*

7   On horseback he seemed to require as many hands as a Hindu god. *Ib*

8   "You're looking nicer than usual," I said, "but that's so easy for you." *Ib.*

9   These marsh fevers drain the energy out of you in bucketfuls, and it trickles back again in teaspoonfuls. *When William Came*

10   She does a dance suggesting the life of a fern. To me it would equally well have suggested the life of John Wesley. *Ib.*

11   She reminds me of garlic that has been planted by mistake in a conservatory. *Ib.*

12   The Canon realises how difficult it will be for the rich to enter the Kingdom of Heaven, and he tries to make up for it by being as nice as possible to them in this world. *Ib.*

13   When you wear a look of idiotic complacency in a Turkish bath it is the more noticeable from the fact that you are wearing nothing else. *Ib.*

14   She is a sort of Catherine the Second of Russia without any of Catherine's redeeming vices. *The Watched Pot*

15 With equal readiness she prescribed rules for the management of the Y.W.C.A. and the Devon and Somerset Staghounds. *Ib.*

16 Matrimony is not reputed to be invariably a bed of roses, but there is no reason why it should be a cactus-hedge. *Ib.*

17 "You think it unlucky to have moonstones?"

"Oh, distinctly, if you've the chance of getting something more valuable." *Ib.*

18 A husband with asthma has all the advantages of a captive golf-ball; you know where to put your hand on him when you want him. *Ib.*

19 A woman who takes her husband about with her everywhere is like a cat that goes on playing with a mouse long after she's killed it. *Ib.*

20 So many people who are described as rough diamonds turn out to be really rough paste. *Ib.*

21 She is not content to have her finger in the pie; she wants the whole pie in her pocket. *Ib.*

22 The suit I've got on was only paid for last month, so you can judge how old it is.

23 There ought to be a law compelling everyone to keep his conscience under proper control. *Ib.*

24 I loathe rice pudding, it's so wholesome. *Ib.*

25 He's the kind of idiot who comes up to you in a Turkish bath and says "Isn't it hot?" *Ib.*

26 You seem to have a good head for business – other people's business. *Ib.*

27 It's generally understood that a rich man has some difficulty in entering the Kingdom of Heaven; the House of Commons is not so exclusive. *Ib.*

28   I hate babies. They're so human – they remind me of monkeys. *Ib.*

29   Sparrowby is one of those people who would be enormously improved by death. *Ib.*

30   She was a good cook, as cooks go, and as cooks go, she went. *Reginald*

31   You can't expect a boy to be vicious till he's been to a good school. *Ib.*

32   Unlike the alleged Good Woman of the Bible, I'm not above rubies. *Ib.*

33   She's desperately anxious to do the wrong thing correctly. *Ib.*

34   A little inaccuracy sometimes saves tons of explanation. *The Square Egg*

J. D. SALINGER

Jerome David Salinger (1919–), American novelist, won acclaim with *The Catcher in the Rye* (1951), the cult novel about an awkward and precocious teenager. Later books include *Seymour: an Introduction* (1963).

1   The more expensive a school is, the more crooks it has. *The Catcher in the Rye*

2   There were pills and medicines all over the place, and everything smelled like Vick's Nose Drops. *Ib.*

3   You don't have to think too hard when you talk to a teacher. *Ib.*

4   Almost every time somebody gives me a present, it ends up making me sad. *Ib.*

5   That guy was as sensitive as a goddam toilet seat. *Ib.*

6   It's really hard to be room-mates with people if your suitcases are much better than theirs. *Ib.*

7   He was the kind of phoney that have to give themselves *room* when they answer somebody's question. He stepped back, and stepped right on the lady's foot behind him. *Ib.*

8   I don't even like *old* cars... I'd rather have a goddam horse. A horse is at least *human*, for God's sake. *Ib.*

9   I have one of those very loud, stupid laughs. I mean, if I ever sat behind myself in a movie, I'd probably lean over and tell myself to please shut up. *Ib.*

10   I hope to hell when I *do* die somebody has sense enough to just dump me in the river or something. Anything except sticking me in a goddam cemetery. *Ib.*

11   A confessional passage has probably never been written that didn't stink a little bit of the writer's pride in having given up his pride. *Seymour: an Introduction*

12   I resented like hell filing out of the theatre just because some playwright was forever slamming down his silly curtain. *Ib.*

HARRY SECOMBE

Sir Harry Donald Secombe (1921–), Welsh comedian and notable singer, first came to notice as a member of the BBC comic radio team *The Goons* (1949–60). He has also appeared frequently on TV, films, and stage (e.g. as Mr Pickwick). He has written a novel, *Twice Brightly* (1974), and an embellished autobiography *Goon For Lunch* (1975).

1   I had measles so quickly on top of chicken-pox that the spots were fighting each other for space. *Goon For Lunch*

2   I had a great respect for all animals, having been kicked by a cow in Cardigan on holiday. *Ib.*

3   When I first became a choirboy my idea of God was of a large, forbidding old gentleman with a fat round face and silver hair, who looked remarkably like the Vicar. *Ib.*

4 We live in the age of the half-truth, the slightly bent statistic, the party manifesto. *Ib.*

5 His profile reminded me of an Easter Island statue. *Ib.*

6 When Don Quixote tilted at a windmill he had a horse on which to make his getaway – all I had was a railway timetable. *Ib.*

7 It was a bed-sitting-room – and the only sitting room was on the bed. *Ib.*

8 Head waiters, particularly on the Continent, single me out for special inattention. *Ib.*

9 "Waiter, there's a fly in my soup."
"Don't worry, sir, the spider on the bread roll will get him." *Ib.*

10 The blaze of indifference of a first house Saturday re-awakens the suspicion that there are more worthwhile things to do than try to dredge laughs from reluctant throats. *Ib.*

11 The author wishes to thank himself for contributing the illustrations to this book.

W. C. SELLAR & R. J. YEATMAN

Walter Carruthers Sellar (1898–1951) collaborated with Robert Julian Yeatman (1897–1968) to write a send-up of conventional history as taught in schools, *1066 and All That.* Sellar was educated at Fettes College and Oxford, and was a schoolmaster. The book was so successful that several similar books on other subjects followed.

1 The first date in English history is 55 B.C., in which year Julius Caesar landed at Thanet... Caesar was compelled to invade Britain again the following year (54 B.C. not 56, owing to the peculiar Roman method of counting). *1066 and All That*

2 William I invented a system according to which everybody had to belong to somebody else, and everybody else to the King. This was called the Feutile system. *Ib.*

3 The Pope decided to put the whole of England under an Interdict: i.e. he gave orders that no one was to be born or die or marry (except in church porches). *Ib.*

4 The war was called the Hundred Years War because the troops signed on for a hundred years or the duration. *Ib.*

5 Richard's cousin Lancaster (spelt Bolingbroke) quickly mounted the throne and said he was Henry IV, Part I. *Ib.*

6 James I slobbered at the mouth and had favourites; he was thus a Bad King. *Ib.*

7 The Petition of Right said that it was wrong for anyone to be put to death more than once for the same offence. *Ib.*

8 Napoleon ought never to be confused with Nelson, in spite of their hats being so alike. *Ib.*

9 The second part of the Napoleonic War was fought in Spain and Portugal and was called the Gorilla War owing to the primitive Spanish method of fighting. *Ib.*

10 History is now at an end; this History is therefore final. *Ib.*

11 A first edition limited to one copy and printed on rice paper and bound in buck-boards and signed by one of the editors was sold to the other editor. *Ib.*

12 Most people go through life eating the wrong food. The effect is disastrous: imperceptibly but inevitably they become the wrong people. *And Now All This*

13 Always get up from the table feeling as if you couldn't eat another mouthful. *Ib.*

14 The North Pole being a purely imaginary erection, there will be nothing there except you when you arrive. *Ib.*

15   The object of all Modern Exploration is, of course, to lecture with a terrific cinema film when you get back. *Ib.*

16   (Test Paper)

Mount Everest is 29,002 feet high. Do you consider this sufficient?

17   The uncontrollable impulse to knit something, which comes to all women sooner or later...is due basically to a *craving for excitement. Ib.*

18   If you are addicted to Knitting while Eating, you should exercise some caution...especially with macaroni. *Ib.*

19   Holland is a low-lying country full of low, lying people whose main object in life is to deceive the English by holding *Dutch auctions,* displaying *Dutch courage,* and talking *Double-Dutch. Ib.*

20   When setting out on a photographic holiday always provide yourself with two cameras, one to leave in the train going, and the other to leave in the taxi going back. *Ib.*

21   For every one person who wants to teach there are approximately thirty who don't want to learn. *Ib.*

22   To confess that you are totally ignorant about the Horse is social suicide: you will be despised by everybody, especially the horse. *Horse Nonsense*

23   You will never achieve a blaze of colour unless you have a greenhouse, some green fingers, and of course a huge orange-and-blue umbrella. *Garden Rubbish*

24   Clay clings magnificently to boots, spades, socks, etc., so that the garden is gradually transferred to the toolshed, bootscraper, or your own bedroom. *Ib.*

25   The secret of weeding is never to begin. *Ib.*

26   *How to tell which way the wind is blowing.* Wet your whistle, hold up one finger in the air, and keep your eye on the weathercock. *Ib.*

27 All the Gardening Encyclopedias, Diaries, Manuals, Articles, Magazines...are addressed to GARDEN-LOVERS. There is simply no literature, no help, and evidently no hope for people who merely *like* having a garden. *Ib.*

TOM SHARPE

Tom Sharpe (1928–), educated at Lancing College and Cambridge, spent several years as social worker, teacher, and history lecturer. His humorous novels, often marked by violent action, include *Blott on the Landscape* (1975) and *Porterhouse Blue* (1974), later presented as TV serials.

1 I've yet to come across a Liberal Studies lecturer who wasn't a crank, a pervert, or a red-hot revolutionary. *Wilt*

2 She was dressed with a simple scruffiness that was beyond Eva's moderate income. *Ib.*

3   Mrs Catterway prided herself on being an advocate of progressive education, in which role she had made a substantial contribution to the illiteracy rate. *Ib.*

4   In spite of what some people say, lecturers in Technical Colleges are members of a profession, if only marginally. *Ib.*

5   He decided that spiritualism might after all have something to be said for it, though you almost always found yourself in touch with a Red Indian who was acting by proxy for an aunt. *Ib.*

6   We're used to libel actions. They're run-of-the-mill for us. We pay for them out of petty cash. *Ib.*

7   The Vicar sat nodding incessantly like a toy dog in the back window of a car. *Ib.*

8   He hardly ever gets home until after eight and he always has an excuse about the Open University. It's nothing of the sort, or if it is it's some divorce student who wants extra coition. *The Wilt Alternative*

9   My experience of foreign students is that they come over here to do a lot more than learn the English language. *Ib.*

10   Wilt emerged into the street feeling, if not on top of the world, at least half way up it. *Ib.*

11   He tried to think of something that ryhmed with Irmgard...There was yard, sparred, barred, and lard. None of them seemed to match the sensitivity of his feeling. *Ib.*

12   I'm lumbered with lecturers who couldn't keep order if the students were in straitjackets. *Ib.*

13   Just say I'm suffering from a virus. Nobody knows what a virus is but it covers a multitude of ailments. *Ib.*

14   There's nothing worse than an introspective drunk. *Ib.*

15   You can do anything with hypnotism. I once saw a hypnotist turn a man into a plank and sit on him. *Indecent Exposure*

16　He had so decimated the wild life that even the foxes...found it difficult to make ends meet, and brought meets to an end by moving off. *The Throwback*

17　By paying one of the instructors danger money...Lockhart had got the hang of driving. *Ib.*

18　"You appeared to be born with measles. A wrong diagnosis, I confess, but understandable in that I have seldom if ever been confronted by a baby born in a stinging-nettle patch." *Ib.*

19　Where other colleges seek academic excellence in their freshmen, Porterhouse more democratically... concentrates upon the evidence of wealth. *Porterhouse Blue*

20　The Dean's pen held in his mottled hand crawled slowly across the paper like some literate but decrepit tortoise. *Ib.*

21　The sight of the Dean in his dressing-gown holding the knotted end of an inflated contraceptive had about it a nightmare quality. *Ib.*

22　His conviction [was] that if a little knowledge was a dangerous thing, a lot was lethal. *Ib.*

23　Edward the Seventh had twice paid visits to Handyman Hall, on each occasion seducing Mrs Handyman in the mistaken belief that she was a chambermaid. *Blott on the Landscape*

24　He went along to the bathroom and wrestled with the intricacies of a gas-fired geyser which had evidently set its mind on asphyxiating him or blowing him up. *Ib.*

25　He liked to think of himself as a self-made man. I have always thought it an extremely presumptuous phrase. *Ib.*

GEORGE BERNARD SHAW

George Bernard Shaw (1856–1950), Irish dramatist, was born in Dublin but lived most of his life in England. His first writing success was as a music critic, but plays, accompanied in print by lengthy prefaces, brought him his greatest fame.

1   I think the Hallelujah Chorus might be improved by steeping in boiling water for ten minutes or so. *Bernard Shaw and Mrs Patrick Campbell: Correspondence*

2   Twice I have seen *The Judgment of Solomon*...the baby was evidently howling all through; so that Solomon would have been justified in having it cut in half merely to stop its noise. *Ib.*

3   (*Caesar and Cleopatra*)
    Cleopatra said "It is dark and I am lonely" with such convincing naturalness that a sympathetic electrician consoled her instantly with a flood of limelight. *Ib.*

4   My sister will tell you lies about my childhood: the relations of great men always do. *Ib.*

5   I saw a *Femme Fatale* who was a fine figure of a woman but so hard that she wouldn't have been fatal to anything in my house except a black beetle if her foot happened to tread on it. *Ib.*

6   I had so little taste for the Victorian womanly woman that in my first play I made my heroine throttle the parlour-maid. (Preface to Lillah McCarthy's *Myself and Friends*)

7   I was officially classed for many years as a pernicious blackguard...because I used my art to expose the real roots of prostitution. *Everybody's Political What's What*

8   I never resist temptation because I have found that things that are bad for me do not tempt me. *The Apple Cart*

9   A man learns to skate by staggering about and making a fool of himself. Indeed, he progresses in all things by resolutely making a fool of himself. *Advice to a Young Critic*

10 *Arms and the Man* was so completely misunderstood that it made my reputation as a playwright. *Ib.*

11 Since I have given you all this advice, I add this crowning precept, the most valuable of all: NEVER TAKE ANYBODY'S ADVICE. *Ib.*

12 Physically there's nothing to distinguish human society from the farmyard except that the children are more troublesome and costly than chickens. *Getting Married*

13 LENTULUS. Your Christian religion forbids you to strike me.
    FERROVIUS. On the contrary, it commands me to strike you. How can you turn the other cheek if you are not first struck on the one cheek? *Androcles and the Lion*

14 If the Government decided to throw persons of unpopular or eccentric views to the lions in the Albert Hall or the Earl's Court stadium, can you doubt that all seats would be crammed? *Ib.*

15 A miracle is an impossible thing that is none the less possible. *Back to Methusaleh*

16 Our democratic public men...never believe anything they say themselves, and naturally they can't believe anything anyone else says. *Ib.*

17 When a stupid man is doing something he is ashamed of, he always declares that it is his duty. *Caesar and Cleopatra*

18 I'm only a beer teetotaller, not a champagne teetotaller. *Candida*

19 The British soldier can stand up to anything except the British War Office. *The Devil's Disciple*

20 When our relatives are at home we have to think of all their good points or it would be impossible to endure them. *Heartbreak House*

291

21   You have been boiled in bread and milk for years and years, like other married men. *Ib.*

22   The surest way to ruin a man who doesn't know how to handle money is to give him some. *Ib.*

23   He's always breaking the law. He broke the law when he was born: his parents were not married. *Major Barbara*

24   He knows nothing and he thinks he knows everything. That points clearly to a political career. *Ib.*

25   Marry Ann, and at the end of a week you'll find no more inspiration in her than a plate of muffins. *Man and Superman*

26   If you go to Heaven without being naturally qualified for it, you will not enjoy yourself there. *Ib.*

27   My way of joking is to tell the truth. It's the funniest joke in the world. *John Bull's Other Island*

28   Time enough to think of the future when you haven't any future to think of. *Pygmalion*

29   What is life but a series of inspired follies? *Ib.*

30   Democracy substitutes election by the incompetent many for appointment by the corrupt few. *Maxims for Revolutionists*

R. B. SHERIDAN

Richard Brinsley Sheridan (1751–1816), dramatist and politician, was born in Dublin but educated at Harrow. He was at one time owner of Drury Lane Theatre and a Whig M.P., but his fame rests on his two great comedies, *The Rivals* (1775) and *The School for Scandal* (1777).

1   'Tis safest in matrimony to begin with a little aversion. *The Rivals*

2   A circulating library in a town is an evergreen tree of diabolical knowledge...Depend on it, those who are so fond of handling the leaves will long for the fruit at last. *Ib*

3   I own I would rather choose a wife of mine to have the usual number of limbs...and although *one* eye may be very agreeable, the prejudice has always run in favour of two. *Ib*

4   If I reprehend anything in this world, it is the use of my oracular tongue. *Ib.*

5   She's as headstrong as an allegory on the banks of the Nile. *Ib.*

6   To have an unmannerly fat clerk ask the consent of every butcher in the parish to join John Absolute and Lydia Languish, spinster! Oh, that I should live to hear myself called Spinster! *Ib.*

7   The surest way of not disgracing your ancestors is to keep as long as you can out of their company. *Ib.*

8   A man may think an untruth as well as speak one. *Ib.*

9   These outlandish allemandes and cotillion dances...Mine are true-born English legs. They don't understand the curst French lingo! *Ib.*

10   The newspapers are the most villainous – licentious – abominable – infernal...Not that I ever read them. *The Critic*

11   I open with a clock striking, to beget an awful attention in the audience. *Ib.*

12   No scandal about Queen Elizabeth, I hope. *Ib.*

13   All that can be said is, two people happened to hit upon the same thought – and Shakespeare made use of it before me, that's all. *Ib.*

14 When a heroine goes mad, she always goes into white satin. *Ib.*

15 Why can't you ride your hobby-horse without desiring to place me on a pillion behind you? *Ib.*

16 I loved her until I found she wouldn't love me, and then I discovered she hadn't a good feature in her face. *The Duenna*

17 He has the worst fault a husband could have – he's not my choice. *Ib.*

18 If a daughter you have, she's the plague of your life:
No peace shall you know, though you've buried your wife.
Ib.

19 You are no honest fellow if love can't make a rogue of you. *Ib.*

20 The character of a nun is a very becoming one at a masquerade; but no pretty woman in her senses ever thought of taking the veil for above a night. *Ib.*

21 There's no possibility of being witty without a little ill-nature.
The School for Scandal

22 When she has finished painting her face she joins it on so badly to her neck that she looks like a mended statue. *Ib.*

23 When an old bachelor marries a young wife, what is he to expect? 'Tis now six months since my wife made me the happiest of men – and I have been the most miserable dog ever since. *Ib.*

24 When I say an ill-natured thing, 'tis out of pure good humour. *Ib.*

25 "I'll swear her colour is natural: I have seen it come and go."
"I dare swear you have: it goes off at night, and comes again in the morning." *Ib.*

26 There's no advantage in not knowing him, for he'll abuse a stranger just as soon as his best friend. *Ib.*

27 I hate militia officers: a set of dunghill cocks with spurs on. *St Patrick's Day*

28 Give me the bold upright youth who makes love today, and has his head shot off tomorrow. *Ib.*

29 (Reply to a political opponent)

The Right Honourable gentleman is indebted to his memory for his jests, and to his imagination for his facts.

N. F. SIMPSON

Norman Frederick Simpson (1919–), a Londoner, was educated at Emanuel School and London University, and has been a teacher and lecturer. A leading figure in the theatre of the absurd, his fantastic comedies include *One Way Pendulum* (1959) and *The Cresta Run* (1965).

1 There's somebody at the door wanting you to form a government. *A Resounding Tinkle*

2 If he's a criminal, he's in plain clothes – that's all I can say. *Ib.*

3 I don't think my lungs hit it off, Doctor. They're at daggers drawn practically the whole time. *Ib.*

4 Your circulation sounds like a mobile iron foundry. You need a silencer for it. *Ib.*

5 The small of my back is too big. *Ib.*

6 Sleep whenever you can with your eyes closed. Keep off strong poisons of all kinds. And breathe. Breathe all the time. *Ib.*

7 I've known people buy a bath sponge and do calculations to show that two-thirds of the sponge is made up of holes. And it galls them to think that two-thirds of what they've paid good money for isn't really there. *Ib.*

8 I want to be made up to look like an electronic computer. *Ib.*

9   Sanity is an illusion caused by alcohol deficiency. *Ib.*

10   He picked up an imaginary chair yesterday...and when he sat down on it, it just crumpled under him. *Ib.*

11   Critics are trained to find meanings, and even if there are no meanings to be found they rarely come unprovided with spare meanings. *Ib.*

12   He went to Dr Bunch and complained about his ribs, and told him they seemed to be giving him claustrophobia. *The Hole*

13   I eat merely to put food out of my mind. *Ib.*

14   If we've got to have five hundred weighing machines in the house, I'd just as soon they did sing. *One Way Pendulum*

15   Knocked down a doctor? With an ambulance? How could she? It's a contradiction in terms. *Ib.*

16   She wouldn't go anywhere without her camel. If she wasn't on top of it she was walking along beside it. She rode to hounds on it more than once. *Ib.*

17   I'm as blind as a bat with my eyes closed. *Ib.*

18   There isn't anything we can do about it now. You should have thought of all this before you were born. *Ib.*

19   On the last occasion he took a life he was warned that complaints had been lodged. *Ib.*

20   Not only were you as drunk as a wheelbarrow, but you were quite incapable of falling flat on your face when asked to do so. *Ib.*

21   From the forty-three victims you killed – not a word. Not one of those forty-three has felt under any obligation to come forward and speak for you. *Ib.*

22   Arthur is an ineffectually self-important man in his middle forties, who sets far greater store by being master in his own house than he would if he were. *Ib.*

23   A man can hardly expect to have much success in keeping vital secrets from other people if he isn't capable of keeping them from himself. *The Cresta Run*

24   You were thinking of taking up ladies' hairdressing...And you had a dream about opening up one morning, only to find that the entire female population had gone bald overnight. *Ib.*

DONALD SINDEN

Donald Sinden (1923–), experienced English actor, both in comedy and in classical roles, is the author of two autobiographical books, *A Touch of the Memoirs* (1982) and *Laughter in the Second Act* (1985).

1   Not only am I colour-blind, a non-swimmer, and a non-dancer, but I can sing out of tune better than anyone else. *Laughter in the Second Act*

2   I had to pirouette. If I began facing front, I always ended up facing the back of the stage. To overcome this difficulty, the choreographer arranged for me to begin facing the back. It made no difference. I still finished facing the back of the stage. *Ib.*

3   "The BBC" [said Peter Willes] "can assume that their viewers have read *Great Expectations*; we [in ITV] must assume that our viewers have never heard of Dickens." *Ib.*

4   Seventeen years ago I was young and the world was my oyster. Now I feel as if I had an allergy to shellfish. *Ib.*

5   (With the Royal Shakespeare Company)

When we had donned our cumbersome armour and begun to wield the mighty swords, the fight appeared to be between two lumbering dinosaurs. *Ib.*

6 "How is *Good Night Vienna* doing in Lewisham [Hippodrome]?" "As well as *Good Night Lewisham* would do in Vienna!" Ib.

7 Boris was about six feet two inches tall and of massive proportions...To my Anglo-Saxon embarrassment he took to picking me up and kissing me on both cheeks each time we met. *Ib.*

8 I once asked a group of ladies if, when watching a programme, they liked to hear a studio audience. "Oh yes" they replied; "it gives us some idea of when to laugh!"

SYDNEY SMITH

Sydney Smith (1771–5), clergyman, author, and wit, was educated at Winchester and Oxford, became a curate in 1794, and was later made a canon of St. Paul's. He became prominent in literature and politics, and helped to found the *Edinburgh Review*.

1 Macaulay has occasional flashes of silence that make his conversation perfectly delightful.
(Quoted in Lady Holland's *Memoir*)

2 No one minds what Jeffrey says...Why, a week ago I heard him speak disrespectfully of the Equator! *Ib.*

3 There are three sexes – men, women, and clergymen. *Ib.*

4 Marriage resembles a pair of shears, so joined that they cannot be separated, often moving in opposite directions, yet always punishing anyone who comes between them. *Ib.*

5 The Smiths never had any arms, and have invariably sealed their letters with their thumbs. *Ib.*

6   I never read a book before reviewing it; it prejudices a man so. (Quoted in Pearson's *The Smith of Smiths*)

7   Poverty is no disgrace – but it is confoundedly inconvenient. *Wit and Wisdom*

8   The heat was so dreadful that I found there was nothing for it but to take off my flesh and sit in my bones. *Ib.*

9   Whoever drinks a tumbler of London water has more animated beings in his stomach than there are men, women, and children on the face of the globe. *Letter*

10 I look upon Switzerland as an inferior sort of Scotland. *Ib.*

TOM STOPPARD

Tom Stoppard (1937–), English journalist and playwright, was born in Czechoslovakia. His first play, *Rosencrantz and Guildenstern are Dead* (1967) was a success and led to others, e.g. *Jumpers* (1972); *The Real Thing* (1982).

1   Eternity's a terrible thought. I mean, where's it going to end? *Rosencrantz and Guildenstern are Dead*

2   No point in looking at a gift horse till you see the whites of its eyes. *Ib.*

3   Life is a gamble, at terrible odds. If it was a bet, you wouldn't take it. *Ib.*

4   A Chinaman...a philosopher, dreamt he was a butterfly, and from that moment he was never quite sure that he was not a butterfly dreaming it was a Chinese philosopher. *Ib.*

5   "How long have you been a pedestrian?" "Ever since I could walk." *The Real Inspector Hound*

6   She's all cocoa and blue nylon fur slippers – not a spark of creative genius in her whole slumping knee-length-knickered body. *Ib.*

7   To say that the play is without pace, point, focus, interest, drama, wit, or originality is to say simply that it does not happen to be my cup of tea. *Ib.*

8   Sometimes I dream of a bloody *coup d'état* by the second rank – troupes of actors slaughtered by their understudies, magicians sawn in half by indefatigably smiling glamour girls, cricket teams wiped out by marauding bands of twelfth men... *Ib.*

9   Not only can I sing better than they can jump, I can probably jump higher than they can sing. *Jumpers*

10   This is a British murder inquiry and some degree of justice must be seen to be more or less done. *Ib.*

11   No problem is insoluble given a big enough plastic bag. *Ib.*

12   "I'm something of a logician myself."
     "Really? Sawing ladies in half – that sort of thing? *Ib.*

13   [There's] a telling extract from *Tarzan of the Apes* in which the boy Tarzan, seeing his face for the first time in a jungle pool, bewails his human ugliness as compared to the beauty of the apes among whom he has grown up. *Ib.*

14   The monk who won't walk in the garden for fear of treading on an ant doesn't have to be a vegetarian. *Ib.*

15   Quick, fetch me a half-witted cab you hansom fool! *On the Razzle*

16   Shakespeare out in front by a mile and the rest of the field strung out behind trying to close the gap. *The Real Thing*

JONATHAN SWIFT

Jonathan Swift (1667–1745), satirical author and cleric, was born in Dublin of English parents. He became Dean of St Patrick's, Dublin, in 1713. A good deal of his satire was political, e.g. *Drapier's Letters* (1724). His writings include *The Battle of the Books* (1704) and the famous *Gulliver's Travels* (1726).

1   Never tell a lie to your master or mistress, unless you have some hopes that they cannot find it out. *Directions to Servants*

2   When you have committed a fault, be pert and insolent, and behave as if you were the injured person. *Ib.*

3   If the groom be drunk or absent and the butler be told to shut the stable door, he should have the answer ready: "An't please your honour, I don't understand horses." *Ib.*

4   The stoical scheme of supplying our wants by lopping off our desires is like cutting off our feet when we want shoes. *Thoughts on Various Subjects.*

5   Every man desires to live long, but no man wishes to be old. *Ib.*

6   Venus, a beautiful, good-natured lady, was the goddess of love; Juno, a terrible shrew, the goddess of marriage. *Ib.*

7   Old men and comets have been reverenced for the same reason: their long beards and their pretences to tell fortunes. *Ib.*

8   Promises and pie-crust are made to be broken. *Polite Conversation*

9   He was a bold man that first ate an oyster. *Ib.*

10 I wonder what fool it was that first invented kissing. *Ib.*

11 Satire is a sort of glass in which beholders generally discover everybody's face but their own. *The Battle of the Books*

12 A man who had a mind to sell his house, carried a piece of brick in his pocket, which he showed as a pattern to encourage purchasers. *Drapier's Letters*

13 Only take this rule along,
    Always to advise her wrong;
    And reprove her when she's right;
    She may then grow wise for spite.
    Daphne

14 So, naturalists observe, a flea
    Hath smaller fleas that on him prey;
    And these have smaller fleas to bite 'em,
    And so proceed *ad infinitum.*
    On Poetry

DYLAN THOMAS

Dylan Marlais Thomas (1914–53), Welsh poet, achieved posthumous success with a radio play, *Under Milk Wood* (1954), after making a considerable reputation with his poetry, e.g. *Deaths and Entrances* (1946). Sadly, alcoholism led to his early death in America.

1 Before you let the sun in, mind it wipes its shoes. *Under Milk Wood*

2 In Salt Lake Farm Mr Utah Watkins counts, all night, the wife-faced sheep as they leap the fences on the hill, smiling and knitting and bleating just like Mrs Utah Watkins. *Ib.*

3 He kissed her once by the pigsty when she wasn't looking and never kissed her again although she was looking all the time. *Ib.*

4 Here's your arsenic, dear
   And your weedkiller biscuit. *Ib.*

5 Oh, isn't life a terrible thing, thank God! *Ib.*

6 I don't want persons in my nice clean rooms breathing all over the chairs. *Ib.*

7 Nothing grows in our garden, only washing. *Ib.*

8 The floorboards had squeaked like mice as I climbed into bed, and the mice between the walls had creaked like wood. *A Visit to Grandpa's*

9 "There's no sense in lying dead in Llanstephan," he said. "The ground is comfy in Llangadock; you can twitch your legs without putting them in the sea. " *Ib*

10 He wore long combinations in the summer with his name stitched in red on them. *Extraordinary Little Cough*

11 A shop full of herbs and curtained holes in the wall, where old men with backache and young girls in trouble waited for consultations. *Ib.*

12 He would soon be leaving for London to make a career in Chelsea as a freelance journalist; he was penniless and hoped, in a vague way, to live on women. *Where Tawe Flows*

13   "I stayed with a couple in Palmer's Green...They used to
      leave messages for each other on the toilet paper every
      single day." *Ib.*

14   It had been such a ferocious night that someone in the
      smoky snipped-pictured bar had said he could feel his
      tombstone shaking even though he was not dead. *Quite
      Early One Morning*

15   As someone cruelly pointed out in print, I looked, anyway,
      like an unmade bed. *A Visit to America*

16   She was so silly that, even when she was fifteen, we had told
      her to eat soap to make her hair crinkle...and she did. *The
      Followers*

17   I can never remember whether it snowed for six days and six
      nights when I was twelve or whether it snowed for twelve
      days and twelve nights when I was six. *Memories of Christmas*

18   She looked at the three tall firemen in their shining helmets,
      standing among the smoke and cinders, and she said:
      "Would you like something to read?" *Ib.*

19   I remember a man came here with a monkey. Called for 'alf
      for himself and a pint for the monkey. *Return Journey*

20   The oldest and boldest...smoked the butt-ends of cigarettes,
      turned green, went home, and had little appetite for tea.
      Reminiscences of Childhood

JAMES THURBER

James Grover Thurber (1894–1961), notable American
humorist and cartoonist, worked on *The New Yorker* for many
years. His books include *My Life and Hard Times* (1933), *Men,
Women and Dogs* (1943), and *Lanterns and Lances* (1955), among
many others.

1   The gentlemen were helped on with their coats by one of
those slim, silent waiters with the cold and fishy eye of an
art critic. *The Middle-Aged Man on the Flying Trapeze*

2   "I never sleep in a hotel...they burn down,"she told us. *Ib.*

3   Each move was as difficult as getting a combative drunken
man out of the nightclub in which he fancies he has been
insulted. *Ib.*

4   Pigeons can be understood only when you understand that
there is nothing to understand about them. *Ib.*

5   Dorothy had begun, when she was quite young, to finish
sentences for people. Sometimes she finished them
wrongly, which annoyed the person who was speaking,
and sometimes she finished them correctly, which
annoyed the speaker even more. *Ib.*

6   I suppose the high-water mark of my youth was the night the
bed fell on my father. *My Life and Hard Times*

7   Aunt Gracie was confident that burglars had been getting into
her house every night for forty years...She always claimed
that she scared them off before they could take anything
by throwing shoes down the hallway. *Ib.*

8   My mother was comparatively at peace with the telephone,
except, of course, during storms, when for some reason or
other she always took the receiver off the hook. *Ib.*

9   Her own mother lived the latter years of her life in the
horrible suspicion that electricity was dripping invisibly all
over the house...out of empty sockets. *Ib.*

10   Muggs [the dog] was always sorry, Mother said, when he bit
someone, but we could never understand how she figured
this out. He didn't act sorry. *Ib.*

11   Early to rise and early to bed
Makes a male healthy and wealthy and dead.
Fables for Our Time

12 You can fool too many of the people too much of the time. *Ib.*

13 It is better to have loafed and lost than never to have loafed at all. *Ib.*

14 Ashes to ashes, and clay to clay, if your enemy doesn't get you your own folks may. *Further Fables for Our Time*

15 Though statisticians in our time have never kept the score, Man wants a great deal here below, and Woman even more. *Ib.*

16 Those who live in castles in the air have nowhere to go but down. *Ib.*

17 "If it weren't for me the sun would never rise," bragged the Rooster. "Nobody would get up."
"If it weren't for me there wouldn't *be* anybody," said the Stork. *Ib.*

18 Blessed are the rich, for they can pay their way into the Kingdom of Heaven. *Ib.*

19 Men of all degrees should form this prudent habit:
Never serve a rabbit stew before you catch the rabbit. *Ib.*

20 (Cartoon caption)

"You wait here and I'll bring the etchings down."
Men, Women and Dogs

21 No man...who has wrestled with a self-adjusting card-table can ever quite be the man he once was. *Let Your Mind Alone*

22 I have not actually known Thurber for fifty years, since he was only forty-eight on his last birthday, but the publishers felt that "fifty" would sound more effective than "forty-eight"...a point I was too tired to argue about. *My Fifty Years with James Thurber*

23 Thurber's boyhood was pretty well devoid of significance. He fell down a great deal during this period, because of a trick he had of walking into himself. *Ib.*

24   She developed a persistent troubled frown which gave her
      the expression of someone who is trying to repair a watch
      with his gloves on. *The Beast In Me and Other Animals.*

PETER TINNISWOOD

Born in Liverpool, Peter Tinniswood began his writing career
on the *Sheffield Star* (1958). He has written novels, plays, and
the TV series *I Didn't Know You Cared*. His humorous *Long Room*
tales are usually related as if by a prejudiced, cricket-loving,
wife-hating Brigadier, with frequent (often unflattering)
references to well-known people, especially cricketers.

1   Above us the rooks caw hoarsely in the elms for all the world
     like a massed choir of Robin Jackmans appealing for lbw.
     More Tales From a Long Room.

2   Let us walk through the churchyard with its gravestones...and
     its monument to those brave British lads...with its simple
     and moving inscription: "Died of Drink". *Ib.*

3   The vast majority of passengers on a cruise liner are there
     against their will. *Ib.*

4   Is there any greater joy known to man than the slow
     pad-padding through the rooms of a house shorn of the
     odious omniscient presence of its mistress? *Ib.*

5   I still feel a deep and brooding resentment towards the lady
     wife who insisted on my being present at our wedding. *Ib.*

6   I presented her with a doctor's note to the effect that I had a
     deep-seated allergy to spats. *Ib.*

7   The lady wife snored heavily in the conjugal container, for all
     the world like a simmering tank locomotive at rest in some
     drowsy branch-line siding.*Ib.*

8   All their natural country instincts came flooding out –
     baseness, mendacity, and kleptomania. *Tales from Witney
     Scrotum*

9   Christopher Martin-Jenkins and Neil Durden-Smith were standing there next to the bar skittles, playing with each other's hyphens. *Ib.*

10   Hush. Walls have ears. That's why it's so damnably difficult to stick anaglypta to them. *Ib.*

11   It was two days ago, on a blissful urban early summer's morning of sleet, incipient hail, and cloying billowing car exhaust fumes, that I walked to my nearest sorting office. *Ib.*

12   How skilful the [printer's] make-up, with scarcely a headline upside down. *Ib.*

13   He had single-handedly scaled Everest on no less than fourteen occasions, and sailed the Atlantic in similar fashion on nineteen occasions (the last three without a boat). *The Brigadier's Brief Lives*

14   I like women with gaps in their front teeth. They are so damnably useful when it comes to scraping carrots. *Ib.*

SUE TOWNSEND

Sue Townsend (1946–) formerly worked as a dress-shop assistant and as a community worker. She has had several plays staged, mainly at fringe theatres, and won a TV bursary in 1979. She is best-known for *The Secret Diary of Adrian Mole* (1982), later shown on TV, and its sequels.

1   My father is in a bad mood. This means he is feeling better. *The Secret Diary of Adrian Mole*

2   Now I *know* I am an intellectual. I saw Malcolm Muggeridge on television last night, and I understood nearly every word. *Ib.*

3   If I was the loneliest person in the world...I would ring the speaking clock; that talks to you every ten seconds. *Ib.*

4   Bert's brother-in-law's uncle once lived next door to a tea lady at Broadcasting House, so Bert knows all about the BBC. *Ib.*

5   He said he didn't hold with divorce. He said he was married for thirty-five miserable years so why should anybody else get away with it? *Ib.*

6   I hadn't actually tasted whisky before and I never will again...If it was in a medicine bottle people would pour it down the drain. *Ib.*

7   I asked the Careers teacher which O levels you need to write situation comedy for television. He said you don't need qualifications at all, you just need to be a moron. *Ib.*

8   I shook the vicar's hand when we were outside. It was like touching dead leaves. *Ib.*

9   My father saw the headmaster today and told him if he didn't allow me back in school...he would protest to his M.P. The headmaster asked who his M.P. was. My father didn't know. *Ib.*

10 My father wanted to know every detail about the baby. I said she took after him. Half-bald and angry-looking. *The Growing Pains of Adrian Mole*

11 "Don't even think of getting married until you've spent a few months sharing a bedroom with a bird. If she leaves her knickers on the floor more than three days running, forget it." *Ib.*

12 How could any English person want to live abroad? Foreigners can't help living abroad because they were born there, but for an English person to go is ridiculous, especially now that sun-ray lamps are readily available. *Ib.*

BEN TRAVERS

Ben Travers (1886–1980), educated at Charterhouse, was a leading writer of farces, particularly for the Aldwych Theatre, London. They were designed generally for a regular cast including Ralph Lynn, Tom Walls, and Robertson Hare, and included *Rookery Nook* (1926) and *Thark* (1927).

1   My bed goes up and down in the middle like the hump of a camel. *A Cuckoo in the Nest*

2   "To any decent-minded person there's nothing wrong in your sleeping on the floor of my room"
    "Yes, but where's the decent-minded person?" *Ib.*

3   When a man gets left alone with a car there's always trouble. If the car doesn't go wrong, the man does. *Rookery Nest*

4   She makes her husband trot about after her, wearing his little straw hat and looking like a rabbit at a stoat's tea-party. *Ib.*

5   "I suppose it's because human nature is so cruel that people always think the worst."
    "No, it's because the worst is most likely." *Ib.*

6   Don't stand there like a small-sized lamp-post with no light on top. *Thark*

7   I want you to tell the truth, the whole truth, or something like the truth. *Ib.*

8   "Have you ever met anyone who's seen a ghost?"
    "No, but I've never met anyone who hasn't met someone who has." *Ib.*

9   "Do you walk in your sleep?"
    "If one is asleep, how does one know if one's sleep-walking?" *Ib.*

10   It isn't easy to say what you've seen when all you know is
      you've seen something you don't know what it is. *Ib.*

11   I finished a play just a few months ago and tore it up last
      week! That is the natural process of writing plays – I always
      tear them up, and I think most playwrights ought to do
      the same.
      (Quoted in Michael Parkinson's *The Best of Parkinson*)

12   I can't think of anything more repulsive than the sight of a
      man with nothing on. *The Bed Before Yesterday*

13   Scones make the worst kind of bed crumbs because they have
      butter on them. *Ib.*

MARK TWAIN

Samuel Langhorne Clemens (1835–1910), American
humorous writer under the name Mark Twain, began his
career as a printer and journalist. His travel book *The Innocents
Abroad* (1865) established his reputation, but the most famous
of his many books are *Tom Sawyer* (1876) and *Huckleberry Finn*
(1884).

1   He liked to have a fresh market for his jokes, most of them
     having reached that stage of wear where the teller has to
     do the laughing himself. *A Yankee at the Court of King Arthur*

2   Take a pencil sharpened by any woman. If you have witnesses
     you will find she did it with a knife; but if you take simply
     the look of the pencil you would say she did it with her
     teeth. *Pudd'nhead Wilson Calendar*

3   If you pick up a starving dog and make him prosperous, he
     will not bite you. That is the principal difference between
     a dog and a man. *Ib.*

4   Few things are harder to put up with than the annoyance of a good example. *Ib.*

5   April 1: the day on which we are reminded of what we are on the other 364 days. *Ib.*

6   Cauliflower is nothing but cabbage with a college education. *Ib.*

7   Nothing so needs reforming as other people's habits. *Ib.*

8   Man is the only animal that blushes. Or needs to. *Pudd'nhead Wilson's New Calendar*

9   In our country we have three unspeakably precious things: freedom of speech, freedom of conscience, and the prudence never to practise either. *Ib.*

10 The modern French duel...is one of the most dangerous institutions of our day. Since it is fought in the open air the combatants are nearly sure to catch cold. *A Tramp Abroad*

11 The cross of the Legion of Honour has been conferred upon me. However, few escape that distinction. *Ib.*

12 His voice was like the distressing noise which a nail makes when you screech it across a window-pane. *Ib.*

13 The Heidelberg museum keeper said my German was very rare, possibly unique, and wanted to add it to his museum. *Ib.*

14 German books are easy to read when you hold them before the looking-glass or stand on your head. *Ib.*

15 Harris went to sleep at once. I hate a man who goes to sleep at once. There is a sort of indefinable something about it which is not exactly an insult and yet is an insolence. *Ib.*

16 I lay abed and rested the remainder of that Sunday, but I sent my agent to represent me at the afternoon service, for I never allow anything to interfere with my habit of attending church twice every Sunday. *Ib.*

17 A hotel chambermaid has nothing to do but make beds and fires in fifty or sixty rooms, bring towels and candles, and fetch several tons of water in prodigious metal pitchers. She does not have to work more than eighteen or twenty hours a day. *Ib.*

18 He said he had noticed that a clergyman at dinner without any breeches was almost sure to excite remark. *Ib.*

19 We bought a bottle of beer. At any rate they called it beer, but I knew by the price that it was dissolved jewellery. *Ib.*

20 I can *understand* German as well as the maniac who invented it, but I *talk* it best through an interpreter. *Ib.*

21 He said that Turner's Slave Ship floundering about in that fierce conflagration of reds and yellows reminded him of a tortoise-shell cat having a fit in a platter of tomatoes. *Ib.*

22 (Leonardo da Vinci)

    They spell it Vinci and pronounce it Vinchy. Foreigners always spell better than they pronounce. *The Innocents Abroad*

23 In Pisa Michael Angelo designed everything but the old shot-tower, and they would have attributed that to him if it had not been so awfully out of the perpendicular. *Ib.*

24 We have seen famous pictures until our eyes are weary...We have seen thirteen thousand St Jeromes, and twenty-two thousand St Marks, and sixty thousand St Sebastians. *Ib.*

25 A swarm of swarthy, noisy, lying, shoulder-shrugging, gesticulating Portuguese boatmen, with brass rings in their ears and fraud in their hearts, climbed the ship's sides. *Ib.*

26 Man is the only creature that has a nasty mind. *Autobiography*

27 By trying we can easily learn to endure adversity. Another person's, I mean. *Following the Equator*

28 A lie is halfway round the world while truth is putting its boots on.

29 Whenever I enjoy anything in art it means that it is mighty poor. *At the Shrine of St Wagner*

PETER USTINOV

Peter Alexander Ustinov (1921–), actor, playwright, producer, novelist, and notable raconteur, is of foreign extraction but was born and educated in London. His plays include *The Love of Four Colonels* (1951) and *Romanoff and Juliet* (1956). *Dear Me* (1977) is his autobiography.

1   There is nothing more boring in this world than someone else's love story, especially if you are told it by a parrot. *Dear Me*

2   Othello, clutching his handkerchief and rolling his eyes, has always struck me as a bit of an ass. *Ib.*

3   An astonishing number of international games were invented by the British, who, whenever they are surpassed by other nations, coolly invent another one. *Ib.*

4   The advantages of Catholicism were shamelessly expressed...Mlle Chausat attempted to force her way into Heaven, using me as a battering-ram. *Ib.*

5   The toilet paper was composed of quartered sheets of typing paper, with holes in one corner...These were covered in messages, many of them marked "Secret", and some of them "Most Secret". *Ib.*

6   Rowing seemed to me a monotonous pursuit, and somehow wasteful to be making all that effort to be going in the wrong direction. *Ib.*

7   (At Westminster School)
I was given the clothes of an undertaker, together with a furled umbrella, in order, so the school brochure explained, to distinguish the boys from City of London Bank messengers. *Ib.*

8   At my selection board interview...I told the officer I was interested in tanks. His eyes blazed with enthusiasm. "Why tanks?" he asked keenly. I replied that I preferred to go into battle sitting down. *Ib.*

9   I got the impression that most of the non-commissioned officers had a vocabulary of ten words, used in an infinity of ungrammatical patterns. *Ib.*

10 A diplomat these days is nothing but a head waiter who's allowed to sit down occasionally. *Romanoff and Juliet*

11 The English have been here on several occasions on the pretext that we were unfit to govern ourselves. They were invariably followed by the French on the pretext that we were unfit to be governed by the English. *Ib.*

12 Babies are so damned selfish. They scream just whenever they feel like it. *Halfway Up the Tree*

JOHN VANBRUGH

Sir John Vanbrugh (1664–1726), English architect, designer of Castle Howard in Yorkshire and Blenheim Palace, was also a leading comic dramatist, contemporary with Congreve. His chief plays were *The Relapse* (1696), *The Provok'd Wife* (1697), and *The Confederacy* (1705).

1   Thinking is to me the greatest fatigue in the world. *The Relapse*

2   LORD FOPPINGTON. These shoes hurt me just below the instep.
    SHOEMAKER (feeling his foot). My lord, they *don't* hurt you there.
    FOPPINGTON. I tell you, they pinch me execrably.
    SHOEMAKER. My lord, I have worked for half the people of quality in town these twenty years, and *I* should know when a shoe hurts and when it doesn't! *Ib.*

3   I'm the worst company in the world at church. I'm apt to
     mind the prayers or the sermon. *Ib.*

4   A man must endeavour to look wholesome at the theatre, lest
     he makes so nauseous a figure in the side-box that the
     ladies are compelled to give their attention to the play. *Ib.*

5   Once a woman has given you her heart – you can never get rid
     of the rest of her body. *Ib.*

6   "Your father designs to defer my happiness – our marriage – a
     whole week."
     "A week! Why, I shall be an old woman by that time!" *Ib.*

7   It is the intent and business of the stage
     To copy out the follies of the age;
     To hold to every man a faithful glass,
     And show him of what species he's an ass.
     The Provok'd Wife

8   What cloying meat is love – when matrimony's the sauce to it.
     Ib.

9   'Tis as hard to persuade a woman to quit something that
     makes her ridiculous as to prevail with a playwright to see
     a fault in his play. *Ib.*

10   I'd sooner undertake to teach sincerity to a courtier, honesty
     to a lawyer, or even humility to a parson, than discretion
     to a woman who's determined to play the fool. *Ib.*

11   If there were no men in the world I should be no longer
     dressing than I am saying my prayers. *Ib.*

12   As if a woman of education bought things because she
     wanted them! *The Confederacy*

13   She's but a scrivener's wife, but she lives as well, and pays as
     badly, as the stateliest countess. *Ib.*

14   I understand myself better than to accept letters when I
     don't know who they are from! *Ib.*

15   If you want my opinion of these matters – I don't think a husband can ever be in the right! *Ib.*

GORE VIDAL

Gore Vidal (1925–), American novelist and critic, often involved in politics. His books include the novel *Myra Breckinridge* (1968) and several books of criticism.

1   For certain people after fifty, litigation takes the place of sex. *Evening Standard (1981)*

2   Politics...the deliberate use of words not for communication but to screen intention. *Esquire (1970)*

3   There is something about a bureaucrat that does not like a poem. *Sex, Death and Money*

4   It makes no difference who you vote for. The two parties are really one party, representing four percent of the people.

5   Whenever a friend succeeds, something within me dies. *Sunday Times Magazine (1973)*

6   Every president of the U.S. has somehow been found to descend from Edward II.
     (Quoted in *Observer*)

7   I'm all for bringing back the birch, but only between consenting adults.
     (On TV's *Frost Programme*)

8   Photography is the "art form" of the untalented. *New Statesman (1978)*

9   Never have children; only grandchildren. *Two Sisters*

10   He will lie even when it is inconvenient, the sign of the true artist. *Ib.*

11   He is the only genius with an IQ of 60. *Andy Warhol*

12   Nobody with that awful wife and those ugly children could be anything but normal.

13   The Italians [demonstrated] once again their astonishing ability to cope with disaster which is so perfectly balanced by their absolute inability to deal with success. *Matters of Fact and Fiction*

14   Democracy is supposed to give you the feeling of choice. (Quoted in *Observer*, 1982)

KEITH WATERHOUSE

Keith Waterhouse (1929–) is the son of a Leeds greengrocer. He worked in a cobbler's shop, an undertaker's, and a garage before entering journalism and becoming a writer. His most famous novel, *Billy Liar*, was made into a stage play and a musical, and was also filmed. He has written freely for *Punch*.

1   He approached the substantial lips gingerly, as if edging into a swamp...They were wet and cold, like fresh fish. *The Bucket Shop*

2   He had thin lips and a slight squint and looked like a demonstrator in a Gas Board showroom. *Ib*

3   She had once heard a semi-drunken peer say on TV that marriage without infidelity was like a salad without dressing. *Ib.*

4   I did not care for her face: the scrubbed honest look, as healthy as porridge. *Billy Liar*

5   I put on the intellectual act, sloping one shoulder down, and trying to look as though the record under my arm was *Under Milk Wood. Ib.*

6   Some of the women at the round tables stared at me like cows waiting to be milked. *Ib.*

7   He was doing the quickstep as it might be performed by a kangaroo. *Ib*

8   He's worked on a liner, so he told me. It should have been the Titanic. *Billy Liar on the Moon*

9   "If I had my way no motor-car would be allowed in Shepford unless a Labour councillor walked in front of it, singing the Red Flag." *Ib.*

10   "Taking things" she used to call it, with the distaste of a maiden lady finding a french letter in her bed. *Ib.*

11   He had begun a process of looking me up and down as if I were a cross-bred dog he was thinking of buying or having put down. *Ib*

12   My mother had put on the intense I-can-understand-long-words expression she kept for insurance men and council officials. *Ib.*

13   The Highways Department had succeeded, at one point, in filtering traffic into a one-way cul-de-sac, a kind of motorised sheep-pen from which it was impossible to escape without technically breaking the law. *Ib.*

14   The lift was next to the staircase proper, which in turn was next to the rubbish chute; a convenient arrangement for an arsonist. *Ib.*

15   She crossed her legs and tugged down her skirt: another good touch, for she was not normally one of nature's tugger-downers. *Ib.*

16   Being a potential suicide was enough to make anyone kill himself. *Maggie Muggins*

17   She talked in such an exaggerated, dated drawl that it was like pulling a Mars bar apart, the syllables stretching out in long glucose strands. *Ib.*

18   Losing her virginity – losing it? She'd taken it for a walk in the woods and abandoned it. *Ib.*

19   He liked nothing better than being first with the bad news. *Ib.*

20   The line was terrible...Maggie would have been better off climbing on the tube station roof with a couple of flags and trying to get through by semaphore. *Ib.*

21   She could no longer open her mouth without sounding as if she were trying to get through to a deaf old-age pensioner. *Ib.*

22   I will not say that the primary purpose of Evening Service is to bring the two sexes together...but you could fare worse than to cast your eye about the neighbouring pews whilst at your devotions. *The Collected Letters of a Nobody*

23   Our best-selling postcard of the day was a depiction of six seaside donkeys with the legend, "Now We are Seven". *Ib.*

24   You may inform a lady that she *looks* well, but not *ask* her if she *is* well; ladies like to keep their illnesses to themselves. *Ib.*

EVELYN WAUGH

Evelyn Arthur St John Waugh (1903–66), English novelist, was educated at Lancing and Oxford. His humorous satirical novels, *Decline and Fall* (1928) and *Vile Bodies* (1930) brought him fame; among others was *Scoop* (1938), a journalistic satire. *Brideshead Revisited* (1945) was made into a successful TV series.

1   Mr Salter's side of the conversation was limited to expressions of assent. When Lord Copper was right he said, "Definitely, Lord Copper"; when he was wrong, "Up to a point". *Scoop*

2   Personally I can't see that foreign stories are ever news – not *real* news. *Ib.*

3   Sub-editors busied themselves with their humdrum task of reducing to blank nonsense the sheaves of misinformation ...which whistling urchins piled before them. *Ib.*

4   Lord Copper often gave banquets; it would be an understatement to say that no one enjoyed them more than the host, for no one else enjoyed them at all. *Ib.*

5   News is what a chap who doesn't care much about anything wants to read. *Ib.*

6   I have been in the scholastic profession long enough to know that nobody enters it unless he has some very good reason that he is anxious to conceal. *Decline and Fall*

7   "You will all write an essay on 'self-indulgence'. There will be a prize of half a crown for the longest essay, irrespective of any possible merit." From then on all was silence until break. *Ib.*

8   "Frankly," said the Doctor, "I can think of no entertainment that fills me with greater detestation than a display of competitive athletics, none – except possibly folk dancing." *Ib*

9   I remember at one of our Sports I omitted to offer whisky to the Press, and the result was a most unfortunate photograph. Boys do get into such indelicate positions during the obstacle race. *Ib.*

10 Anyone who has been to an English public school will always feel comparatively at home in prison. *Ib.*

11 "The Welsh," said the Doctor, "are the only nation in the world that has produced no graphic or plastic art...They just sing...or blow down wind instruments of plated silver." *Ib.*

12 Never get mixed up in a Welsh wrangle. It doesn't end in blows, like an Irish one, but goes on for ever. *Ib.*

13 I have often observed in women of her type a tendency to regard all athletics as inferior forms of fox-hunting. *Ib*

14 I have noticed again and again since I have been in the
    Church that lay interest in ecclesiastical matters is often a
    prelude to insanity. *Ib.*

15 The Bookbinding instructor says that a practice is growing
    among the prisoners of eating the paste issued to them for
    their work. They say it's preferable to their porridge. *Ib*

16 Assistant masters came and went...Some liked little boys too
    little and some too much. *A Little Learning*

17 They say the sea's going to be rough, but don't you believe it.
    If you have peace in your heart your stomach will look
    after itself. *Vile Bodies*

18 "We're just thinking of having a little drink. No, not that
    wine, dear, it's what we keep for the police." *Ib.*

19 All my cousins are in lunatic asylums, or else they live in the
    country and do indelicate things with wild animals. *Ib.*

20 All this fuss about sleeping together. For physical pleasure
    I'd sooner go to my dentist any day. *Ib.*

21 It was the second most expensive restaurant in London. It was full of oilcloth and Lalique glass, and the sort of people who liked that sort of thing went there continually and said how awful it was. *Ib.*

22 She admitted that love was a thing one could grow to be fond of after a time, like smoking a pipe. *Ib.*

23 The victor's trophy (for the car race) was a silver-gilt figure of odious design. *Ib.*

24 You never find an Englishman among the underdogs – except in England of course. *The Loved Ones*

25 Most [American] cemeteries, he says, provide a dog's toilet and a cat's motel. *Ib.*

H. G. WELLS

Herbert George Wells (1866–1946), English novelist, was educated at Midhurst Grammar School and the Royal College of Science. His early novels were science-fiction, e.g. *The War of the Worlds* (1898), but his later stories reveal an engaging sense of humour, e.g. *Mr Polly* (1910).

1 His chief holiday was to go to a cricket match, which he did as if he was going to church. *The History of Mr Polly*

2 Uncle Pentstemon was an aged rather than a venerable figure. Time had removed the hair at the top of his head and distributed a small dividend of the plunder in little bunches carelessly and impartially over the rest of his features. *Ib.*

3 "Wimmin's a toss-up," said Uncle Pentstemon. "Prize packets they are, and you can't tell what's in 'em till you took 'em home and undone 'em." *Ib.*

4 "I brought 'er a nice wedding present, what I got in this passel. Vallyble old tea-caddy that uset' be my mother's. What I kep' my baccy in for years and years – till the hinge

at the back got broke." *Ib.*

5   You cannot pursue people about the streets of a watering-place, compelling them either by threats or importunity to buy flannel trousers. *Ib.*

6   She cooked because food had to be cooked, and with a sound moralist's entire disregard of the quality or the consequences. *Ib.*

7   If our community was anything more than a feeble idiot, it would burn most of London and Chicago, for example, and build sane and beautiful cities. *Ib.*

8   Mr Polly wondered what the horse thought of him, and whether it really liked being held and patted on the neck, or whether it only submitted out of contempt. *Ib.*

9   Mr Polly struck a vein of humour in telling them how he learnt to ride the bicycle. He found the mere mention of the word "wobble" sufficient to produce almost inextinguishable mirth. *Ib.*

10 To ride a bicycle properly is very like a love affair: chiefly it is a matter of faith. *The Wheels of Chance*

11 Until the cyclist can steer with one hand, contemplative flies stroll over his face and trifle absently with its most sensitive surfaces. *Ib.*

12 Anyone who has ever ridden a cycle of any kind will bear witness that the things are unaccountably prone to pick up bad habits. *Ib.*

13 There is no greater contempt in the world than that of shop men for shop girls, unless it be that of shop girls for shop men. *Ib.*

14 All drapers have to be of a sanguine disposition, or else they could never have the faith they show in the beauty, washability, and unfading excellence of the goods they sell you. *Ib.*

15   If you had noticed anything about him, it would have been
     chiefly to notice how little he was noticeable. *Ib.*

16   A conscientious and normally stupid schoolmaster perceived
     the incipient talent and nipped it in the bud by a series of
     lessons in art. *Ib.*

17   The human nose is at best a needless excrescence. *Ib.*

18   The Anglo-Saxon genius for parliamentary government
     asserted itself; there was a great deal of talk, and no
     decisive action. *The Invisible Man*

19   Every time Europe looks across the Atlantic to see the
     American eagle, it observes only the rear end of an
     ostrich. *America*

20   He found that a fork in his inexperienced hand was an
     instrument of chase rather than capture. *Kipps*

21   All other callings have a certain amount of give and take; the
     house-agent simply takes. *Ib.*

22   We're in a blessed drainpipe, and we've got to crawl along it
     till we die. *Ib.*

23   He was inordinately proud of Britain and abused her
     incessantly. *Mr Britling Sees It Through*

24   The uglier a man's legs are the better he plays golf. *Bealby*

25   A man who eats like a pig ought to look like a pig. *The Truth
     About Pyecraft*

26   He had read Shakespeare and found him weak in chemistry.
     The Lord of the Dynamos

27   In his mouth are Lies in the shape of false teeth. *Love and Mr
     Lewisham*

MAE WEST

Mae West (1892–1980), American stage and film actress, script writer, and sex symbol, enjoyed a successful theatrical career before making the first of her many films, *Night After Night* (1932). Other films included *I'm No Angel* (1933) and *Come On Up* (1946).

1   "Goodness, what beautiful diamonds!"
"Goodness had nothing to do with it, dearie."
Night After Night

2   When I'm good I'm very, very good – but when I'm bad I'm better. *I'm No Angel*

3   I was once so poor I didn't know where my next husband was coming from. *She Done Him Wrong*

4   When women go wrong, men go right after them. *Ib.*

5   It's better to be looked over than overlooked. *Belle of the Nineties*

6   A man in the house is worth two in the street. *Ib.*

7   If you're the backbone of your family, they'd better see a chiropractor. *Goin' to Town*

8   Give a man a free hand and he'll try and put it all over you. *Klondike Annie*

9   Between two evils, I always pick the one I never tried before. *Ib.*

10   Keep a Diary and one day it will keep you. *Every Day's a Holiday*

11   That's a guy so crooked he uses a corkscrew for a ruler. *Ib.*

12   I avoid temptation, unless I can't resist it. *My Little Chickadee*

13   "I went up to the Count's room last night. Did I do wrong?"
"How do I know? Don't you remember?" *The Wicked Age*

14 I used to be Snow White, but I drifted.
(Quoted in Fergus Cashin's *Mae West*)

15 *Diamond Lil* is like *Hamlet*, but funnier. *Ib.*

16 My life is an open book. All too often open at the wrong page. *Ib*

17 The censors wouldn't even let me sit on a guy's lap, and I've been on more laps than a table-napkin. *Ib.*

18 If I asked for a cup of coffee, someone would search for the double meaning. *Ib.*

19 To err is human, but it feels divine.

20 Marriage is a great institution, but I'm not ready for an institution yet.

KATHARINE WHITEHORN

Katharine Whitehorn (1926–), English journalist, was educated at Glasgow High School and Roedean (from where she ran away). She has worked for various journals, but is best known as an *Observer* columnist and as author of humorous books, e.g. *How to Survive Children* (1975).

1 We still buy cotton frocks in April as a folk magic to bring on summer. *Observer (August 1966)*

2 Why do born again people so often make you wish they'd never been born the first time? *Ib.*

3 Have you ever taken anything out of the clothes basket because it had become, relatively, the cleaner thing? *Ib. (August 1964)*

4 A food is not necessarily essential just because your child hates it. *How to Survive Children*

5   The easiest way for your child to learn about money is for you not to have any. *Ib.*

6   There's a grand old tradition that patients should be sewn-up and not heard. *How to Survive in Hospital*

7   The ladies of the lamp are not keen on their wards looking like a camp for migrant fruit-pickers.*Ib.*

8   They wake you up to give you your sleeping pills. *Ib*

9   Spring gardening advice always tells you what you ought to have done last autumn. *Ib.*

10 It might be marvellous to be a man – then I could stop worrying about what's fair to women and just cheerfully assume I was superior. *View from a Column*

11 How do you ever get credit for the things you manage not to say? *Ib.*

12 I learned to accept that if you walked past the bowler's arm they hung you upside down by your toenails in the pavilion. *Ib.*

13 The suggestion that people sleep together without being married no longer calls automatically for instant denial and the smelling-salts. *Ib.*

14 I would have thought it would at least be easier to remember (or even check) whether you had or had not inserted a suppository than it is to remember if you've swallowed a pill. *Ib.*

15 The self-appointed representative of the underdog...will see a connection with the plight of the underprivileged or the woes of the Third World, even if you're only trying to decide the date of the next committee meeting. *Ib.*

16 I yield to no one in my admiration of the office as a social centre, but it's no place actually to get any work done. *Sunday Best*

OSCAR WILDE

Oscar Fingall O'Flahertie Wills Wilde (1854–1900), Irish poet, playwright, and wit, attended university at Dublin and Oxford. His fiction includes *The Picture of Dorian Gray* (1891). Three of his plays mix wit with a serious plot, but his last, *The Importance of Being Earnest* (1895) is pure comedy. A trial and conviction for homosexuality darkened his later life.

1   Who are the people the world takes seriously? All the dull people, from the Bishops down to the bores. *Lady Windermere's Fan*

2   I won't hear of it raining on your birthday! *Ib.*

3   I can resist everything except temptation. *Ib.*

4   There are lots of people who say I have never done anything wrong in the whole course of my life. Of course, they only say this behind my back. *Ib.*

5   Australia must be so pretty with all the dear little kangaroos flying about. *Ib.*

6   London is full of women who trust their husbands. One can always recognize them. They look so unhappy. *Ib.*

7   Nowadays we are all so hard up that the only pleasant things to pay are compliments. *Ib.*

8   Hopper is one of Nature's gentlemen – the worst type of gentleman I know. *Ib.*

9   There is a great deal of good in Lord Augustus. Fortunately it is all on the surface. *Ib.*

10   A man who moralizes is usually a hypocrite, and a woman who moralizes is invariably plain. *Ib.*

11   Whenever people agree with me I always feel I must be wrong. *Ib*

12 Experience is the name everyone gives to their mistakes. *Ib.*

13 "It's no use talking to Tuppy. You might just as well talk to a brick wall."
"But I like talking to a brick wall. It's the only thing that never contradicts me." *Ib*

14 London is too full of fogs – and serious people. Whether the fogs produce the serious people or whether the serious people produce the fogs, I don't know. *Ib.*

15 I was in hopes Lord Illingworth would have married Lady Kelso. But I believe he said her family was too large. Or was it her feet? *A Woman of No Importance*

16 American women are wonderfully clever in concealing their parents. *Ib.*

17 Twenty years of romance make a woman look like a ruin; but twenty years of marriage make her something like a public building. *Ib*

18 You can't make people good by Act of Parliament – that's something. *Ib.*

19 We in the Lords are never in touch with public opinion. That makes us a civilized body. *Ib.*

20 Lord Illingworth told me this morning that there was an orchid in the conservatory as beautiful as the seven deadly sins. *Ib.*

21 The English country gentleman galloping after a fox – the unspeakable in pursuit of the uneatable. *Ib.*

22 One should never trust a woman who tells one her real age. *Ib.*

23 "I adore silent men."
"Oh, Ernest isn't silent. He talks the whole time. But he's got no conversation." *Ib*

24 After a good dinner one can forgive anybody, even one's own relations. *Ib.*

25 Duty is what one expects from others, it is not what one does oneself. *Ib*

26 You should study the Peerage. It is the one book a young man about town should know thoroughly, and it is the best thing in fiction the English have ever done. *Ib.*

27 Moderation is a fatal thing. Nothing succeeds like excess. *Ib.*

28 I love talking about nothing. It is the only thing I know anything about. *An Ideal Husband*

29 They actually succeeded in spelling his name right in the newspapers. That in itself is fame, on the continent. *Ib.*

30 In England people actually try to be brilliant at breakfast. *Ib.*

31 I always pass on good advice. It's the only thing to do with it. *Ib.*

32 To love oneself is the beginning of a lifetime romance. *Ib.*

33 My doctor says I must not have any serious conversation after seven. It makes me talk in my sleep. *Ib.*

34 It is a very ungentlemanly thing to read a private cigarette case. *The Importance of Being Earnest*

35 It is very vulgar to talk like a dentist when one isn't a dentist. It produces a false impression. *Ib.*

36 The truth is rarely pure and never simple. *Ib.*

37 To be born, or at any rate bred, in a handbag seems to me to display a contempt for the ordinary decencies of life. *Ib.*

38 It is awfully hard work doing nothing. *Ib.*

39 To lose one parent may be regarded as a misfortune; to lose both looks like carelessness. *Ib.*

40 I hope you have not been leading a double life, pretending to be wicked and really being good all the time. That would be hypocrisy. *Ib.*

41 No woman should ever be quite accurate about her age. It looks so calculating. *Ib.*

42   I dislike arguments of any kind. They are always vulgar and often convincing. *Ib.*

43   The only way to get rid of a temptation is to yield to it. *The Picture of Dorian Gray*

44   A man cannot be too careful in his choice of enemies. *Ib.*

45   A little sincerity is a dangerous thing, and a great deal of it is absolutely fatal. *The Critic as Artist*

46   Nothing is worth knowing that can be taught. *Ib*

47   A poet can survive everything except a misprint. *The Children of the Poets*

48   He had one of those characteristic British faces that once seen is never remembered.

KENNETH WILLIAMS

Kenneth Williams (1926–88), a Londoner, became known as a comic voice on radio (e.g. in *Hancock's Half Hour* and *Round the Horne*), and acted in many stage plays and films (e.g. the *Carry On* series).

1   I'm so mean I've got a burglar alarm on my dustbin. *Just William*

2   My teeth are so full of lead fillings my head keeps falling forward. People think I'm nodding but I'm just top-heavy. *Ib.*

3   Just because you've made your bed, you don't have to lie in it – you can get out and remake it. *Ib.*

4   I complained to John Law, "I've got quite enough on my plate as it is," but he said, "What plate? Audiences eat out of your hand." *Ib.*

5   I have no physical co-ordination; my feet start waltzing "one-two-three", but invariably they stray into "one-two-three-four". *Ib.*

6   I have never met anyone who was indifferent to their
        publicity. *Ib.*

P. G. WODEHOUSE

Sir Pelham Grenville Wodehouse (1881–1975) was the
outstanding British comic novelist of his time, possessor of a
very individual humorous style, and creator of such notable
characters as Bertie Wooster and the omniscient manservant
Jeeves. After the Second World War Wodehouse lived in the
United States.

1   He spoke with a kind of what-is-it in his voice, and I could see
        that, if not actually disgruntled, he was far from being
        gruntled. *The Code of the Woosters*

2   The secretary drew the curtain, and the sunshine, having
        called without an appointment, was excluded. *Heavy
        Weather*

3   On the lawn there was peace – the perfect unruffled peace
        which in this world seems to come only to those who have
        done nothing whatever to deserve it. *Ib.*

4   A sort of glaze had some over his eyes, causing them to
        resemble two pools of cold gravy. *Ib.*

5   He looked at me as if I were some sort of unnecessary product
        which the cat had brought in after a ramble among the
        local ash-cans. *The Inimitable Jeeves*

6   Jeeves's pick-me-up will produce immediate results in
        anything short of an Egyptian mummy. *Ib.*

7   In the woods beyond the river a nightingale had begun to sing
        with all the full-throated zest of a bird conscious of having
        had a rave notice from the poet Keats. *Ring for Jeeves*

8   She went through her capital like a drunken sailor. I don't
    know if she ever endowed a scheme for getting gold out of
    sea-water, but, if not, that's the only one she missed. *Big
    Money*

9   It was a two-storey edifice...constructed of bricks which
    appeared to be making a slow recovery from a recent
    attack of jaundice. *Ib.*

10 Some people prefer their bad news broken to them gently.
    Others would rather that you poured it over them like a
    pail of water. *Ib.*

11 I have a headache that starts at the soles of my feet and gets
    worse all the way up. *Piccadilly Jim*

12 She was the type of woman whom small, diffident men seem
    to marry instinctively, as unable to help themselves as
    cockleshell boats sucked into a maelstrom. *Ib*

13 Her mouth had the coldly forbidding look of the closed door
    of a subway express when you have just missed the train. *Ib.*

14 Porters skimmed to and fro like water-beetles. *Ib.*

15 The fact that she described the bridegroom-to-be as a
    wretched mummer, a despicable fortune hunter, a
    broken-down tramp, and a sneaking, grafting confidence
    trickster lends colour to the supposition that she was not a
    warm supporter of the marriage. *Ib.*

16 He deposited his hat with the robber band who had their
    cave just inside the main entrance of the restaurant. *Ib.*

17 The detective had a practice of glancing keenly at nearly
    everything. It cost nothing and impressed clients. *Ib.*

18 She would have suspected ulterior motives if he had asked
    her the time. *Ib.*

19 Lord Emsworth had one of those minds capable of
    accommodating but one thought at a time – if that.
    Blandings Castle

20 It is never difficult to distinguish between a Scotsman with a grievance and a ray of sunshine. *Ib.*

21 So lyrically does the Encyclopedia Britannica deal with Glasgow that it covers twenty-seven pages before it can tear itself away and go on to Glass. *Ib.*

22 His attitude was that of one sorely perplexed. So might the early bird have felt if the worm ear-marked for breakfast had suddenly turned and snapped at it. *Ib.*

23 I've had as many as six wasps standing on a plum, rolling their eyes at me and daring me to come on. *Ib.*

24 A ray of sunshine which had been advancing jauntily along the carpet, caught sight of the butler's face and slunk out, abashed.

25 Like all motion-picture magnates, he had about forty-seven guilty secrets, many of them recorded on paper. *Ib.*

26 There was only one man who could have coped adequately with the situation [a children's tea-party] and that was King Herod. *Ib.*

27 He was a tubby little chap who looked as if he had been poured into his clothes and forgotten to say "When!" *Very Good, Jeeves*

VICTORIA WOOD

Victoria Wood (1953–) was born in Lancashire, and holds a university degree in Drama. She has often appeared on TV and on stage both solo and in her own humorous sketches; also occasionally with her husband, a magician (The Great Soprendo).

1 I was hoping to give birth to a seven-year-old girl. *Up To You, Porky*

2   Even drugs would have helped Charlotte Brontë to maintain a more cheerful attitude. In fact, she'd probably not be dead if she was alive today. *Ib.*

3   "You've actually been a prostitute?"
"Yeah, but it was boring. The sex was all right but they kept wanting you to talk to them." *Ib*

4   The secret of my youthful appearance is simply – mashed swede. As a face-mask, as a nightcap, and in an emergency as a draught-excluder. *Ib.*

5   I toured the working-men's clubs with a magic act; I used to close with a song. When I got better at it I used to saw myself in half and finish with a duet. *Ib*

6   In Russia, show the least athletic aptitude and they've got you dangling off the parallel bars with a leotard full of hormones. *Ib.*

7   I think we were more neighbourly in those days. If anyone was ill in bed, the whole street would let themselves in and ransack the parlour. *Ib.*

8   A few dates for the date-minded. The Brontë family moved here some time in the nineteenth century, and lived here for quite a number of years. *Ib.*

9   (In a dress shop)

We don't usually let obese people in the cubicles, in case they sweat on the wallpaper. *Ib.*

10   I know that being hit over the head with an adjustable piano-stool can give you a nasty headache. *Ib.*

11   "Has he got over his divorce?"
"I think so. His wife got custody of the stereo and they sold the children." *Barmy*

12   So you're not double-glazed? It's a marvellous investment. I'm not saying it's cheap, but with what you save in fuel bills you'll have made it back within eighty or ninety years. *Ib.*

13 I sometimes think that being widowed is God's way of telling you to come off the pill. *Ib*

14 "Do you think those new tablets will cure her amnesia?" "Well they might, if she could remember to take them." *Ib.*

15 Attempting to murder you was just a silly way of trying to draw attention to myself. *Ib.*

16 I gave birth to three children, all on the same day. Two of them had dangerously straight hair and had to be rushed immediately to the hairdresser. *Ib.*

17 I can never marry Clifford – I have a terrible disease. I'm allergic to men's pyjamas. *Ib.*

18 Do you think those triplets were really mine? After all, I did only go into hospital to have my ears pierced. *Ib.*

19 Is sexual harassment at work a problem for the self-employed?

ALEXANDER WOOLLCOTT

Alexander Humphreys Woollcott (1887–1943), American literary and dramatic critic, journalist, and broadcaster, was also at one time a *New Yorker* columnist.

1 The audience strummed their catarrhs. *While Rome Burns*

2 The chair...was upholstered in one of those flagrant chintzes, designed, apparently, by the art editor of a seed catalogue. *Ib.*

3 A combination of Little Nell and Lady Macbeth. *Ib.*

4 He imported to the peeling of a banana the elegant nonchalance of a duke drawing a monogrammed cigarette from a platinum case. *Ib.*

5　I am in no need of your God-damned sympathy. I ask only to be entertained by some of your grosser reminiscences.
Letter to a friend

6　All the things I like doing are either immoral, illegal, or fattening.

7　(On Oscar Levant, well-known American broadcaster)

There is absolutely nothing wrong with him that a miracle can't fix.

8　The scenery was beautiful but the actors got in front of it. *New Yorker*

9　To all things clergic
I am allergic

10　(On Christopher Morley)

He became mellow before he became ripe.

TOPIC INDEX

I am much indebted to my wife for help in compiling this Index, which is intended as a useful but simple guide. A few cross references have been given: common sense will suggest many more. Thus Acting obviously suggests Theatre, Coffins suggests Funerals, and Crime invites reference to Murder and Theft.